RICHARD
LION HEART

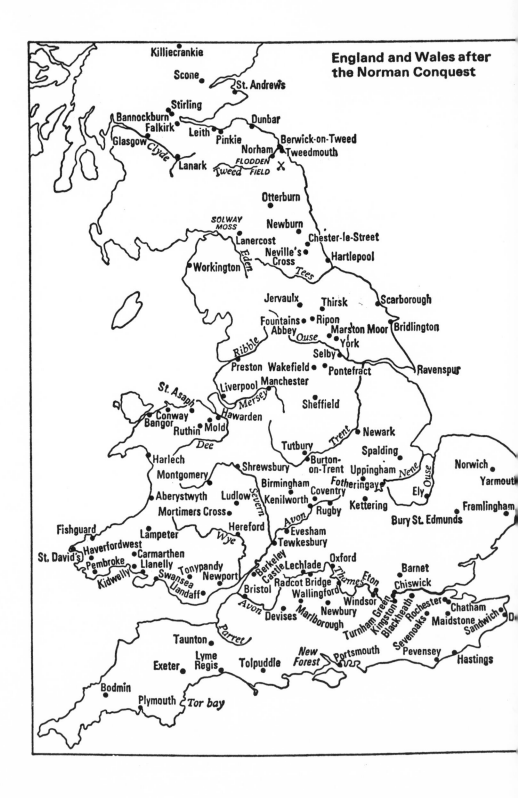

England and Wales after the Norman Conquest

James A. Brundage

RICHARD
LION HEART

Charles Scribner's Sons
New York

*We gratefully acknowledge permission
to use the following maps:*
Pages 2 and 3:
*The World of the
Middle Ages: A Reorientation of
Medieval History* © 1949 John L. LaMonte. Reproduced
by permission of Prentice-Hall, Inc.,
Englewood Cliffs, New Jersey.

Page ii:
English History: A Survey, by Sir
George Clarke. Clarendon Press,
Oxford.

3 5 7 9 11 13 15 17 19   v/c   20 18 16 14 12 10 8 6 4 2

Printed in the United States of America
Library of Congress Catalog Card Number 73-1361
ISBN 0-684-13802-6

For Greg

Preface

My work on this biography began some five years ago, when I first discussed the notion of writing a life of Richard Lion Heart with Professor Goldwin Smith. Since then the pressure of other projects and other commitments has carried my attention to areas and periods quite remote from those in which King Richard lived. Still, I have returned, time and again, to the chronicles and documents of Richard's reign. The time has now come to put my conclusions in writing.

In doing so, I must acknowledge the help of numerous persons and institutions who have aided me in writing this work. The librarians of my own university have been, as always, helpful and accommodating in my search for the materials which I have needed for this book. I have in addition been afforded access to books and working facilities by a large number of other libraries, both in this country and abroad, to all of whom I am grateful. A grant from the Graduate School of the University of Wisconsin-Milwaukee during the summer of 1968 gave me the chance to visit a number of the sites connected with Richard's career in France and Germany, as well as to pursue other research not connected with this project. The secretarial staff of my department have pitched in once more to turn my disordered drafts into presentable typescript. Mrs. Mary Schoultz, Miss Kathy Poplawski, and Mrs. Hazel Kay have borne this burden cheerfully and with great efficiency.

Lastly, I am grateful above all to my wife, Marie, and our children for their patience, understanding, and support while I have been preparing this book.

Contents

RICHARD
LION HEART

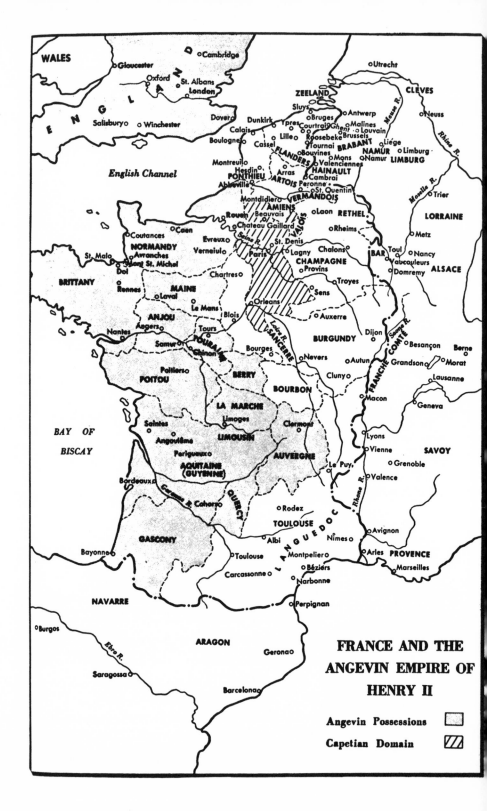

FRANCE AND THE
ANGEVIN EMPIRE OF
HENRY II

Angevin Possessions
Capetian Domain

CRUSADER STATES

Iconium

Marash

E D E S S A
Lost 1144

Edessa

A R M E N I A

Adalia

Mamistra

Tarsus

Seleucia

Alexandretta

Harenc

Antioch
St. Simeon

Aleppo

ANTIOCH

Marra

Laodicea

Kyrenia

Nicosia

Famagusta

Margat

ASSASSINS

Hamah

CYPRUS

Tortosa

Safita

Crac-des-Chevaliers

Homs

Limassol

Archas

Tripoli

TRIPOLI

**SALJUQ
TURKS**

Djebail

Beirut

M E D I T E R R A N E A N

Sidon

Damascus

Tyre

J E R U S A L E M

S E A

Acre

Hattin

Haifa

SEA OF GALILEE

Athlit

Tiberias

Nazareth

Caesarea

Ain Jalut

Arsuf

Naplouse

Jaffa

Lydda

Ibelin

Ramlah

Ascalon

Jerusalem

Gaza

Bethlehem

*DEAD
SEA*

Daron

Damietta

Kerak

Mansourah

Nile R.

Jordan R.

E G Y P T

Montreal

Cairo

*RED
SEA*

Introduction

This is a biography of Richard Plantagenet, king of England, better known as Richard Lion Heart. In it I have attempted to describe the career and character of Richard, but this attempt is subject to certain limitations which are inherent in the nature of the subject and which should be described at the outset. We do not know much about Richard's early life, nor is there any great amount of information about his private affairs at any period of his life. The bulk of the surviving information about Richard deals necessarily with his involvement in public affairs, with his conduct as a king, as a crusader, a warrior and as a political figure. A more intimate view of his inner thoughts and emotions is possible only by inference from his public actions and from episodes which are attested by witnesses of one sort or another, most of them people who knew Richard only slightly. We do possess a handful of letters which Richard wrote or dictated in person, as distinguished from the public documents which were produced by his clerks. He did write at least two poems that tell us something about his ideas and feelings. He also produced some art-works of a kind: his castles and fortifications. These buildings tell us something about him as well.

But aside from such scraps of evidence, we have nothing to give us Richard's view on the world in which he lived and the events in which he took part.

Since this is a biography, I have not attempted to describe in detail the vicissitudes of English government during Richard's reign or to deal with the general political history of Europe in his period, save insofar as these matters impinged upon Richard personally. The evidence suggests very strongly that Richard was quite uninterested in matters of royal administration and government policy, save as they bore directly upon his own immediate concerns. Thus, for example, he was interested in fiscal policy only to the extent that he had to find the money to finance his crusade, to build his castles, and to carry on his wars. It was the results of government operations that interested him, not the means by which those results were obtained. This bias of Richard's is reflected in the way in which this book is constructed.

Similarly, Richard's crusade receives heavy emphasis in this biography, precisely because the crusade was the supreme adventure of Richard's life. Since this was the central incident in Richard's career, the crusade has been made the central episode of this biography of Richard.

This biography is based upon a study of the primary sources for Richard's life. Both narrative and documentary sources have been used, but the bulk of my information has necessarily been drawn from the narrative writers. The main sources of information are mentioned in a bibliographical note at the end of the book, but that note is simply what the title implies: a brief sketch of the most important material, not an attempt to supply either a full bibliography or an exhaustive account of all the works consulted in the preparation of this book.

Because this book has been written primarily for the general reader, as opposed to historians, I have refrained from supplying footnote references. Some scholarly readers may feel that this was an ill-advised decision and that at least

a scattering of notes should have been incorporated to indicate the sources used for the various episodes in the book. I
have resisted the temptation to do this for two reasons. First,
references to sources would be entirely meaningless for a
substantial majority of the readers to whom the book is
directed and might well put some of them off completely. For
whatever reason, a great many people apparently find the
very sight of footnotes, no matter how innocuous, displeasing
and annoying. My second reason for dispensing with annota-
tions is that most of my sources can readily be located by
those who feel the need for them in the books and articles
mentioned in the bibliographical note at the end of this book.
Landon's *Itinerary of King Richard I* and Norgate's *Richard
the Lion Heart*, between them, will supply the bulk of the
necessary references. Any reader who is sufficiently expert to
be able to benefit from a scholarly apparatus will know how
to dig the information out of the materials cited in those two
books and in the other items in my bibliographical note. This
book does not rest upon a body of unpublished manuscript
sources. Rather, it is based upon source material that is already in print. What is new in it is the way in which the story
of Richard's life is told and some of the emphases and in-
terpretations which I have supplied.

Although Richard Lion Heart is one of the best-known
medieval monarchs, there have been surprisingly few biographies of him. Since 1900 there have been exactly two of them
in English which have any claim to be taken seriously. One
of those is Philip Henderson's *Richard Coeur de Lion* (New
York, 1959). Henderson's biography is based upon a considerable amount of reading, almost wholly in the narrative
sources, mainly in translation. His book suffers badly, in my
opinion, from inaccuracies and from anachronisms. In addition, I differ from Mr. Henderson on a substantial number of
points in the interpretation of the sources. Miss Norgate's
Richard the Lion Heart is in an entirely different class. Her
biography of Richard is a painstaking presentation of scholarly

research pursued over many years. It retains great value as a work of scholarship and is well documented. Nonetheless, Miss Norgate's book presents what I take to be essentially a romantic view of Richard's life. With that view I cannot agree. My own reading of the sources bearing on Richard's life suggests a view of his character which is considerably less generous than the one presented by Miss Norgate. Both his personal character and his conduct as a public figure were flawed, in my estimation, by grave deficiencies. At the same time, Richard exemplified in a spectacular way some of the principal virtues of chivalric ideals, which both his contemporaries and later generations have admired. I have tried in this biography to face up to this paradox of Richard's life and to suggest how, if not always why, these contradictory elements in Richard's career fitted together.

Milwaukee, Wisconsin, 1973

ONE

✠──────────────────────────────✠

The Setting

Richard Plantagenet, third son of King Henry II of England, was born at Oxford. His mother, Queen Eleanor, had come to Oxford to stay in the country, at Beaumont Palace, during the last weeks of her sixth pregnancy. There, just within Oxford's city gates, on September 8, 1157, she gave birth to Richard.

The birth of the prince was reassuring to both of his parents. A male heir was both a political necessity and a guarantee of family continuity. Their eldest son, Prince William, a sickly boy, had died the year before Richard was born and their second son, Prince Henry, was still an infant, just two-and-a-half years old. The high risks of infancy in the 1150s were well enough known to King Henry and his thirty-five-year-old wife from the experience of their own relatives. It was comforting to have another son. It would be even more reassuring to have others—and in due course they did. Geoffrey was born the next year after Richard. Then Henry and Eleanor had to wait until Richard was nine years old before another son appeared. In the meantime, however, they had two daughters, named Eleanor and Joan. When John, their last child, was born at the end of 1166, the royal family was complete. In addition, though, King Henry had also sired a bastard son, born of a common whore named Hikenai in 1153. This natural son was named Geoffrey and was raised at the royal court, together with his legitimate half-brothers and sisters.

The heritage of Richard and his brothers was both splendid and frightening. Their father, Henry II, was not only king of England, but also held extensive powers in the French kingdom as well. In 1157, the year of Richard's birth, Henry's fortunes glowed more brightly than ever.

The king was twenty-four years old and bristled with an almost superhuman energy. Physically strong, stocky of build, deep-chested, red-haired, Henry possessed a robust constitution. He was always on the move and perennially scheming to enlarge his power and his lands. His mother, Matilda, was a granddaughter of William the Conqueror. She had once been married to the Holy Roman Emperor. After her first husband's death, Matilda had married Geoffrey Plantagenet, Henry's father. The Plantagenets held territories of considerable extent, even before this marriage, but Matilda brought them the control of the Norman duchy, which vastly extended their power and their importance in Continental politics. A family legend also linked the Plantagenets to an other-worldly power. One of the early members of the family, Count Fulk by name, was rumored to have taken as his wife Melusine, the daughter of Satan himself. Although, according to the legend, Fulk's wife mysteriously disappeared when she was unwittingly brought into the presence of the Eucharist, she left behind two of her children, from whom all the subsequent generations of the family were said to be descended. The story was widely known and, no doubt, widely believed in the twelfth century. Although members of the family might scoff and joke about it—as Richard himself was to do later—the Plantagenet heritage carried with it a sinister reputation, as well as earthly power and distinction.

From Matilda, Henry Plantagenet inherited a claim to

the English throne as well as control of the Duchy of Normandy. From Geoffrey, Henry Plantagenet secured the counties of Anjou and Maine. Normandy, Anjou, and Maine were the cornerstones of Henry Plantagenet's power in France and Henry built splendidly on those foundations. Through a combination of shrewd bargaining, unscrupulous intimidation, and bloodthirsty military campaigns, Henry enlarged his holdings steadily, winning over the allegiance of one after another of the lesser landholders whose possessions adjoined his own domains.

But beyond any doubt, Henry Plantagenet's finest conquest had been the winning of his wife. Eleanor of Aquitaine was a woman of striking beauty combined with an even more striking wit and a lively personality. Although Eleanor was nearly twelve years older than Henry, the discrepancy in their ages seemed to bother neither of them. Moreover, Eleanor was wealthy, the heiress of Poitou and Aquitaine, those rich, fertile, productive lands which had long been the envy and the despair of the French kings. For although Eleanor and her parents, like Henry and his family, were nominally subjects of the French king, neither Eleanor's nor Henry's family was accustomed to devote much thought or attention to the wishes of their overlord at Paris. For all practical purposes, the French king was powerless to impose his will on the territories controlled by Henry's and Eleanor's families.

Eleanor herself had more than a slight acquaintance with the French capital and its monarch, for before her marriage to Henry Plantagenet, she had for fifteen years been the wife of the French king, Louis the Young. She had married Louis in 1137, when she was fifteen years old. The marriage was a political affair, arranged by their parents with an eye to the mutual advantages which this union might confer on their two families. Neither Louis nor Eleanor, by all accounts, had found much satisfaction in their marriage. Louis had the soul of a monk and found his dual role as monarch and as husband

uncongenial. His heart was in the cloister and his court reflected the monastic, other-worldly predilections of its king.
Eleanor, for her part, was a product of the south of France.
She frankly enjoyed the music and poetry, feasting and flir-
tation which were a part of her background and which were
unwelcome in the chill, sober halls of her first husband's pal-
aces.

Eleanor's marriage to Louis the Young ended in an annulment on March 21, 1152. The legal grounds of the decree
which ended their marriage was consanguinity—a plea that
they were related more closely to each other than was allowed by the law of the twelfth-century Church. The grounds
were technically correct, but then the closeness of their relationship had never been a secret. The real grounds for the annulment of their marriage were quite different, but much
more difficult to define. One factor, certainly, was the fact
that in the fifteen years of their marriage Eleanor had borne
no sons. She and Louis the Young did have two daughters:
Marie, born in 1145 and Alice, born four years later. But
Queen Eleanor had failed to produce a son to inherit the
French throne: this was a failure of capital importance in the
society of mid-twelfth century France. More than this, Louis
was undeniably put off personally by his consort. Incompati-
bility, however, was not the only factor leading to an end of
their marriage. Perhaps more important, King Louis had reason to suspect that his wife had been unfaithful to him.
Stories to that effect were in circulation and were gleefully
reported by contemporary chroniclers. How much truth there
may have been to these rumors, it is not now possible to tell
with any precision, but the rumors themselves were enough
to make King Louis uncomfortable, at the very least, with
Eleanor's continued presence at his court.

Eleanor, for her part, was eager to end a marriage that
had brought her few advantages and much grief. She neither
understood nor cared to understand the springs of piety that
motivated her first husband's activities. Nor did she find ei-

ther the climate or the character of his court agreeable. More
than this we do not know for certain. But there are reasons to
suspect that even before the annulment of her marriage to
King Louis, Eleanor had reached an understanding with the
Plantagenets that she and Henry Plantagenet would be married as soon as she could be freed from her first husband. Gerald of Wales, a contemporary writer who did not care much
for Eleanor, plainly states that she had carried on an affair
with Henry's father, Geoffrey the Fair, before the annulment
of her marriage with Louis the Young. Certainly Henry and
Eleanor had met at the French court while she was Louis's
wife and it is likely enough that they had reached some sort
of compact to marry before the conclusion of the legal formalities which made Eleanor once again free to contract another
marriage. It was ironic that Eleanor was even more closely
related by blood to her new husband than she had been to
King Louis.

In any case, Eleanor and Henry wasted little time. The
annulment of Eleanor's first marriage was pronounced at
Beaugency, near Orléans, on March 21, 1152; eight weeks
later, on May 18, the marriage of Eleanor of Aquitaine to
Henry Plantagenet, count of Anjou, and duke of Normandy,
was celebrated quietly in Eleanor's favorite city, Poitiers.

King Louis was, perhaps, affronted by the suddenness of
his former wife's remarriage, but he had even greater reason
to be alarmed by it on political grounds. For the marriage of
Eleanor to Henry Plantagenet united a disconcertingly large
portion of the French kingdom in the hands of the newly
married couple. Between them, Henry and Eleanor had control of nearly two thirds of the territory of modern France,
while Louis the Young, although he wore the French crown,
in actuality could control somewhat less than half of the remaining third.

The next few years saw steady improvement in the fortunes of Henry Plantagenet. In England, King Stephen's only
son, Eustace, strangled on a dish of eels at Bury St. Edmunds;

his death in 1153 left Henry the chief surviving heir to the English throne. The death of King Stephen on October 25, 1154, opened the way for Henry to take the final steps to secure the English throne. In the midst of a dreadful storm, Henry and his court crossed the channel at the beginning of December. On the Sunday before Christmas, he and Eleanor were crowned by Archbishop Theobald of Canterbury in Westminster Abbey, surrounded by an impressive array of their new subjects, who had come to pay their allegiance to the royal pair, while crowds milled through London's streets shouting, "Long live the king."

Once the ceremonials of coronation and anointing had sealed his new position as monarch, Henry set out on the demanding task of welding his new domains onto his old ones. His position as king of England meant no diminution of Henry's interest in his Continental possessions. Rather, he was determined to create out of the union of his English kingdom with his French possessions a new power bloc which could rival even the most powerful European monarchies in every department of government—military, administrative, and financial alike.

The first imperative stage in realizing this goal was to create an administration for England that would enable the king to delegate many items of business to his trusted men, thus freeing the monarch to concentrate on the pursuit of his designs in France. England was for Henry a source of revenues, of men, and of the royal dignity which enabled him to claim a rank equal to that of his Continental rivals. But England was never the real center of his attention and his energies. Rather, it was a valuable resource which he could exploit in the pursuit of his larger designs. Hence the creation of an administrative system to control the realm and to tap its assets was a primary consideration in the politics of his reign.

The reign of Stephen had been a disaster for the government of England. The fecklessness of the monarch and the weakness of his position had made it possible for his powerful subjects to seize many of the powers of the crown itself without any effective opposition from the king. "Every great man built him castles and held them against the king," writes the Anglo-Saxon chronicler, "and they filled the whole land with these castles." From these fortified centers they could both defy the king and oppress his subjects with impunity. "I know not how to, nor am I able to tell of, all the atrocities nor all the cruelties which they wrought upon the unhappy people of this country," one of them wrote. "It lasted throughout the nineteen years that Stephen was king, and always grew worse and worse."

To repair the fortunes of the English crown required vigor, strength of mind and character, an abundance of imagination and the will to translate design into reality. Henry Plantagenet possessed all of these qualities and he used them with great skill during the first decade of his reign in England. His court was boisterous, busy, and always on the move. One of his officials described its life:

> If the King has decided to spend the day anywhere, especially if his royal will to do so has been publicly proclaimed by herald, you may be certain that he will get off early in the morning, and this sudden change will throw everyone's plans into confusion. . . . You may see men running about as though they were mad, urging on the pack-horses, driving chariots one into another, and everything in a state of confusion. . . . His pleasure, if I may dare to say so, is increased by the straits to which his courtiers are put. After wandering about three or four miles in an unknown forest, frequently in the dark, we would consider our prayers answered if we found by chance some mean, filthy hut. Often were there fierce quarrels over these hovels, and courtiers fought with drawn swords for a lodging that it would have disgraced pigs to fight for.

Out of all the confusion of the day-to-day life of his court, Henry slowly, persistently, tirelessly brought new order into the life of his English realm. In this process he relied heavily on the services of three men: Theobald, archbishop of Canterbury; Robert, earl of Leicester, who was his justiciar; and Thomas Becket, his chancellor. Of the three, King Henry was closest to Becket. The king and his chancellor were inseparable. They played chess with each other, dined together, spent days together in the hunting fields. But most of all they worked hand in glove at the business of administering Henry's English kingdom. Together they haggled with the Scots over the demarcation of the boundaries of the northern counties and with the Welsh over England's western frontiers. Together they dealt with the problems of coinage, together they sounded out the nobility of the kingdom to make sure that Henry's eldest son would be accepted as king in his turn upon his father's death.

The English kingdom was the financial heart of Henry's empire. From its mines flowed the silver which paid his armies and from its sheep runs came the wool which supplied the growing textile mills of Flanders with raw material. The island kingdom produced men, too, who could be enlisted to fight in Henry's Continental wars, to bolster the manpower of his armies in France. Although England's borders required guarding—in the west against the Welsh and in the north against the Scots—still the threats to its safety were minor when compared to the dangers which constantly faced Henry's Continental domains.

When he was in England, Henry devoted much of his time and energy to the task of centralizing the administration of the kingdom and combating the perennial tendency of his English barons to make themselves independent of the royal government. From the beginning of his reign, Henry made strenuous and successful efforts to assure that the castles of the English kingdom were in the hands of garrisons whose first loyalty was to the king. It was a fixed principle of his policy to deprive potential rebels of fortified bases from which they might defy his government. In every county of the realm his sheriffs and the itinerant judges of his courts had the task of maintaining the king's prerogatives intact against local noblemen who might act independently of their monarch. But Henry was not content with the surveillance of local developments by the officers of his government. The king himself was constantly on the road, traveling from one county town to the next. Day after day, week after week he rode through his kingdom, from the lonely sweep of the Yorkshire moors, through the gloomy, cold fastness of Northumbria, down through the gentle, green pasturelands of Dorset and Devon in the south. Everywhere he was on the watch, inquiring, inspecting, prodding his royal servants to greater alertness in minding their master's interests. There was little that evaded his sharp gaze and even less eluded the shrewd grasp of his accountants in the Exchequer, where his sheriffs came, as regularly as clockwork, to prove their accounts to Henry's clerks.

In all of these affairs Queen Eleanor had only a small role. She and her children lived for the most part a secluded life and joined King Henry on special occasions only. Surrounded by the women of her household and her husband's female relatives, active participation in larger affairs seems to have been limited to the supervision of her own domains in France, which she visited as often as she could.

Henry was also actively involved in strengthening his position in France, at the same time that he was mending his fences in England. He claimed title to the overlordship of the peninsula of Brittany shortly after the death of his brother, Count Geoffrey of Nantes, in 1157. Meeting resistance from the Breton nobility, he overwhelmed them in a stormy campaign. Following this, he expended vast sums of money in building and strengthening a chain of fortified castles throughout his French domains. Having shown his strength, he was willing to negotiate an agreement with the French king in 1158; an agreement which involved the betrothal of King Louis's daughter Margaret to Henry's eldest son, young Henry, who was then three years old. As a part of the bargain, Louis agreed to turn over to King Henry the castles of the Vexin, a strategically vital region separating Normandy from France proper. The possession of this frontier territory was necessary to make Henry's control of Normandy more secure. During much of the next two years, Henry was involved in a complex series of forays and negotiations whose main aim was to secure more firmly his control of the Vexin and to strengthen his position in the south of France.

The decade of the 1160s was one in which Henry's attention centered mainly on England. From his accession in 1154 until the death of Archbishop Theobald of Canterbury in 1162, Henry had relied heavily upon his chancellor, Thomas Becket, as the mainstay of his English administration. When Theobald died, Henry determined that Becket should succeed him as primate of the Church in England. Henry's aim in this maneuver seems relatively clear. He had discovered that Becket was a man he could rely upon, an administrator and politician of great finesse and large experience. With such a man in the See of Canterbury, Henry had good reason to believe that he could count upon the new archbishop's loyalty and political skills to ease any opposition within the English Church to the policies of the crown.

Tensions between the prelates of the Church and King Henry had been building up slowly since the time of Henry's coronation. There was a feeling among many of the bishops that the king had acted both unwisely and beyond his legitimate powers in neglecting to nominate bishops to dioceses which had been left vacant by deaths. The king's reason lay mainly in the fact that during such vacancies the revenues which ordinarily would have gone to the bishop reverted instead to the king. By holding dioceses vacant, Henry was quite simply increasing his own income. His temptation to do so was obvious enough, but conscientious churchmen had good reason for feeling that Henry was enriching the crown at the expense of the spiritual well-being of his subjects.

The king, for his part, had a growing list of complaints against the Church. In particular he was disturbed by the wide-ranging activities of the Church's courts. Both the canon lawyers and the ecclesiastical judges were steadily widening the area of their work in the twelfth century and they were doing so at the expense of the royal courts and the king's jurisdiction. In addition, the courts of the Church claimed exclusive jurisdiction over clerics, no matter what kind of crime they might be accused of. The clerical class was a large and extremely important segment of the population. Admission to the ranks of the clergy involved merely a brief ceremony and the clipping of the candidate's hair in the style peculiar to the clergy. In return for this minor inconvenience, the ceremony had the effect of bestowing on the new cleric a handsome list of privileges, without putting him under any serious obligations. Many twelfth- and thirteenth-century clerics were only marginally involved in the service of the Church and found their real employment and careers in the service of the monarch or of some other powerful prince or nobleman. The effect of the jurisdictional claims of the Church's courts was to exempt this large, prosperous, and important class of the king's subjects from the laws of the land. This exemption was in Henry's eyes a glaring abuse which required correction; in this and other matters he hoped to secure easier cooperation from Thomas Becket than from any alternative candidate who might be named to the See of Canterbury.

Here Henry's calculations foundered. He failed to anticipate that Becket, once he was named archbishop, would become as ardent a champion of ecclesiastical prerogatives as he had previously been of royal prerogatives. But in fact the assumption of his new office changed Becket quite radically. He became stern, severe, and ascetic in his private life, stubborn and unbending in his defense of the rights (as he saw them) of the Church and churchmen in general and of the See of Canterbury in particular.

The result was a head-on collision between the archbishop and the king. Within a few months of Becket's nomination as archbishop the two men were at odds. They clashed first at Westminster in October, 1163, when Becket refused to give the "clear answer" that Henry required to a demand that the jurisdiction of the ecclesiastical courts be cut back in some areas. At the beginning of 1164 they clashed even more violently at Clarendon, when Becket refused to put his seal to the constitutions for the English Church which Henry's lawyers had drawn up.

Nine months later Becket found himself haled before a royal court at Northampton, charged with contempt, fined £300, and threatened with further exactions which were clearly beyond his power to pay. When he refused to submit to the king's command that he not appeal this matter to the pope, Becket fled in disguise, crossed the Channel, and took refuge under the patronage of King Louis of France. From there Becket appealed to the pope for support, while in England Henry confiscated the archbishop's possessions, rounded up all of Becket's relatives whom he could find, exiled them, and forbade Becket himself to return to England.

The archbishop's exile continued for six years. Attempts were made at various points to patch up the quarrel between the king and his former chancellor. Becket pressured his foe by excommunicating first the king's principal servants and finally Henry himself. Henry retaliated by bringing pressure to bear on the pope to urge Becket to submit and by doing everything in his power to persuade the French king to withdraw his support from the intransigent archbishop. Finally the two antagonists met together in "Traitor's Meadow" near Frétival on July 22, 1170. There they went through a formal reconciliation, although it is clear that there were serious reservations on both sides. On the first of December in that year, Thomas returned at last to England. He and the king were reconciled, but neither had forgiven the other for what had happened.

The climax of the quarrel came quickly. Thomas refused upon his return to Canterbury to withdraw the excommunications which he had pronounced against the archbishop of York and the bishops of London and Salisbury for the help they had given Henry. These three prelates hurried to Henry's court near Bayeux on Christmas Eve to complain. This new eruption of the quarrel enraged Henry. In his fury he burst out: "What a parcel of idle cowards I have nourished in my house, that no one can be found to avenge me on this upstart clerk!"

Four knights of his household took the king's outburst as the archbishop's death warrant. Secretly they left the court, crossed the Channel to England by separate ships, and met at Saltwood to make their final plans. On the evening of December 29, they butchered the archbishop at the foot of the altar in his cathedral church at Canterbury.

No event of the twelfth century so profoundly shocked Western Christendom as the murder of Thomas Becket. Vengeance for the murder rained down upon King Henry in abundance. The pope excommunicated the killers at once and placed Henry's French possessions under interdict. Henry was saved from excommunication only by a timely promise to submit to whatever penance the pope thought fit for his part in the affair.

Henry's first reaction to the news of Becket's murder was one of stunned grief, as much for himself, perhaps, as for Thomas Becket. Henry was terrified that he would be blamed for what had happened. He shut himself up alone in his room for three days, and refused to eat. His courtiers feared that he might kill himself in the throes of his hysterical behavior. When he emerged from seclusion, however, Henry came slowly to his senses. After making a statement in which he denied any complicity in the assassination, Henry decided to leave Normandy. He had long planned to visit Ireland and took this opportunity to do so. As a result, it was impossible for the pope's representatives to contact him for over six months and by the time of his return, in April, 1172, the anger of those who blamed him for Becket's death had cooled off.

Henry made his formal peace with the pope's representatives on May 21, 1172, at Avranches. He agreed that he would dispatch a sum of money sufficient to support 200 knights for a year's service in the Holy Land, that he would take the crusader's cross himself (though later he went back on this promise and founded three monasteries instead), that he would freely allow appeals to Rome against his decisions, and that he would recompense the See of Canterbury and those who had supported the archbishop for the losses which they had suffered during his quarrel with Becket.

The submission of Henry II at Avranches in 1172 marked a turn in the fortunes of the king. During the years that followed, he was increasingly preoccupied with schemes to strengthen his position in France. He also began to grapple with the problem of settling the future of his dynasty by providing for the fortunes of his sons.

TWO

✠————————————————————✠

Duke of Aquitaine

Three weeks after Henry's reconciliation with the Church at Avranches, his son Richard was solemnly enthroned in the abbot's chair in the church of St. Hilary at Poitiers. His enthronement symbolized Richard's recognition as duke of Aquitaine and heir to his mother's rich, strategically placed holdings in the south of France. Richard, who was three months shy of his fifteenth birthday, had come of age.

Richard was clearly Eleanor of Aquitaine's favorite child. He had spent most of his life up to this point at her court, centered at Poitiers, the administrative capital of the sweet, lush county of Poitou. From the city of Poitiers, which she had newly refurbished and rebuilt, Eleanor supervised all of her lands in the south of France. Her Aquitainian possessions were administratively separate from those of her husband and from her comfortable residence in the center of Poitiers Eleanor governed her inherited lands almost as an independent sovereign. There Richard was more at home than he was anywhere else in the world.

Poitou and the whole of Aquitaine to the south of it was green and fertile. Watered by its ample river systems, which spread and branched like veins and arteries through the land, Aquitaine was prodigiously abundant. Its crops had been legendary since before the time of Julius Caesar. Split up as it was into crazy-quilt patterns of natural divisions by its waterways in the west and by its mountain systems farther to the east and south, the very land itself favored the growth of feudal divisions among its rulers. A complex multitude of feudal states had grown up in the region since the passing of Charlemagne, the last monarch who had been able to link Aquitaine effectively into a larger political whole. Each of these feudal enclaves was fiercely independent of the others. Their rulers tended to be haughty noblemen, spurred on by ambition to build up their own domains at the expense of their neighbors. The result was that Aquitaine's history consisted for the most part of a murky maze of petty wars. The region was only tenuously held together by a traditional allegiance to the family of Queen Eleanor, but within this framework the shifting marriage alliances and feuds among the nobility often reduced the politics of the region to near anarchy.

Every nobleman who had any hope of achieving and retaining independence of action symbolized his ambition by building himself a castle. The landscape was cluttered with these private fortresses, many of them tiny, often amounting to little more than a stone manor house surrounded by a wall. Small and insignificant as many of them were, these structures embodied their owners' dreams of independence and symbolized their claims to self-sufficiency. Such claims were not entirely fantastic, for even the smaller castles, if stubbornly and skillfully defended, could withstand the attack of an army several times the size of the garrison holding the fort. A feudal lord who hoped to subdue the owner of such a castle might find it necessary to spend days or even weeks besieging the castle of a well-entrenched adversary. Even if the siege were successful in taking the castle, there was sure to be another similar fortress, belonging to an equally stubborn neighboring nobleman, just a few miles away. In order to gain control of a large block of land, a potential conqueror had to face the prospect of subduing the feudal proprietors of each little castle, one by one. This process was expensive, time-consuming, and vexatious. It was far simpler and less expensive, as Eleanor knew and as she taught her sons, to play off one baron against another, using promises of military or economic assistance, land grants, mineral rights, marriage alliances, and even outright bribes, as conditions warranted. From his youth, Richard was schooled in the intricate, bemusing politics of his Aquitainian homeland. The intrigues and tortuous bargaining of the court at Poitiers, where he was brought up, were an integral part of his life from an early age.

Emotionally and culturally Richard was a Poitevin through and through. The French of Poitou was his native language, the one which he preferred to use whenever possible. Indeed, although he became England's king, he never learned the English language well enough to speak it. He was, however, a competent, if not always fastidious, Latinist. Unlike most of his contemporaries, even those of high rank and royal lineage, he was literate, for, as a boy, he was carefully educated, as were all of his brothers and sisters. The family of Henry II and Eleanor of Aquitaine was highly unusual, even unique, in its devotion to learning and literature in an age when literacy was very nearly a monopoly of the clergy—and not even all clerics were in fact able to read easily, although the Church theoretically required them to be able to do so.

At Eleanor's court, Richard had learned not only to speak and write in Poitevin French, but he also learned to appreciate and to imitate the poetry and music which was popular at the court. Eleanor's court was the birthplace of courtly romance and Richard grew up in a household that placed a high value on the ability to frame compliments in elegant verse, to turn phrases prettily, and to pay one's allegiance to a lady in song. His great-grandfather, William IX of Aquitaine, had been a poet of considerable skill, as well as a well-known roué, who had suffered excommunication because of the notoriously lax morals of his court. The delight of Eleanor's family in delicate, sensuous verse was a significant part of Richard's childhood world.

If Richard had learned to appreciate and to create poetry at his mother's court, he also picked up there another characteristic both of Eleanor's family and of his father's family: a delight in fighting, a mastery of its skills, and a sense of the way in which a forceful warrior could use his skills to secure what he wanted. The knife in the guts, the armor smeared with brains, the horse's fetlocks spattered with red mud—these were just as much a part of Richard's Poitevin heritage as the poems in which his grandfather had celebrated his adultery with the wives of two of his neighbors.

Certainly Richard began his apprenticeship to the art of warfare when he was very young. The one area in which it was absolutely essential for the boys of the royal household to excel was the mastery of the skills of a knight, a professional fighter on horseback. And if there was anything that fascinated and satisfied Richard throughout his life, it was the employment of his training as a warrior and the thrill of carrying off a feat of arms with consummate skill. The military skills which he began to learn as a child were comparatively complex and his apprenticeship was correspondingly long and arduous. Basic to everything else was a mastery of horsemanship, particularly of the knack of guiding the mount and retaining complete control while engaging in violent maneuvers: gallops, quick turns, sudden halts. Above all, Richard had to learn to master the shock of encounter, when his lance met his opponent's body and concentrated the full weight and force of his own body, his horse's body, his armor, and his velocity on a single tiny point: the point where his lance hit the enemy. The shock of encounter can fairly be compared to the shock of being hit by a truck or a railroad train. Remaining in his saddle, while swerving to avoid being carried into head-on collision with his opponent and his horse, was a skill which required long hours of training and concentrated practice. Likewise it was no simple matter for Richard to learn how to parry the thrusts of an assailant and to avoid being spitted on his lance, while he struck the enemy directly with his own weapon. In addition, there were other skills to be mastered: the use of the sword, both on horse and on foot, the use of the mace and the war axe, the employment of defensive measures against all of these weapons—these were the tools of Richard's trade and he took to them with an enthusiasm and enjoyment which lasted all of his life.

Mastery of the skills of a fighter was essential for any nobleman in the world in which Richard lived. For the son of a king, however, other military skills were also necessary. He must not only be able to fight, he must also be able to lead others in war, to command the obedience of his men, to direct the tactical development of a battle, and to plan the strategy of a campaign. For these matters, too, Richard turned out to have a notable flair and he took to them more easily and more eagerly than any of his brothers. In his fascination with military matters, Richard clearly followed his father's example, for Henry II was also a superb master of the military arts, a consummate knight and warrior.

More generally, it might be added, the society in which Richard grew up valued the achievements of a feudal warrior above almost anything else. The knight was not only a utilitarian soldier, skilled and strong enough to triumph over his opponents on the battlefield; he was also, in Richard's day, in the process of being transformed into a benevolent social figure. The emergence of ideas about chivalry, which began to become a significant factor in European social thought during Richard's childhood, broadened and modified the feudal warrior's role in the scheme of things. The chivalric poems which Richard undoubtedly heard sung at Poitevin firesides during his youth, pictured the knight as a protector of the more defenseless classes of society: of women, the clergy, monks, nuns, orphans, widows, and the poor. The concept of knightly honor, of the knight's duty to seek out and destroy evil persons and oppressors, was something that Richard grew up with from an early age. So, too, the idea of the knight as a defender of Christendom and of religion from its enemies was often reiterated in the songs and stories which molded Richard's youthful view of the world. A knight must be brave, bold, fearless, and aggressive in his dealings with those who threaten the peace and tranquillity of his dependents and his subjects. He must be loyal to those above him in the social hierarchy. He had a positive obligation to seek out the wicked and to do battle with them. To shirk such duties was to dishonor oneself, one's family, and one's peers. Toward his subjects and his family the knight was honor-bound to be generous, open-handed, kind, and forgiving. Knights were not, however, expected to be men of culture and academic learning. It was sufficient if they could say their prayers and if they knew by heart a few songs and poems about deeds of arms and valiant warriors. Intellectual values had only a small, subordinate role in the scheme of things accepted by chivalric society. In this respect Richard and his family were different from the rest of their society.

If Richard received much of his training in chivalry and in military affairs from the men belonging to his father's household, he also received instruction from members of his mother's court in other matters. Whatever religious training and instruction he received in the beliefs and practices of the twelfth-century Church apparently did not influence him very deeply. Still, Richard was never suspected of harboring any yearnings to become a convert to Islam, as both his father and his youngest brother, John, were reported to have done. Richard's fidelity to Latin Christendom was unquestioned in his own lifetime and while his recorded actions may indicate that his practice of Christian moral principles in his own career was somewhat haphazard, his life-long adhesion to the Christian faith was well attested.

When Richard was enthroned as duke of Aquitaine in 1172, he entered for the first time into the tortuous political life of his father's empire. No part of that empire was less placid than Richard's new duchy and the boy-duke was soon deeply embroiled in a highly dubious tangle of enmities and alliances.

In March of 1173 his eldest brother, Henry, deserted his father's court and made his way to the court of his family's staunchest enemy, King Louis VII of France. Young Henry was the heir-apparent to the English throne and to the choicest portions of the Angevin domains on the Continent as well. His position as heir-apparent had been consecrated three years earlier, in 1170, when Henry II had insisted, against strong opposition, that young Henry be crowned as king of England. Such a coronation, while the ruling king was still alive, was almost unprecedented, but the elder Henry would tolerate no opposition to his plan and the coronation had duly taken place. Henry II's motive in this was to make sure that if he were to die unexpectedly, his nobles and his subjects would have no excuse for upsetting his eldest son's succession to the crown. Since the coronation of the young king, Henry II had employed him from time to time as a military commander, but had carefully refrained from granting him any independent power. It was the young king's resentment of his father's evident lack of trust which caused him finally to flee to the court of the French king. There young Henry summoned his brothers, Richard and Geoffrey, to join him and all three agreed to ally themselves with Louis of France against their father. Presumably young Henry persuaded his younger brothers to join with him in rebellion by convincing them that their father was treating all of them unjustly. He argued that their father ought to furnish them with large estates and a greater share in the governance of the English kingdom and his other holdings. In this course of action, the three brothers were probably encouraged and aided by their mother, Eleanor. Certainly she attempted to join her sons at the court of King Louis, her first husband, but she was caught on the road, disguised as a man. Her husband, the elder Henry, was understandably furious and jailed Eleanor forthwith. She remained in confinement and under guard for the next sixteen years, until after her husband had died.

Richard, meanwhile, remained with his brothers at the court of Louis VII through much of the rest of 1173 and it was during this period at the French court that he was knighted by King Louis. The ceremony formally confirmed Richard's status as a full-fledged military man. Now he faced the problem of how to secure his own sphere of action, independent of his father. Richard's only realistic hope of doing this lay in Aquitaine, where he had spent his youth and where he was now duke. There, if anywhere, he might hope to rally support behind him from the nobles of the region. He was one of them, after all, and shared with them a fierce urge to be independent of the rule of outsiders, even of his own father. Before the end of the year Richard returned to Aquitaine to try to convince the barons of the south to support him against King Henry.

In Aquitaine Richard found few allies who were brave enough to court the disfavor of his father by siding openly with their young duke. When he attempted to enter the town of La Rochelle, in order to align its citizens publicly with the rebel forces, Richard found the town gates slammed shut in his face. Not all of his efforts were as unrewarding as this one. In May of 1174 he succeeded in taking the town of Saintes by force, although his troops were soon ousted from the city by his father's army. The summer of 1174 saw the rebels falter and fail on all sides. King Henry's counterattacks against his treacherous sons met with one success after another, while Richard's brothers fell to quarreling with each other and reproached their patron, King Louis, for not assisting them more effectively.

By September Richard was disillusioned with the plot which he had unwisely supported. Shortly after his seventeenth birthday he met his father in Poitou. Richard fell to the ground and lay with his face in the dirt at his father's feet, while he asked Henry's forgiveness for his treachery. Henry lifted his dust-covered son to his feet, kissed him, and granted him forgiveness. Then the two returned to Poitiers together.

By this time both Henry the Young King and Geoffrey had given up the struggle as well. At the end of September a peace settlement was concluded between King Henry and his three sons at Montlouis in Touraine. The sons promised obedience to their father and the younger two did homage to him as well. The eldest son, Henry the Young King, was not required to do homage, since he had already been crowned as king in anticipation of his inheriting the English throne; his father believed that one monarch should not do homage to another.

Following the formal peace ceremonies at Montlouis, Richard returned to Poitou. During the next two years he was busy with affairs in Aquitaine, whose barons were even more restive and rebellious than usual, following the revolt of King Henry's sons. During the greater part of 1175 and 1176, then, Richard was engaged almost constantly in fighting one or another of the turbulent and quarrelsome noblemen of the south. In doing so he was acting essentially as his father's agent, since at the peace of Montlouis the elder Henry had reasserted his authority over Aquitaine, thus bypassing Richard's nominal authority in that area. These campaigns were, on the whole, successful and added significantly to Richard's expertise as a fighter and as a commnader of troops. His constant campaigning was interrupted briefly by a visit to England in the spring of 1176. Richard spent the Easter holidays at his father's court and presumably sought his father's advice about the conduct of future campaigns in the south of France. Following this short respite, Richard returned once again to Poitou and resumed fighting there. By the end of the year he had humbled the most significant of his enemies in the northern portions of Aquitaine and early in 1177 he began still further campaigns in Gascony. There he again piled up an impressive record of successful engagements, which led him down to the foothills of the Pyrenees. One after another he forced the Navarese and Basque noblemen to submit to him and to pledge their obedience to his father's authority. Those who resisted were bludgeoned into acquiescence, either by threats or by physical attacks on their castles and towns.

In June of 1177, Richard joined his father and King Louis of France at Nonacourt on the Norman frontier, near Tillières. Their discussions dealt with preparations for the forthcoming crusade. The meeting was of unusual interest, from Richard's point of view, since one of the principal topics of discussion was a proposal for Richard's marriage to Alice, the daughter of Louis of France and his second wife, Constance of Castile. Richard had been betrothed to Alice since 1169, when he was twelve years old and she was nine. By now the betrothal had been in effect for eight years and the French monarch was becoming increasingly impatient to see his daughter's future firmly settled. King Henry was less anxious to commit his son to the alliance implied by the proposed marriage and the meeting at Nonancourt was supposed to settle the matter once and for all.

King Henry managed to cloud the issue and postpone a final settlement once again. This he did by proposing to the French king that they should jointly agree to go on crusade, a proposal that was dear to Louis's heart and to which he eagerly assented. Since they were to participate as comrades in the crusade, Henry then proposed that he and the French king lay aside all of the disagreements outstanding between them until after they had returned. To this King Louis reluctantly agreed and accordingly the problem of Richard's marriage was left open indefinitely.

The next eleven months were a respite for Richard from the constant fighting of the four preceding years. During much of this time, King Henry was on the Continent, making leisurely arrangements for the crusade. Richard's inactivity was doubtless a result of his father's presence on the scene. Henry was dealing with the Aquitainian nobility personally and Richard had no part to play so long as his father was actively involved in Aquitainian affairs. When Henry returned to England in July, 1178, Richard again took up the task of maintaining Angevin control in the south of France. Once again he led an army into Gascony, made a show of force, and discouraged potential mutineers by demonstrating on a handful of unlucky victims the fate in store for those who defied the Angevin rulers.

Richard's successful siege of Taillebourg in the spring of 1179 was one of the high points of his early career. This redoubtable fortress on the Charente River, near Cognac, had the reputation of being impregnable, perched as it was high on a forbidding crag, completely inaccessible on three sides and sturdily fortified on its remaining flank. Three sets of walls, one inside the other, protected it. Within the walls a strong and resolute garrison waited, equipped with every variety of weapon then in use and supplied with ample stocks of food and water. On the first of May, Richard settled down resolutely to test the determination of the defenders. With cold, calculating dispatch he began by applying a scorched earth policy to all the farms and villages in the vicinity of the castle. Livestock and food were seized by his army. Animals that they could not use or did not need were butchered and their corpses were left to rot. Houses and barns were set afire. Crops in the fields were put to the torch. Then Richard and his army settled down to wait.

The citizens of Taillebourg were horrified. They were unprepared for the display of ruthlessness which they witnessed from the walls of their fortress and they were shocked beyond measure by the devastation of their homes and possessions. On May 8 they sallied out to test Richard's defenses, hoping to take his army by surprise. Richard, however, was expecting this move and put up a vigorous defense. Then, when the citizens tried to return to the safety of the fortress, he outflanked their forces and pushed his way ahead of them through the walled redoubt. After two days of bloodshed and plundering, Taillebourg capitulated and Richard put his army to work knocking down its walls, leveling the fortress to the ground.

The capture of supposedly impregnable Taillebourg shocked and horrified Richard's remaining enemies in Aquitaine. The resistance to his army collapsed in most parts of the duchy, as tales of the butchery at Taillebourg spread through the land. Richard's reputation as a military man was established.

A few weeks later he received his reward. Returning to England, he visited the tomb of Thomas Becket at Canterbury and then rode on to his father's court. Henry received him with honor and agreed to allow Richard free exercise of his powers in the county of Poitou.

The years immediately following Richard's victory at Taillebourg were comparatively quiet. There were sporadic problems, to be sure, but nothing to compare with the hectic campaigns of the preceding period. In 1181 there was a minor outbreak of trouble in Gascony once again, but Richard put this down quickly. It was not until 1182 that warfare again occupied him on a major scale. This time the center of the problem was in Périgord and the Limousin. Richard had insisted in recent months that it was his right as a feudal lord in the region to determine the succession of fiefs. Lands held from him should not simply be passed on to the heirs of a deceased vassal, Richard claimed. Rather, the heirs should petition him for permission to claim the estates of their deceased parents and it was his right either to grant permission

for the estate to go to a particular heir, or else to select someone else to receive it. The barons of the region were incensed
at Richard's claims. Richard, they thought, was trying to deprive them of control over their rightful possessions and to
impoverish their children. A group of barons joined forces to
resist the execution of Richard's policy and the result was a
full-fledged war between the rebellious barons and their
young count. Again, Richard's reaction was sudden and vigorous. Catching the rebels by surprise, he set in motion a
lightning campaign against a select number of strong points
which he took ruthlessly. By the summer of 1182 the resistance collapsed and Richard's authority was reestablished.

At Christmastime, 1182, Richard joined his father's
court in Normandy for the holiday season. The Plantagenets
were not really a family in a modern sense of the term. They
were a group of ambitious, able, and ruthless individuals who
happened to be related to one another and who had some political and economic interests in common. Both their marriages and their quarrels were far more commonly based
upon calculations of political advantage than they were upon
sentiment or affection. At their Christmas reunion in 1182,
Richard met with an unwelcome surprise. His father now
demanded that Richard do homage to Henry the Young King.
The elder Henry's demand apparently was based on a fear
that, when he himself died, Richard might attempt to go his
own way and thus tear apart the Angevin empire which had
been so carefully put together through decades of fighting,
scheming, and negotiation. Richard at first flatly refused to
comply with his father's wishes; but, after a brief quarrel, he
backed down. His resistance to the demand, however, offended his elder brother, who was meanwhile busily attempting to make common cause with both the Aquitainian
barons and with Richard's other brothers in order to subvert
Richard's position. The Christmas party broke up amid quarrels, recrimination, and mutual suspicions, many of them
well founded.

Richard's temper, which was never remarkable for its evenness, broke through. After hurling threats and insults at his elder brother, Richard hurried back to Aquitaine to put his defenses in order. It was well for him that he did so. Henry the Young King and his brother Geoffrey had secretly made agreements with a discontented group of Aquitainian barons and in February they all joined forces against Richard. As a first objective they laid siege to a fortified church at Gorre, a short distance south of Limoges. There Richard took them unawares. Using a small castle near Poitiers as a secret base, he assembled his forces and with them made a forced march to Gorre. His surprise attack was successful and devastating. The opposing force was unable to defend itself and large numbers of them were killed on the spot. Many of the rest were taken prisoner and these captives were dragged to Aix, where Richard drowned some of them, slit the throats of others, and blinded the rest.

The success of Richard's tactics in this first encounter was not enough, however, to discourage his brothers. Escaping from the disaster of Gorre, they were able to rally other supporters to their standards. A large part of their support came from mercenary troops whom they hired, but they secured help also from the king of France and from Aquitainian noblemen who held grudges of various kinds against Richard. The struggle dragged on through the spring of 1183. Then at the beginning of June Henry the Young King fell ill with dysentery. His condition deteriorated quickly. On June 11 he died.

The death of young Henry spelled the end of the coalition against Richard. Its members deserted the cause as quickly as they could and began to consider how best they could pacify their opponent.

For Richard was now the eldest surviving son of the Angevin house and the heir-apparent of Henry II.

THREE

The Heir-Apparent

When his elder brother, Henry, died in 1183, Richard was just three months short of his twenty-sixth birthday. Handsome and strongly built, with long legs and a surprising reach in his muscular arms, Richard presented a commanding figure, well suited to inspire admiration, while his already impressive record in combat also warranted a wary respect from those who dealt with him.

His character was as striking as his appearance, although in his manner he was less prepossessing than in his looks. He had showed himself impetuous and self-willed in his earlier dealings both with the barons of Aquitaine and with his father. But by now Richard had learned something of his parents' skill in appealing to the self-interest of his opponents and actively enjoyed the game of pitting one Aquitainian baron against another. He was personally proud and vain, as well, and dearly loved the pomp and display of court ceremonies and ecclesiastical rituals, especially those which cast him in the starring role. But if he was vain, devious, and self-centered, he was also extraordinarily brave, generously endowed with the kind of physical courage which is indifferent to personal danger and scornful both of possible perils and of actual hurts. He had already proved his audacity of mind as a commander and was to display repeatedly throughout his career his resourcefulness and quick-wittedness on the field of battle. Danger sharpened his mind and provoked him to use it with an efficiency that he was rarely able to achieve when he had to deal with more routine tasks in more placid circumstances. Although he was skilled at using other people to achieve his goals, he never displayed in the council chamber or the counting room the same level of application and intelligence that he often manifested amid the screams, dust, and stench of the battlefield.

During these years another, darker side of Richard's character began to take shape. Contemporary writers furnish us with no details, but Richard we know chose men, rather than women, as his usual sexual partners. As a boy he had been very close to Queen Eleanor and was always her favorite son, brought up in the predominantly feminine environment of the queen's court at Poitiers. This may well have been a conditioning factor of some importance in shaping Richard's psyche. Queen Eleanor's fall from his father's favor and then her confinement under close guard probably also affected Richard very intimately. Never close to his father, Richard may have come to dislike him intensely during these years and this, too, may have been related to his growing homosexual inclinations.

The death of Henry the Young King further complicated Richard's relationship with his father. Previously Richard had been a younger son, whose succession to the throne was problematical; now he was the heir-apparent and, barring accidents, could expect to succeed Henry II eventually as ruler of the widespread Angevin domains and thus as one of the major political powers of the European world. For the time being, however, Richard doubtless hoped to enjoy at least some measure of the independence and personal authority which Henry the Young King had been given during his lifetime. Henry II, as it happened, felt differently. His experience with young Henry had taught him the dangers of allowing his heir-apparent too much independence and he was not anxious to repeat that unhappy experience. His other son, Geoffrey, who might have caused trouble, died suddenly in 1186. But there was a still younger son, John, who had to be considered. Up to now John had had no share in the Angevin domains marked out for him and hence was sometimes known as John Lackland. Now, after the death of Henry the Young King, the elder Henry thought that he might be well advised to give Poitou and the rest of Aquitaine to John, as his lieutenant. This would have two advantages from Henry's viewpoint. First and foremost, it would limit the independence of Richard, since Richard would no longer have a base for independent action in the Poitevin territory. This in turn might discourage any further rash rebellions. In addition, such a settlement would provide John with an inheritance, although Henry seems to have envisioned a different arrangement than he had made with Richard when he had become duke at Poitiers. Henry contemplated making himself the formal ruler of Aquitaine and employing John simply as his agent in charge of the region. In that way he would not give John any significant scope for independent action, but could exercise a continual surveillance over his activities.

Richard was dismayed at these plans. Instead of granting him a greater measure of freedom and a larger field of action, his father's scheme would deprive him of the independence which he had already achieved, in great part through his own efforts, in the south of France. Moreover, this would be done at his expense in order to provide for John, a younger brother who was clearly his father's favorite and for whom Richard never much cared. Both personal antagonism and political calculation conspired to keep Richard and John at odds with each other so long as their father was alive.

There was, in addition, another consideration. Richard, as count of Poitou (he had been invested as count in 1172), was ruler of lands that belonged to the Angevin family as a part of his mother's inheritance. Richard and Eleanor had always been very close and it is more than likely that Richard bitterly resented his father's high-handed disposition of his mother's property, especially since Eleanor was now kept constantly under what amounted to house arrest.

The seeds of tension between Richard and his father had been planted three years earlier, with the death of Geoffrey; they germinated and grew luxuriantly in the months that followed the death of Henry the Young King. And as Richard and his father found their interests more and more at odds, the importance of a third interested party increased. That third party was the new king of France, Philip Augustus.

Philip was only fifteen years old. Although he was young and relatively inexperienced, Philip was nobody's fool. Clever and scheming by nature, Philip was keenly aware that both his own personal interests and those of his kingdom could best be served by sowing dissension among his enemies. His principal enemies, as he also well knew, were the English king and his sons. Between them, Henry II and his sons had more or less effective control over nearly two thirds of the French kingdom, while Philip could realistically claim control over only about half of the remaining third. Clearly the French king could benefit by weakening the power of his Angevin rivals and by creating situations where the French king could intervene in the quarrels and dissensions which erupted within the Angevin domains. A frontal assault on the Angevin territories was likely to be worse than useless. Philip was, in any case, no match for either Henry II or Richard as a general or as a warrior. Besides, he seems to have had a personal aversion to fighting; unlike Richard, he took no joy in doing battle on the field. He could and did fight effectively when he had to, but he usually chose other means of obtaining his objectives where that was possible. By temperament and choice he was a diplomat and manager, rather than a warrior and knight. Physically, too,

Philip was no match for the men of the Angevin family. Although reasonably strong and well built, he lacked the physical force and presence of his Angevin foes. Still, despite his shortcomings, Philip was a man to be reckoned with—a cool, careful, quick-witted and resourceful antagonist.

In order to rearrange the internal organization of his French domains, Henry II needed the consent of the young French king. Philip was, after all, at least nominally Henry's overlord for his French domains. Beyond this, there were other outstanding issues which Henry required Philip's cooperation in resolving. In December, 1183, the two kings met to discuss these matters and reached agreements on a number of them in almost unprecedented harmony. For his part, Henry agreed to do homage formally to Philip for all of his French territories, thus acknowledging the French king's suzerainty openly and unambiguously. This was something that Henry had previously been unwilling to do. He agreed to it now because he needed concessions from Philip on other matters. One of them was the matter of the dowry of Philip's sister, Margaret, the widow of Henry the Young King. In return for the elder Henry's promise to pay the widow an annual pension, Philip agreed that Henry might retain control of Gisors and the Norman Vexin—territories Henry actually controlled anyway, but which he was legally obliged to return to the French king upon the death of the younger Henry. Now Henry secured an open recognition of his title to these lands, on condition that they be counted as a part of the dowry of Alice, King Philip's other sister, who was engaged to marry Richard.

The engagement between Alice and Richard had been entered into fourteen years earlier, but the marriage had still not taken place and there was no immediate prospect that it was going to take place soon. Meanwhile, Alice had been living at Henry's court and there were widespread rumors that her prospective father-in-law's relations with young Alice were something more than paternal. She was commonly believed to be sharing his bed and the reports which circulated so freely were probably true. In any case, Philip Augustus was anxious, as his father had been before him, to see Alice's situation regularized. In this he may have been moved by brotherly feelings and anxiety about his sister's future. He was also motivated—of this we can be certain—by political considerations. Richard was remarkably indifferent to the whole business. There is no indication that he cared for Alice in any way at all. He was certainly not eager to marry her and he seems to have played no significant part in the complex negotiations which were going on to determine the future of his fiancée. When King Henry, at his meeting with Philip Augustus in 1183, indicated that he would rather see Alice married to John than to Richard, Philip Augustus was, if anything, somewhat relieved. No doubt this accounts for his readiness to come to terms over the question of the dowry.

After closing his negotiations with Philip Augustus, Henry rode to Le Mans, where he celebrated Christmas. At Le Mans Henry again approached Richard to try to work out an agreement with him on the future alignment of the Angevin territories in France. Apparently Henry's proposal was, in effect, that Richard take control of Normandy and Anjou, under the direct supervision of his father. In return for this, Henry demanded that Richard give up Aquitaine, so that the southern duchy could be set aside as an inheritance for John. Richard, while willing enough to accept Normandy and Anjou, flatly refused to give up any part of his interest in Aquitaine. Henry threatened and blustered, but Richard refused to listen. Henry softened his tones, became his most reasonable self, argued, even pleaded for Richard to change his mind. Richard still refused. He would not, he declared, give up any part of Aquitaine so long as he was alive; and, so saying, left his father's court.

Henry, whose temper was always close to the boiling point, erupted. Richard was a fool and a knave to refuse obedience to his father, Henry declared. Now, Henry turned to

John, his favorite son, and told him to invade Aquitaine and take what he wanted by force.

Henry's words may not have been completely serious: they were uttered in a fit of rage and frustration. But John was prepared to take them very seriously indeed. Over the next several months he went about making preparations for an attack on Aquitaine, enlisting the help of his half-brother Geoffrey in the enterprise. In June of 1184 they struck, as soon as their father had crossed the Channel to England, where he had urgent business to attend. The expedition of John and Geoffrey was in the main a plundering and looting foray; the two brothers were more concerned with taking booty than with securing substantial territorial gains. The clash was short-lived and never developed into a major contest, principally because King Henry, upon hearing of it, abruptly commanded his sons to lay down their arms and to meet with him forthwith in England. After a stern dressing-down, Henry demanded that they forgive one another and make peace, perhaps forgetting or conveniently ignoring the fact that he himself was in a very real way the cause of the whole affair.

Richard spent the rest of 1184 in England and was allowed to return to France only after Christmas. He sailed from Dover to Wissant and on his way to Poitou passed some time with Geoffrey, who was currently in Normandy. After this meeting, which was not likely to have been a friendly one, Richard continued on to Poitou.

His sojourn there was neither peaceful nor long. In April of 1185 Henry summoned Queen Eleanor to join him in Normandy. When Eleanor had arrived, Henry sent word to Richard that he was to give all of his Poitevin holdings back to his mother, since it was her property that he was holding. If Richard failed to comply, Henry added, then Eleanor and a sizable army would take Poitou away from him by force.

To this ultimatum Richard gave in. He surrendered Poitou to his mother's representatives and then returned to

Normandy to settle in quietly as a member of his father's court. His docility is surprising, in view of his earlier defiance of Henry's commands, but it is also quite possible that Richard counted upon his mother to prevent Henry from going through with the plans he had announced earlier of giving Aquitaine to John. Richard was Eleanor's favorite son, much as John was Henry's favorite, and Richard may well have calculated that his mother would see to it that her dowry was not carved up for John's benefit.

Externally at least, Richard's future was left vague and undecided for nearly a year, while he remained at his father's court, obedient and submissive, at least outwardly, to his father's wishes. Early in March of 1186 there was another conference between King Henry and Philip Augustus at Gisors. The conference covered much of the ground that the two kings had agreed upon more than two years earlier, in December, 1183. The only significant difference was that the new agreement in 1186 specified once again that Richard was to marry Alice, Philip Augustus's sister. What brought about this change is difficult to say. Certainly it was not a result of any renewed interest in the marriage on Richard's part, for Richard seems already to have made overtures to King Sancho of Navarre with a view to arranging a marriage between himself and Sancho's daughter Berengaria. It is more likely that the resurrection of the project to marry Richard to Alice was a result of second thoughts on Philip Augustus's part. Even if Richard was a notably reluctant candidate for Alice's hand, Philip may have decided that he would make a more appropriate husband for her than would his younger brother, John. In any event the renewed engagement of Richard and Alice was incorporated in the treaty of 1186, amid mutual guarantees of good wishes and peaceful intentions between the French and English kings. Following his meeting with Philip Augustus, Henry prepared to return to England. Just before his departure, he summoned Richard to his side, gave him a large sum of money, and ordered him to use it to wage war upon Henry's enemies in the south of France.

Richard now returned to Poitou with his father's commission in his pocket and with a large treasury in his pack train to engage in his favorite sport: war. He focused his campaign on the lands of Count Raymond of Toulouse and, with a numerous following of knights and foot soldiers, conquered a portion of Raymond's territory, in the county of Quercy. Count Raymond, taken by surprise, was unable to fight off Richard's onslaught and retreated steadily in the face of the advancing forces. Philip Augustus, to whom Raymond appealed for help, was seemingly indifferent to the situation and took no significant steps to check Richard's forces. The fighting continued haphazardly through the summer and fall of 1186, but came to a virtual standstill in the winter of 1186–87. In the spring of 1187 Philip Augustus finally intervened. He met with Henry and Richard at Gué St. Rémy early in April, 1187, but no agreement was reached between them. Following this, both sides began to prepare for a full-scale encounter.

At this point, Henry divided his forces into four divisions. The southern division of the army he gave to Richard, who thus became the operational commander of the English forces on the southern front during the subsequent hostilities. John was given command of another division, which was supposed to operate in conjunction with Richard's forces, while the other two divisions, commanded by William of Mandeville and Richard's half-brother, Geoffrey, were concentrated on the northern and central frontiers of the Angevin domains.

Philip Augustus was likewise preparing for all-out combat. He chose to concentrate his attack in the south, in the county of Berry. There he besieged Richard and John at Châteauroux and prepared for a pitched battle. At the last moment a peace agreement was patched up and a two-year truce was made. Richard played a major role in negotiating the truce and the papal legate assisted in defining the final terms, by which peace between the French and English kings was to be guaranteed for two years.

After these negotiations were completed, Philip Augustus invited Richard to join his party for a time and friendship between the two ripened quickly and warmly. They spent long hours in one another's company, eating at the same table and even sharing the same bed. Richard's father was at first astounded and then alarmed—not perhaps because of any fear for Richard's virtue, but rather because he suspected that his overlord and his son might be conniving together against him.

Peremptorily Henry summoned Richard back to join his court and Richard reluctantly agreed to come. First, however, he stopped at Chinon, where he took all of the money he could find in the Angevin treasury and brought it with him into Aquitaine, where he spent it in repairing his castles and laying in supplies against a siege. After a brief delay, he then rejoined his father and they reestablished an uneasy peace between them, with Richard doing homage to Henry for the lands which he held.

While Richard was near Tours in November of 1187 he received word of an event which was to change the course of his career and to provide the great adventure of his life. The messengers who came to him that evening near Tours brought word of the invasion of the Holy Land by Saladin and the massacre of the Latin armies defending the Holy Land by Saladin's forces. All of this had occurred in the previous July, but news of these events only reached France at the end of October or the beginning of November.

The morning after he learned of these events, Richard took the cross and made his vow as a crusader to deliver the Holy Land from the Muslim invaders.

Henry was at this point in Normandy. News of Richard's action reached him quickly and he was profoundly dismayed. For several days he kept to himself and refused to see anyone. Henry had good reason to be disturbed. The making of a crusade vow and the taking of the cross were actions that carried with them a heavy freight of responsibility, which was not easily shrugged off. It might be possible to delay embarking on the crusade, but the pope was making it increasingly difficult for crusaders to evade their obligations. The responsibilities were particularly serious for the heir to such an empire as Henry of Anjou's. As a crusader, Richard was obligated by law and by common expectation to raise an army and to go to Palestine. The costs involved would be heavy, the time invested would be long, and the perils were exceedingly great. Richard's action in becoming a crusader could well upset the whole chain of provisions which Henry had been making for the preservation of his English kingdom and his French domains.

A few days later Richard came to his father to inform him in person of what he had done. Henry reproved him for having taken so serious a step without consultation, but promised his support in making arrangements for the fulfillment of Richard's vow.

Philip Augustus was also disturbed when he heard the news of Richard's proposal to go on crusade. His own plans hinged in part on Richard's availability and if Richard were to depart for the East for an indefinite period, Philip's political calculations might be badly endangered. Philip immediately let his displeasure be known. Richard, he said, must either marry Alice at once, or else Gisors must be given back to him. Otherwise he was prepared to make war upon the Angevins and would devastate Normandy and all their other possessions on the Continent.

In the face of this threat, Henry returned at once to Normandy and hastened to Gisors. There on January 21, 1187, he met with the French king to discuss matters. They were soon joined by Archbishop William of Tyre, who had arrived from the Holy Land to secure aid for the Latin states.

Upon learning of the conference of the two kings at Gisors, the archbishop had hurried there to try to persuade them to join in the defense of the holy places. The prelate's eloquence and persuasiveness were fired by his own experiences in the East and by a vivid consciousness of the dangers which Saladin's invasion posed for the remaining outposts of Latin Christendom there. He was an able preacher, but on this occasion he seems to have surpassed even the wildest expectations, for he succeeded in persuading both Henry and Philip to join the crusade. A more unlikely pair of partners in the crusade would be difficult to imagine, but somehow William brought it off, for both of the kings accepted the cross from his hands. Perhaps they were persuaded by the vision of the cross which appeared in the sky that day and which we are told was seen by many people, laymen as well as clerics.

However that may be, arrangements for the implementation of the royal crusading vows began at once. Henry and Philip agreed that they would set out for the East a year from the date on which they had taken the cross and both kings then retired from the conference site to begin their preparations.

Henry rode from Gisors back to Le Mans, where he met at once with Richard and a quickly assembled council of bishops and lay barons. At this meeting the basic plans for the crusade were worked out. First came the matter of financing the expedition. The members of the group agreed that an extraordinary, indeed unprecedented, scheme for raising money would be needed in order to raise sufficient funds to carry out the proposed campaign. Jointly they agreed upon a plan. Although not entirely novel in every detail, the scheme involved a more extensive system of fund raising than any previously attempted. What was planned was the levy for three years of a general tax of one tenth of the value of the income and movable property of Henry's subjects, including the clergy. This Saladin tithe, as it came to be called, was to be collected in each parish. Those who failed to pay were to suffer excommunication. It was supposed to be self-assessing: each parishioner was to decide how much he owed under the provisions of the law and then to turn that amount over to the authorities of his parish, who, in turn, were to forward it for the use of those who joined in the crusade. Crusaders themselves were, naturally, exempted from paying the Saladin tithe, which was a significant inducement to persuade men to participate in the expedition. The provisions governing the Saladin tithe were an innovation of major importance, for with the Saladin tithe we have the beginning of a system of general direct taxation on a large scale, the ancestor of most modern revenue tax systems.

The council at Le Mans was concerned with other matters, too, that would advance the cause of the crusade. The council laid down regulations against gambling and excessively lavish clothing, with the aim both of reducing luxury spending and also of setting a proper moral climate for the crusade. Other enactments dealt with the privileges which the crusaders were to enjoy. They were exempted from paying interest on their loans and were granted a moratorium on the repayment of the principal as well. Beyond this, they were granted a series of tax exemptions and were excused from a variety of feudal services while they were on crusade. In addition the council discussed other arrangements for the commencement of the expedition and the governance of the realm during the absence of the king.

Once the meeting at Le Mans had concluded its work, King Henry departed for England and the machinery for preaching the crusade and recruiting men to participate in it was set in motion. Teams of crusading preachers were organized and sent systematically to canvas the population and to enlist as many as possible in the ranks.

Meanwhile, Richard had returned to Poitou, where a fresh crisis was brewing. Although Richard had evidently planned to devote himself mainly to making preparations for his own departure on crusade, the barons of the south viewed the distractions caused by his desire to leave for the Holy Land as an opportunity to raise once again the banner of revolt. The uprising was led by Aimar of Angoulême, Geoffrey of Rancogne, and Geoffrey de Lusignan, all of them perennial troublemakers and frequent opponents of Richard. At least one contemporary writer saw more sinister overtones in this rebellion than in the others which Richard had faced in the south of France. According to Gerald the Welshman, King Henry himself was the moving force behind the southern rebellion. Henry encouraged the insurgents there, Gerald says, in order to dissuade Richard from participating in the crusade. Possibly, too, Henry may have seen another rebellion in Aquitaine as a means of encouraging Richard to give up his claims to the area and to fall in with Henry's plans to assign part of Aquitaine to John.

Whatever support and encouragement the rebels may have had from Richard's father, they fought a bitter and devastating war. The original rebels were soon joined by Count Raymond of Toulouse, who stepped up the pace of the fighting and contributed an ample fund both of men and of bitterness to the struggle. Thanks to Raymond's activities, the war enlarged its scope to include attacks not only on Richard's soldiers, but also against merchants, pilgrims, and other noncombatants, who were normally supposed to be immune from the unwelcome attentions of hostile armies.

Richard retaliated by capturing and imprisoning Peter Seilun, a member of Count Raymond's household. Peter was apparently held in close confinement and suffered harsh treatment from Richard. Upon learning of this, Count Raymond complained to Philip Augustus. Raymond invited Philip to intervene in the war, alleging that Richard had attacked his lands and that this violated the terms of the truce which was supposed to be in effect between the Angevins and the French crown. Philip responded to Raymond's appeal by visiting Aquitaine in person. He seems to have made a genuine effort to patch up peace in the region, but he soon discovered that the malice and hatred between the parties to the struggle was something that could not be papered over with any compromise settlement that he could devise. He returned to his own territories, frustrated in his attempt to act as a peacemaker; but he did send a messenger to King Henry, asking him to restrain Richard and to see that amends were made for the damage that had been done. Henry replied noncommittally, stating that he took no responsibility for Richard's actions in this affair.

Richard, meanwhile, was doing quite well on his own. A quick thrust into the county of Toulouse was paying off handsomely. He had taken seventeen castles belonging to the count and was whipping his forces into positions from which he could besiege Toulouse itself. At this point, his campaign was interrupted by threats from another quarter.

However sincere Philip Augustus may have been in his earlier attempts to make peace in Aquitaine, he was now preparing to launch his own attack upon the Angevin lands in the north of France. With the aid of the warrior-Bishop of Beauvais, Philip of Dreux, Philip Augustus commenced a two-pronged attack upon the Angevins. While his kinsman, the fighting bishop, led an attack on Normandy, King Philip advanced into Touraine and Berry and by June 16 had captured Châteauroux.

King Henry was forced to return immediately from England to deal in person with the deteriorating situation on the Continent. After sending on ahead a fruitless plea for a settlement of the widening struggle, he arrived in Normandy on July 11, 1188. Henry invaded the French kingdom on August 30, 1188, leading a mixed force of English and Welsh troops. Now it was King Philip's turn to feel the brunt of a two-pronged attack. Henry advanced through Mantes, Ivry-la-Bataille, and Danville toward Philip's headquarters, burning towns, fields, and villages as he went. Richard at the same time disengaged his forces from his struggle with Raymond of Toulouse in order to counterattack Philip Augustus's forces in Berry, thus threatening Philip's armies from the south.

After three days of hard fighting, the French king had seen enough. He proposed a peace conference at Gisors, but when the parties met there they were unable to agree. Smarting with rage and frustration, Philip cut down the giant elm tree between Gisors and Trie which had for years marked the conference site for discussions between the French and English monarchs.

In the following weeks the tempo of the war quieted rapidly, in large part because Count Theobald of Blois, the count of Flanders, and other major noblemen of France refused any longer to participate in the conflict. They had pledged themselves to accompany their king on the crusade and were unwilling to take part in a war against other Christians, they said, at least until after they had returned from Jerusalem. Under pressure from his own supporters, then, Philip Augustus agreed to meet once more with King Henry and to try to reach agreement with him.

The two kings conferred briefly at Châtillon-sur-Indre on October 7, but this meeting was as unproductive as the earlier one in September. Terms were proposed for a settlement, but no agreement could be reached on the details. After a short colloquy both sides retired from Châtillon-sur-Indre without having arrived at any concord. During the next several weeks Richard made a bid to intervene. He offered to submit the quarrel between himself and the count of Toulouse to the judgment of the king of France—an offer that Henry strongly disapproved—but Philip insisted that this was not a sufficient concession and demanded that further conditions, whose nature we do not know, be imposed. Richard would not agree and negotiations were again broken off.

Another meeting between Henry and Philip took place at Bonmoulins, near Soligny, on November 18. This time Richard was in attendance. He conferred privately before the meeting with Philip Augustus and apparently they struck a secret bargain. Without consulting his father, Richard offered to do homage to Philip Augustus not only for Poitou, but also for Normandy, Anjou, Berry, Toulouse, Le Mans, and the other territories belonging to the Angevins in France. Although Richard inserted a saving clause, reserving his first fealty to his father for these lands, the message was clear. Unless Henry was willing to accede to Richard's demands, Richard was prepared to join with Philip Augustus in order to get what he wanted.

When Richard made a public offer of his fealty to Philip at the conference between the two kings, Henry seems once again to have been taken completely by surprise. He had not believed that his son would so openly defy him or that Richard would ally himself so clearly with the traditional enemies of the Angevin family. Quickly he offered Philip Augustus a cease-fire to last until St. Hilary's Day, January 13, 1189. When Philip assented to this, Henry turned and stalked away from the meeting. Philip turned to his counselors and strode off in the opposite direction with them, while Richard went his own way. Bystanders saw in the break-up of the conference a graphic portent of things to come.

Henry, Richard, and Philip each took his own course after Bonmoulins. None of them trusted either of the other two, but none of them was willing to take the first step into further open warfare. The closing weeks of 1188 and the opening months of 1189 were marked by nervous waiting and half-hearted, abortive negotiations by all of the parties involved. When the end of the truce period arrived on St. Hilary's Day, Henry pleaded illness and failed to attend the scheduled conference. Another meeting was set for February 2, but this conference also failed to materialize and Henry proposed that a further meeting be held at Easter. At that time he and Philip Augustus conferred briefly, but failed to reach a settlement. Other meetings, equally unproductive, took place between Henry and Richard. Two papal legates, one after the other, sought to mediate the quarrel, without notable success. The second legate, John of Anagni, did manage to secure half-hearted consent to an arrangement by which he and four other prelates would hear the demands of the parties and would try to arbitrate their differences. A joint meeting between the arbitrators and the parties took place near La Ferté Bernard during the week of May 28, 1189. This meeting brought only a hardening of the lines of disagreement. Philip and Richard demanded that Henry make a formal settlement of the succession on Richard, that Richard at long last be formally married to Princess Alice, and that John be required to join the crusade and accompany the expedition to Jerusalem. In return, the lands which Henry had lost during the previous two years would be handed back to him. Henry rejected these proposals and submitted a counter-proposal, which shocked and angered both Philip and Richard. Henry now submitted that Alice should be married to John and that John be given the lands that Richard demanded.

It is difficult to believe that Henry seriously meant to bargain. Certainly he could not have believed that his proposal was likely to appeal very strongly to Philip Augustus, much less to Richard. With such wide, irreconcilable differences between the parties, there was no chance that any arbitrators, no matter how skilled, could negotiate any bargain, no matter how astute, between the parties. In fact there were even suspicions that John of Anagni, the papal legate and chief arbitrator, had been bribed by Henry. Amid charges and counter-charges the meeting broke up in disarray.

Hostilities erupted immediately. While Henry was still riding back toward Le Mans, where the major part of his field army was stationed, Philip Augustus attacked and took the castle of La Ferté. In short order he was able to master the rest of the castles around Le Mans with the aid of Richard, who had also brought his armed followers to the peace conference. On June 12 Richard and Philip attacked Le Mans itself. The city was Henry's birthplace and he had just promised the citizens that he would remain there. Now he was forced to flee for his life from his native city, with the buildings of the lower town blazing about him. Richard personally did not participate in this attack on his father's stronghold. He supervised the actions of his troops, but felt apparently that filial respect required that he refrain from actual participation in the action. On this account he very nearly lost his own life, when a group of Henry's men while fleeing from the burning city doubled back and charged at him, even though he was unarmed. At the last moment their leader, William Marshall, spitted Richard's horse, instead of Richard, upon the point of his lance, and tumbled Richard into the dust.

After the capture of Le Mans, the attack on Henry's positions continued unrelentingly. The successes that Richard and Philip enjoyed were partly due to the disgust of Henry's followers with the scheme to substitute John for Richard in the plans for the succession to the Angevin domains. In any case, Henry was on the run. He headed first to the north, then doubled back to Chinon, where he holed up with a small supporting force. By now Henry was seriously ill, burning with fever, and debilitated. Meanwhile, the campaign rolled on. Tours was besieged on July 1 and fell to Philip Augustus two days later. With the fall of Tours, Henry clearly saw that further resistance was useless. On July 4 the ailing king surrendered.

The defeat was humiliating. As he lay on his bed, the peace terms were dictated to him. Henry was required to give back his French possessions to Philip Augustus, who would then return them to him on exceedingly harsh terms. Henry was required to promise a heavy cash payment of 20,000 marks to Philip. He had to agree that all of his barons, both in England and in France, would swear to accept Richard as his heir. Henry was not to take revenge on any of those who had deserted his service in order to help Richard and Philip during the recent hostilities. Any failure on Henry's part to respect the surrender terms would cancel the allegiance which his subjects owed to him. Meanwhile a number of Henry's most cherished cities would remain in the hands of Philip and Richard until they were satisfied that Henry had complied fully with their demands.

To all of this, the fever-ridden king agreed. Then he was handed a list of those who had joined forces with Philip and Richard against him, so that he would know for certain whom he had agreed to pardon. When Henry came to John's name on the list, he sat up in bed and gazed fiercely about at those present. "Is it true," he asked, "that John, my very heart, whom I have loved before all my sons, and for whose advancement I have endured all these ills, has deserted me?" He was told that this was true.

Lying back on his bed, Henry turned his face to the wall. This was the end and Henry knew it. "Now let all things go as they will," he groaned, "I care no longer for myself or for anything else in the world."

A short time later, Richard came to his father's bedside. Honor demanded—and the surrender terms had stipulated—that Henry must be reconciled with his son by giving him the kiss of peace. The ceremony was formally enacted. Father and son embraced. As Henry settled back on his bed, Richard turned to leave the room. On his way out, Richard heard his father mutter: "God grant I die not before I have worthily revenged myself on you!" They never met again.

Two days later, on July 6, 1189, Henry died at Chinon. Richard learned of his death while he was with Philip Augustus at Tours, celebrating their victory. Henry's bastard son, Geoffrey, was the only one of Henry's sons to have been present at his father's deathbed.

Henry's burial was to take place at the abbey of Fontevrault. The king's body was carried there on the shoulders of William Marshall and a handful of other loyal followers, who honored their allegiance to Henry even in death. The rest of his household made off with Henry's last remaining possessions and even stripped the clothes from his body.

Henry might have been buried naked, save that one of the young squires of his household donated his short cloak to cover the dead monarch. His attendants had to go out begging to borrow a ring to put on his finger as he lay in his coffin.

When Richard came to the abbey church for his father's funeral, some of those present swore that Henry's corpse began to bleed from the nostrils, a sign, they said, that Richard was his father's murderer.

The next day the old king was buried in his borrowed finery at Fontevrault. He is still there, covered by a funeral effigy, in company with Queen Eleanor and Richard.

FOUR

Preparations for the Crusade (1189–1190)

The first year of Richard's reign as king was dominated above all by his preparations for the crusade expedition which was the focal point of his whole career. Within one year, almost to the day, of King Henry's death, Richard was to depart from Western Europe on an adventure whose outcome no one could predict. Before he left, it was essential to lay a solid foundation for the crusade expedition itself. It was a year of hectic activity and almost incessant work of the kind that Richard least enjoyed. Nonetheless, it was absolutely essential to the success of his crusade that the work be gotten through. Even Richard, whose capacity for administrative detail and taste for systematic planning was virtually nil, could appreciate the need for the labors which occupied the first year of his rule as king.

Richard's first act upon his father's death, while Henry's body still awaited burial at Fontevrault, was to dispatch messengers to England. They carried Richard's instructions to release his mother, Queen Eleanor, from captivity and to appoint her as his representative in England until he could make the journey to his new kingdom in person.

After Henry's funeral, Richard dealt immediately and

harshly with those who had participated in the revolt against his father. With splendid inconsistency, he attacked those who, a few days earlier, had been his allies. He made it clear to the court which now surrounded him that the rebels could expect no mercy from him. The only exception to the rule was Richard's younger brother, John. To him Richard was prepared to act magnanimously and when John appeared at court, Richard received him with honor and permitted him to accompany the royal household into Normandy.

Once the ceremonies attendant upon King Henry's funeral were completed, Richard moved immediately to consolidate his claims to his new inheritance. His haste was entirely natural, for succession to the throne by inheritance was a novelty in England and Richard's title might have been challenged if he had not soon secured its acknowledgment by the magnates of his new domains.

His first move was to secure his title to the Norman duchy at Rouen, where he was formally girded by the archbishop with the sword symbolizing his new office. While he was at Rouen he also took care of some familial arrangements. He formally bestowed the county of Mortain upon his brother John. He also confirmed to his half-brother Geoffrey his intention to carry out a promise that Henry II had made, namely that Geoffrey should become archbishop of York.

As soon as these matters had been dispatched, Richard hurried to meet with Philip Augustus in order to reach a settlement with him. Because of the help he had received from Philip in the past, during his disagreements with his father, Richard must have anticipated that Philip's demands would be set high. They met on July 20 between Chaumont and Trie. In the opening stages of the bargaining, Philip demanded that Gisors be given back to him. This Richard was unwilling to do, but as a counter-offer he renewed his promise to marry Philip's sister Alice, provided that Gisors was left under his control as part of her dowry. Philip was willing to settle for this concession on the territorial issue, but he had further demands to press. He wanted hard cash, as well as promises. Earlier, King Henry had promised to pay him 20,000 silver marks as part of the surrender terms just before his death. Now Philip renewed his demands for this payment; in addition he required that Richard add to it a further sum of 4,000 silver marks, bringing the total payment to 24,000 marks in all. Richard agreed, no doubt reluctantly, to this arrangement.

The other outstanding item to be negotiated concerned the preparations for the crusade. The two kings agreed that they would carry through that project jointly. They discussed some of the details which had to be settled in organizing the expedition and agreed that they would set out on their crusade during the following Lent.

Once they had reached agreement on the arrangements for the crusade, the meeting broke up and the two kings went their separate ways. Richard spent the next three weeks in his Norman duchy, acquainting himself with the duchy and with his new subjects, in order to confirm their adhesion to the new government. Meanwhile his mother, the dowager Queen Eleanor, was making a royal tour of the English kingdom, trooping from city to city, castle to castle, surveying her son's realm and assuring by her presence the loyalty of his English subjects and their willingness to accept Richard as their ruler. She was also much concerned with clearing the jails of their inmates. Having spent the past sixteen years as a prisoner herself, Eleanor was understandably enthusiastic to oversee in person the implementation of a general pardon for all kinds of prisoners, which Richard had authorized her to undertake. The principal condition for the release of large numbers of prisoners was that they swear their allegiance to Richard and Eleanor, undertaking to support the new regime "against all men and women who can live and die," and that they promise to give the new government their support in preserving the peace. This tactic was bound to assure the new king and his mother the enthusiastic support not only of the liberated jailbirds, but also of their families.

On August 13, 1189, six weeks after King Henry's death, Richard and his party sailed from Barfleur to Portsmouth, while his brother John and another group landed at Dover. The two brothers were enthusiastically received in England. There was a widespread hope that Richard would become a reforming king and that he might prove more liberal toward his subjects than his father had been. The liberation of prisoners which had already taken place seemed to justify these hopes and Richard's popularity among his new subjects soared. On the following day at Winchester, he was formally received on English soil by his mother and a large group of court officials, who added to the enthusiasm of the crowds their own assurances of welcome on behalf of the ecclesiastical and official establishment.

Preparations were already in progress for Richard's coronation and his official accession to the throne, but Richard, unlike all of his predecessors since the Conquest, was in no great hurry to be crowned. He had no immediate rivals to contend with, any danger of an insurrection by the nobility seemed to have passed, and therefore there was no need to clap the crown on his head at the earliest possible moment. In contrast to earlier English kings, Richard's coronation was to be the formal ratification of a general acceptance of his succession, not a necessary prerequisite to secure his grasp on a disputed throne.

His progress from Winchester to London, where the coronation was scheduled to take place, was accordingly slow and leisurely. It was marked by scenes of rejoicing and acclamation at every stopping point. From Winchester he went to Salisbury, where he rewarded Andrew of Chauveny for past services by giving him the daughter of Ralf de Deols as his wife and granting him the lands of Châteauroux and Berry. Another faithful aide, upon whom Richard was to rely heavily, was William Marshall, who had been one of the mainstays of King Henry's regime and whose doughty courage and high sense of honor appealed mightily to Richard as well. William was also given a wealthy wife, the daughter and heir of Richard of Clare, earl of Pembroke.

A week later at Marlborough Richard witnessed another wedding. The bridgegroom this time was his brother John, who married Isabel, the daughter and co-heir of Earl William of Gloucester. The marriage was under a cloud, because of the close family relationship between John and Isabel, who were second cousins. On this account the archbishop of Canterbury had already ruled that it violated the laws of the Church relating to consanguinity and had forbidden the marriage to be celebrated. Richard insisted, however, and the ceremony took place despite the archbishop's objections. Richard took the occasion of John's marriage to make a handsome settlement upon him, thus providing him with revenues and social status befitting the brother of a king. John received, among other things, the counties of Gloucester, Nottingham, and Derby, including five major fortified castles, and numerous forests, villages, and all of their inhabitants.

On the day after John's wedding, Richard went to Windsor, where he greeted his half-brother Geoffrey, who had by now been elected archbishop of York. Geoffrey's election had been opposed by Queen Eleanor, who was perhaps reluctant to see her husband's bastard promoted to high office. Several of the leading officials of the English realm had also opposed Geoffrey's promotion on the grounds that he seemed to be entirely unsuited to the role of a bishop and pastor in the Church. Geoffrey was, indeed, an incongruous candidate for the position. He had little training to fit him for the office of archbishop and he was notable neither for his sanctity of conduct nor for his learning and administrative experience. Moreover he was uncommonly ambitious, hotheaded, impatient, quarrelsome, and stubborn. Nonetheless he was the king's brother and if that was his only qualification to be an archbishop, in Richard's eyes it was enough.

Richard had insisted upon the appointment and those who opposed it had reluctantly given way.

From Windsor on September 1 the royal party made its ceremonial entry into London, where the new king was formally received by the city fathers at St. Paul's Church. He then had a day's rest, before embarking on the exhausting ceremonies of his coronation.

The ceremony took place on September 3, 1189, at Westminster Abbey. Archbishop Baldwin of Canterbury officiated. He was assisted by Geoffrey, archbishop-elect of York, and more than thirty other archbishops, bishops and abbots. When the royal procession entered the abbey, it was packed with the leading nobles and officials of the English kingdom. Godfrey de Lucy led the official party, bearing the royal cap, and he was followed by other dignitaries who carried the insignia of the king: his golden spurs, his scepter topped with a cross and another scepter emblazoned with a dove. John, the king's brother, carried one of the ceremonial swords and was accompanied by the earl of Huntingdon and the earl of Leicester, each with an additional sword. After them came six barons and six earls, holding a checkered board on which were piled the royal vestments. Then came Earl William of Aumale, who carried the crown itself. At the end of the procession, under a silken canopy held by four barons, marched Richard, flanked by the bishops of Durham and Bath.

The procession wended its way down the abbey nave toward the high altar. The members of the procession ranged themselves around the sanctuary, while Richard took his place immediately in front of the altar. He commenced the ceremony by taking three formal oaths, guaranteeing his subjects that he would honor the Church and its decrees and maintain it in peace, that he would grant justice to his subjects, and that he would keep the good laws and customs of the kingdom and abolish any that were evil and unjust. Then he took off the robes which he had worn into the abbey and was ritually dressed in the royal vestments. After the archbishop had anointed him with sacred oils and consecrated him as king, he put on the sword of justice and his golden spurs. Then he was led up the steps to the altar, where the archbishop gave him a ceremonial warning that he must respect the promises which he had just uttered in his coronation oaths. Following this solemn adjuration came the coronation itself. The archbishop lifted the crown from the altar and placed it on Richard's head. Then taking the two scepters, he placed one in each of Richard's hands.

With the crown on his head and the scepters in his hands, Richard was led from the altar to the throne, as the choir sang the *Te Deum,* while candlebearers and sword bearers preceded him. Once he had been seated on the throne, the Mass began, during which Richard was attended by the two bishops who had escorted him into the abbey. After the king had received communion and the Mass was ended, Richard was led in procession out the abbey to his apartments, still bearing the royal insignia.

Once the ceremony was completed, Richard put off the heavy, intricate royal robes and crown and substituted for them lighter, more comfortable garments and a simpler crown. Then came another, more light-hearted procession, this one to the banqueting hall, where Richard was seated at a table on a raised dais, surrounded by the archbishops and the other prelates who had participated in the coronation. The lay nobility on this occasion had to dine at other tables.

The state banquet was long, elaborate, and festive. The royal household had outdone itself. More than 5,000 extra dishes had to be bought for the feast, to say nothing of 900 cups and nearly 1,800 pitchers. The joy of the occasion was marred, however, by an unexpected incident.

On the day before his coronation Richard had ordered that no women and no Jews were to be suffered to attend any of the coronation ceremonies or the festivities which followed them. The Jewish community of London, however, was determined to demonstrate its loyalty to the new king. In defiance of the king's order, a delegation of London Jews forced their way into the banquet hall, bearing gifts which they wished to offer to the new monarch. As they attempted to enter the main dining hall, they were attacked by a group of Richard's courtiers, who beat them and stole the presents which they had brought for Richard.

The Jewish leaders were forcibly ejected from the coronation festivities and thrown, bruised and bleeding, into the street. When the crowds milling about the palace saw what was happening, they joined in the fray and set upon the unfortunate Jews once more. Several of the Jews had been killed and the others were only half alive, when the crowd decided to invade the Jewish quarter of the city in order to finish there what they had begun at Westminster. The massacring, burning and plundering continued through the night and into the early hours of the next day, despite an effort by Richard to put a halt to the rioting. Some of the London Jews were able to escape by finding a haven in the Tower, while a few others were hidden by friends. The rest were beaten, raped, murdered, and cremated in the ruins of the Jewish quarter. The example of the capital city was quickly imitated in the provinces. One after another Lynn, Norwich, Lincoln, Stamford, and York saw sickening reenactments of the brutal events in London.

On the day after his coronation, Richard took action against some of the rioters. Three of them were hanged, to be sure, but they were all men who had been overly enthusiastic and had attacked Christians in the general excitement of the night. Still, Richard was offended, since by law the Jews of England belonged to the king and were under royal protection. The attack upon them was an attack both upon royal property and upon the royal prerogatives, neither of which Richard was prepared to sacrifice. Accordingly he issued stern orders for the punishment of those responsible and caused his decree to be published in every county of the kingdom. By the time this was done, however, it was too late to save many of his Jewish subjects and the Jewish communities never completely recovered from the effects of Richard's coronation day.

The ghastly events outside of Westminster, it would seem, had some dampening effect upon the revels celebrating the coronation. They were not sufficient, however, to halt the celebrations, which continued for three days.

Once the coronation was over, it was time for Richard to get down to business. The royal treasury at Winchester had been inventoried as soon as Richard landed in England and the reports of the accountants were gloomy. They had found approximately 100,000 silver marks in ready cash, to be sure, but this sum was not likely to be sufficient to sustain the level of expenditures that Richard could foresee. He already owed 24,000 marks to Philip Augustus and this would soon have to be paid out, reducing the treasury by almost one fourth. Then there were the expenses of the coronation itself, which was as costly as it was lavish. The regular expenses of the court and the administration would soon eat through the rest, unless Richard was minded to economize.

In fact, Richard's plans involved quite the opposite course. He was committed to depart on crusade within a few months and the expenses of this would clearly be enormous. Meanwhile, the ordinary expenses of the royal administration would continue to demand funds, under any circumstances. With the king absent from the country for an indeterminate period, administrative expenses were likely to be greater, not less, than normal. In addition, the generous grants which Richard had already made to John had cut into the revenues of the crown, since the income from the lands which had been given to John had formerly been channeled into the treasury.

Clearly Richard needed to raise money and to raise it on a very large scale indeed if he were to meet his foreseeable expenses. There was no simple way to improve the financial yields from the ordinary resources of the crown. The income from landed property was relatively static and could be increased only slightly, if at all, over any short-term period. Likewise the normal income from fees and licenses was not likely to increase markedly in the ordinary course of events, since these rates were fixed and could not easily or quickly be changed.

In the light of this situation, Richard was going to have to raise his needed revenues by some extraordinary measures. The methods he chose were crude but effective. Richard's solution to his financial problem was to put the offices of the kingdom up for sale. Every sheriff found himself summarily removed from office on one pretext or another, no matter how flimsy. He could regain his position—and the income which went with it—only by paying a substantial fine to the king. Castellans, manorial lords, earls, in short every class and every kind of office holder, found the same sort of thing happening. And as they paid up, the money flowed into Richard's war chest. Nor were office holders the only source for the revenues which he sought. Monasteries found their privileges endangered and paid handsomely to secure a parchment from the king assuring them that they could keep what they had. Cities found that new and more generous charters could be secured in return for handsome payments to the king. Everything, or nearly everything, in the kingdom could suddenly be had, if the price was right. "The king most obligingly unburdened all those whose money was a burden to them," one contemporary wrote, "and he gave to whomever he pleased whatever powers and possessions they chose." When Richard joked one day with his courtiers that "If I could have found a buyer, I would have sold London itself," he was not being entirely facetious. He found, too, that the business of the crusade itself could be made to yield a profit. Many of those who, in the first moments of shock at hearing of the disasters in the Holy Land, had impulsively responded by vowing to go on crusade, were not on second thought so anxious to attempt the journey. They could be relieved of their crusading vows, through the generosity of the king, by contributing sizable amounts to Richard's war chest.

Within a few weeks of Richard's coronation the money was beginning to roll in nicely and considerable sums were already beginning to accumulate in the Exchequer. The bishopric of Ely, to take one example, was vigorously exploited. Its incumbent, Geoffrey Ridel, had died shortly after greeting Richard on his arrival at Winchester. From the bishop's estate Richard was able to confiscate 3,000 marks in cash, as well as goods valued at considerably more than that. In addition, when Richard named one of his favorite attendants, William Longchamp, as bishop to succeed Geoffrey, he also made him chancellor of the realm, for which he was paid £3,000. To take another example, Henry II's old justiciar, Ranulf de Glanvil, with whom Richard apparently had a falling out early in his reign, was deposed from his office and imprisoned. Ranulf regained his freedom, but not his office, by paying Richard £15,000. Ranulf's deputy, Rener, paid an additional 1,000 marks (£666 13s. 4d.) in order to keep in the new king's good graces. To appreciate the enormity of these sums, one must keep in mind that the accountable income of the crown in the last year of King Henry's reign stood at slightly less than £50,000. Obviously Richard's frantic money-raising at the beginning of his reign yielded revenues far in excess of the normal funds which the English king could dispose of.

If the sums raised were very considerable, however, Richard's outlay was just as great, if not somewhat greater. The preparations for the crusade were enormously costly. Material of every kind had to be laid in: 50,000 horseshoes, for example, together with such things as ship fittings, rations, and the like certainly absorbed a considerable part of the revenues which the king was raising. The wages of mercenary soldiers and their equipment were also a considerable item. Professional cavalrymen, largely recruited from Wales, were paid 4 d. a day in wages, while infantrymen received half that amount. Full-fledged knights commanded approximately 1 s. daily. Arrangements of all kinds for provisioning the army and making ready the ships to convey it occupied Richard's days, as well as eating up his revenues as fast as he could raise them.

In addition to his preoccupation with revenues and the outfitting of his crusading expedition, Richard was also involved during the months following his coronation with another set of problems. Before he could set out on crusade, it was imperative that he make arrangements for the governance of his English kingdom during his absence, and for the safeguarding of his Continental possessions as well. The problems in both areas were formidable, but in some senses the solutions to the problem in England were less complex. In part this was true because of Richard's considerable popularity and the absence of any organized opposition to his rule there. In part, too, the institutional structures which Richard found ready-made and functioning in England were reliable and more fully developed than those which he inherited in his French domains, where he had to face the additional fact of the presence of a number of armed and capable opponents.

The arrangements that he made in England showed up some of the basic weaknesses of Richard as a ruler. He had little political wisdom and he was a poor judge of character. His design was, in effect, to partition the control of the kingdom between two justiciars, one of whom would act during the king's absence as his representative in the area north of the Humber River, while the other would concentrate his attention on the south. The geographical demarcation of the two spheres of authority was not clear-cut, however, and in practice each justiciar could easily find a basis for claiming the right to exercise power in the bailiwick of the other. The inevitable result was a conflict between the two, rather than the harmonious balance of authority, which Richard had presumably intended to achieve.

If the principles upon which Richard's provisions for government during his absence were dubious, his implementation of them was very nearly disastrous. For he chose as his two justiciars men who were not only able, but also ambitious and unscrupulous. The justiciar in the north was to be Hugh du Puiset, bishop of Durham, who reputedly paid £10,000 for the appointment. For his justiciar in the south, Richard named William Longchamp, bishop of Ely, who was also chancellor of the kingdom, as well as papal legate to England. As if to assure trouble between the two justiciars, Richard granted control of Windsor Castle to Hugh, while giving Longchamp the Tower of London.

Compounding the problems created by the dual justiciarship was the further difficulty created by Richard's overly handsome treatment of his brother John. Since King Henry's death, Richard had lavished one gift after another on his younger brother. On December 5, 1189, Richard added to his earlier gifts the counties of Cornwall, Devon, Dorset, and Somerset. Despite John's already dismal record of mismanaging his affairs and squandering the gifts which had been bestowed on him, Richard continued to aggravate the problem by giving John more. His actions here are puzzling. Before his death, Richard's father had planned to supplant Richard in favor of John, by endowing the younger brother with almost all of Richard's landed possessions on the Continent. That Richard should resent this was only natural: it would have been equally natural for him to have resented the younger brother whom his father had so outrageously favored and to deprive him of his inheritance after his father's death. Richard did quite the contrary. By the time that he was ready to depart from England on crusade, Richard had made over to John lands which brought in an income of £4,000 a year and more. It has been suggested that in doing so, Richard, who had been a disobedient son during his father's lifetime, was attempting to fulfill his father's designs after his death. It was as if he was attempting to salve his conscience for the guilt which he may well have felt for helping to cause his father's death. His treatment of John may reflect an effort to alleviate a conscious or unconscious feeling that Richard had been a party to parricide. Certainly on any rational basis, his generosity to John made no sense. The lands which Richard gave to his brother in England constituted a very handsome principality, embracing all of the southern coast of England, together with a large portion of the Midlands in addition. The mere existence of such a wide block of lands held by a single individual constituted a virtual invitation to rebellion and a certain danger to the stability of the monarchy.

There were those who took Richard's generosity to his brother as a sign that he did not expect to return to England at all. There were rumors that he was in poor health, which some attributed to an immoderate amount of soldiering during his youth. Beyond this, his actions since his arrival in England could easily be interpreted to indicate that his mind was unsettled, if not actually unbalanced.

Certainly few monarchs could have created so potentially disastrous a situation as Richard did during the first four months he spent in England. At the beginning of his reign, his subjects welcomed him because they hoped that he would tax them less harshly than his father had done. Instead, he multiplied the levies on the populace of the realm and squeezed every penny he could find out of the English kingdom. He had completely unsettled the government, turning out the experienced administrators whom King Henry had placed in office over the years and substituting for them anyone who could pay well enough to secure the king's favor. He had made his bastard half-brother Geoffrey archbishop of York, despite opposition from every level of the English hierarchy. The archbishop of Canterbury, whose moral authority and experience would have been of the highest value in maintaining domestic peace during his absence, was constrained to accompany Richard on the crusade, while hundreds of others were excused from the fulfillment of their crusade vows. Richard created an admirable base of operations for his greedy and untrustworthy brother John and then set off on the perilous and uncertain war far from his kingdom without designating an heir.

When Richard sailed from Dover on December 12, 1189, there was ample reason for his English subjects to wonder in dismay what kind of king it was they had and what prospects the future might hold for the realm.

Richard landed at Calais, where he was met by Count Philip of Flanders, who accompanied him into Normandy. He spent the Christmas holidays at Lyons-la-Forêt and then rode to Nonancourt, where he met in council with Philip Augustus on December 30. Their talks at Nonancourt centered on the preparations for their crusade and the final arrangements which had to be agreed upon before they could depart. They compared notes with one another on the preparations which each had in hand for the expedition and agreed on a date for departure, which was set at the end of the week following Easter, that is April 1, 1190. Other matters discussed were the monarchs' relationships with one another and the safeguarding of their own possessions and those of their subjects while they were on crusade. The principles on which they agreed were relatively conventional ones, in use for half a century or more and dictated by the canon law of the Church. In essence what was involved was an agreement by each monarch that he would respect the property rights of the other and that he would countenance no attack upon the other's possessions until they had both returned from the crusade. They also undertook to guarantee the same rights and protection to each other's subjects. Both kings decreed that their representatives were to supervise the implementation of the guarantees during the absence of their monarchs.

By the middle of January it was apparent to both kings that they had been too optimistic in setting their departure for April 1. On January 13 they met again and agreed to postpone the beginning of their expedition until the Feast of St.

John the Baptist on June 24. Subsequently they agreed to another postponement and rescheduled their departure to July 1, 1190. Meanwhile the preparations for the crusade went ahead at an increasing tempo. In mid-March Richard summoned his mother and a group of English magnates to meet in council with him at Nonancourt. There the arrangements concerning the two justiciars, William Longchamp and Hugh du Puiset, were made final and the king's two brothers, Archbishop Geoffrey of York and Count John, were required to take an oath that they would not return to England during the next three years. The object of this, clearly, was to prevent the king's brothers from encroaching upon his prerogatives while he was on crusade and to leave the justiciars a free hand in conducting the affairs of the kingdom during Richard's absence. Richard was not able, however, to remain consistent in this policy. Queen Eleanor apparently asked him to change his mind and to allow John to return to England. The queen mother considered John to be Richard's natural heir and she wanted John to be on hand in England so that he could take over the government quickly if Richard should happen to die while he was on crusade. In the end Eleanor had her way. Richard released John from his oath and permitted him to return to England. Richard's change of mind was later to bring him a multitude of grief.

At the beginning of April Richard sent Longchamp, his chancellor and chief justiciar, back to England with a commission to attend to some last minute preparations for the crusade. One of the main items of business which the chancellor was commissioned to take care of was to find a sufficient supply of horses for the expedition. He was authorized to requisition four horses from each city in the kingdom and two horses from every manor that belonged to the king. These animals were collected and shipped to Normandy, where they were used by Richard and the forces which he raised on the Continent.

The other principal business with which the chancellor was charged was the raising of ships to transport Richard's forces to the Holy Land. Preliminary orders concerning the requisition of a fleet had been issued long before, but now the actual delivery of the vessels and their dispatch to the departure ports had to be taken in hand. This was Longchamp's job. The terms on which the vessels were secured varied from case to case. Some vessels were already in the king's possession and were in ordinary use for transporting him and his court back and forth from England to Normandy. These smaller vessels had to be refitted and equipped for the longer, more demanding voyage to the East. Other, heavier ships were requisitioned from the port cities in Richard's domains, both in England and on the Continent. Still others were purchased, sometimes at bargain prices. In addition, some ships were donated to the king by individual magnates as their contribution to the crusade.

The greater part of Richard's army planned to travel by sea virtually the whole way from their departure ports to the Holy Land. In June, while Richard was at Chinon, he issued an ordinance to govern the conduct of the fleet and of the soldiers who sailed in his ships. The ordinance was relatively elementary in the cases for which it provided, but it was framed to cover some situations which Richard evidently foresaw as likely problems during the journey.

Whoever shall kill a man on ship-board, the king wrote, shall be bound to the dead man and thrown into the sea. If he shall slay him on land, he shall be bound to the dead man and buried in the ground. If any one shall be convicted by lawful witnesses of having drawn a knife with which to strike another, or shall strike another so as to draw blood, he shall lose his hand. Also, if he shall give a blow with his hand without drawing blood, he shall be plunged three times into the sea. If any man shall curse, swear, or revile his fellows, he shall pay an ounce of silver for each offence. A thief convicted of robbery shall have his head clipped, just like a champion, and boiling pitch shall be poured on it and the feathers of a cushion shall be shaken upon him, so that he may be recognised and he shall be put ashore the first time the ship touches land.*

The ordinance is eloquent, both in the type of behavior that it seeks to regulate (and which Richard presumably foresaw as causing trouble) and in the forthright way in which culprits are to be dealt with. Richard further appointed five justiciars—two bishops and three laymen—to sail with the fleet and to act as the commanders of the crew and the army while they were at sea.

Other things, too, demanded his attention. In the late spring of 1190 Richard made a journey into Aquitaine and still farther south into the county of Bigorre in the Pyrenees. There he made a show of force, to remind his subjects that his claims to their loyalty were still in force and that he was prepared to make use of his prerogatives. In the process he attacked and captured an outlaw nobleman, William of Chis, who had been molesting pilgrims passing through the Pyrenees on their way to Santiago de Compostella. Richard had William hanged in order to make the moral of the incident plain to his subjects.

But Richard had other reasons for his journey into the south, beyond simply hanging an errant bandit. His father had discovered in the last years of his life that Normandy and Aquitaine were increasingly difficult to control. The French king had over the years gradually grown more successful in finding allies in Berry and Touraine. With the increase of French royal authority in this central area, the possibility of holding Normandy and Aquitaine together grew progressively dimmer. Richard was quite clever enough to see the point of these developments. With the help of his mother and

---

* *Gesta Regis Ricardi I*, s.a. 1190, ed. W. Stubbs, pp. 110–111.

her still formidable prestige, Richard began to make alliances in the south. He could no longer afford the luxury of making enemies there indiscriminately. Instead he slowly but consistently began to change the center of power within the Angevin empire. During Henry II's lifetime that center had been located in Normandy. Under Richard the center shifted to Aquitaine.

There were other matters to be seen to as well. He founded two small monasteries during the months before embarking on the crusade. One of them was the Augustinian house of Lieu-Dieu, near the mouth of the river Jard. This monastery was endowed with the lordship of Talmont, once a part of Eleanor of Aquitaine's dowry. The other was the priory of St. Andrew of Gourfaille in the Vendée. The foundation of these two religious houses embodied Richard's hopes that the monastic communities of his new monasteries would intercede for him with God and would thus help to assure the success of his crusade.

June 18 found Richard back at Chinon, where there were some final details to be taken care of prior to his departure. Richard was busy for a week with various matters at Chinon—granting charters, issuing last minute commands, and generally wrapping up his administrative business. On June 24, he moved to Tours. There, three days later, he was formally invested with the pilgrim's insignia of purse and staff by the archbishop of the city. Now Richard had technically become a pilgrim and was on his journey to the Holy Land.

Leaving Tours on June 27, he made his way slowly to Vézelay, reaching there on July 2. At Vézelay he met Philip Augustus and the kings spent two days readying for their joint departure, accompanied by their retinues, court officials, servants, and friends. On July 4, 1190, they set out at last on the great adventure. The anniversary of King Henry's death fell two days after their departure.

FIVE

✠————————————————————————————✠

Richard's Crusade: From Vézelay to Famagusta (1190–1191)

From Vézelay the two kings followed a leisurely road south to Lyon, which they reached on July 10. At Lyon they and their combined parties crossed the Rhône River. They planned to follow the east bank of the Rhône in their passage farther south. When the major part of their followers had passed over the river the bridge the forces were using suddenly collapsed. It was a narrow wooden structure, set on pilings in the river and seemingly the congested traffic of the crusading force with its heavy supply wagons overburdened it. The casualties were numerous: several persons were killed, more were injured in the mishap. The crowds of crusaders trapped on the west bank of the river and isolated from the rest of the force proceeded to build a bridge out of boats, which Richard ordered his men to requisition from the communities up and down the river.

After this unsettling incident, Richard's party separated from the one led by Philip Augustus. While King Philip's forces headed for Genoa, where Philip had made arrangements for sea transport, Richard and his followers meanwhile set out for Marseille. Richard had directed the justiciars of his fleet to meet him there and the fleet itself had set out from

English ports four months earlier, soon after Easter. Part of the fleet had stopped on the way in Portugal, where the soldiers had briefly disembarked and lent their assistance to the Portuguese king, who was engaged in his own crusade against the Iberian Moors.

The delay of the naval forces en route was, of course, unknown to Richard. He reached Marseille on July 31 and was disappointed to find that his fleet had not yet arrived. At Marseille he waited for a week, expecting the fleet to arrive at any time. When the fleet had still not appeared by August 7, Richard's patience gave out. He leased two large transport ships and twenty smaller vessels and set sail in them with his court and immediate followers. He had earlier agreed with Philip that their two armies would rendezvous at Messina in Sicily and Richard now set out in that direction. He deliberately held down the speed of his journey, in the hope that his own fleet would soon catch up with his hired ships, but in this he was disappointed.

Richard's journey down the Italian coast was slow, but it was not without interest. Coasting at a leisurely pace, he reached Genoa on the thirteenth of August, then made for Portofino, where he spent five days. By the twentieth of August he was at Pisa, where he made a brief stop and where the bishop of Rouen joined the royal party. Sailing from Pisa, he disembarked for a few hours at Piombino, where he took the opportunity to mount a horse for a change and cantered down the coast a few miles, pacing his fleet, which continued on its way while the king paralleled its course on land. When he reached the castle of Piombino he rejoined his ships and they set out again under fair winds. On August 25 he reached the mouth of the Tiber River and sailed a short way upstream. There he had his ships moored, while he dealt with a party of clerics who had come to greet him on behalf of the pope and to invite him to visit the city of Rome, which was only some sixteen miles away. Richard was not inclined to be entertained. He was irritated by a number of minor snags in his recent dealings with the papal court and he took this chance to complain loudly and in bad humor about all of them to the bishop of Ostia, Cardinal Octavian, who headed the papal delegation. His list of complaints was garrulous and the king was obviously in a bad humor. The Roman curia, he fumed, had taken advantage of him and had charged exorbitant fees for processing his recent requests for favors. Petulantly he refused the pope's invitation. Instead he again mounted a horse and rode off from Ostia through the forested paths of the Selva di Nettuno to the castle of Nettuno, where he rejoined his small band of ships and reembarked. They continued their journey down the coast and on the twenty-eighth of August arrived at Naples. There Richard spent ten days, resting and sightseeing in the vicinity of the city. On September 8 he resumed his journey once again, this time by land and rode thirty-one miles to Salerno. He took advantage of his visit to this ancient city, long famous for its skilled medical practitioners, to seek advice about his own health. The local doctors were flattered to be consulted and Richard took five more days to secure their opinions. He sought their counsel about the best methods of dealing with the hazards to be encountered in the East and the most efficacious medicines for counteracting the various ills which he was subject to. In truth, Richard seems to have been something of a hypochondriac, at least when he had nothing more pressing or more interesting to worry about, and was perpetually concerned with the state of his physical well-being. The Salerno physicians gave him an opportunity to indulge in one of his minor hobbies and, if they were unable to do much of real value for his body, no doubt they provided some reassurance for his mind.

While Richard was at Salerno he at last received some news about his fleet. It had arrived at Marseille, according to the report, on August 22 and after a week's layover had sailed directly for Messina. This was the news Richard had been waiting for. As soon as he learned of it he set out for Messina, though not in unbecoming haste. On this stage of his journey he traveled by land, wending his way through Amalfi, Scalea, Santa Eufemia and Mileta. At Bagnara he was joined by his servants, who had come on from Messina to meet him. On September 22 he reached the outskirts of Messina, where he camped for the night, and on the next day he made his formal entry into the city.

Richard's arrival at Messina was a performance calculated to awe and impress both the local magnates and their followers and also the crusading army itself. For this occasion, Richard mustered his resources of showmanship and bravado in order to outshine King Philip Augustus, who had entered the city quietly and with minimal display a week earlier. Richard, in contrast, pulled out all the stops. Trumpets and clarions were massed to sound the signal of his arrival. Armor was polished until it shone. Ships were drawn up to escort King Richard and his party. At the signal to commence the trumpets let out a blast which rocked the town and terrified its inhabitants. Amid the calls of the brass instruments, Richard's army debarked from the ships and marched into Messina, clashing their swords and bucklers to add to the noise and to augment the impression of the English king's power and wealth.

The local notables lined up on the shore to witness the event and were suitably gratified by the din and display of the arrival. As soon as King Richard came ashore, Philip Augustus stepped forward from his place in the crowd to greet him. Philip was followed by a delegation of the Sicilian nobility, headed by Reginald de Moyac, who conducted Richard and his aides to his own house where a banquet was prepared for them. It was all very much to Richard's taste and satisfied his liking for the theatrical gesture. But there were also practical considerations involved. The display of Richard's arrival was calculated to forcefully impress both upon the Sicilians and the rest of the crusading forces Richard's wealth and power. It was, in short, a bid to establish a psychological ascendancy over the situation at Messina and over Philip Augustus in particular.

This was a competition that Philip Augustus could not win and apparently he knew it. Instead of trying to outdo Richard in the kinds of displays that delighted Richard, Philip chose to play a discreet, waiting role. He embraced Richard warmly upon his arrival and kissed him to show his delight at the English king's arrival. The French and English armies mingled with one another and onlookers were impressed by their apparent unity of purpose and their mutual friendliness.

The outward signs of harmony and friendliness carried over into the next several days. On August 24, Richard and Philip met again at Richard's lodgings in Messina to confer about their future plans. The meeting was marked by abundant signs of sweetness and light between the two monarchs. It seemed, according to one writer, "That such was the mutual delight and affection between them that their love for each other could never be dissolved or violated."

King Tancred of Sicily also went out of his way to demonstrate his good will toward Richard, both by his personal attitude and also by allowing Richard's sister, Queen Joan, to join her brother on the crusade. Joan was the widow of the late King William of Sicily. Although William's aunt, Constance, who was married to Henry VI of Germany, claimed the right to inherit the Sicilian throne, she and her husband were unpopular with the Sicilian nobility. The nobles had chosen Tancred as their king in defiance of Constance's hereditary claims and, with the backing of the nobility, Tancred was now in control. As the reigning king, Tancred insisted that the dowager queen, Joan, was subject to him. By allowing her to accompany Richard, Tancred was granting Richard a favor of some significance. But Richard was not entirely satisfied. In addition to his sister's person, he also wanted the dowry she had brought with her to Sicily. He demanded that Tancred return the dowry to him, along with Joan, but this Tancred refused to do. The dowry was too valuable to part with. It included not only Joan's own property, but also the legacy that her husband, King William, had left to her. Of all this, the most that Tancred was willing to turn over was Joan's own furniture for her bed chamber and a lump sum of 2,200 pounds of gold. Richard was far from satisfied with the settlement, but for the time being he accepted it. Richard's reunion with his sister was witnessed by Philip Augustus, whose face lighted up so conspicuously at the sight of Joan that rumors were put about that he intended to marry her himself.

On September 30, the day after his reunion with Joan, Richard accompanied her across the straits to Bagnara, which he occupied. After lodging Joan in the castle there, Richard returned on the following day to Messina.

Shortly after his return, the atmosphere of good-will at Messina turned sour. The immediate cause of the trouble appears to have been Richard's occupation of a Greek monastery on an island in the straits separating Italy from Sicily. Richard took over the monastery in order to use it as a warehouse to store the weapons and other supplies he had brought with him from England. The populace of Messina, who were in large part of Greek descent, were appalled at this conversion of a house of prayer into an armory. They may even have suspected that his occupation of the monastery together with the garrisoning of Bagnara by Richard's troops who were guarding Queen Joan, presaged a plot by Richard to take over the island of Sicily.

The storm broke quickly. On October 3 there were disturbances in Messina between the local populace and Richard's troops. The citizens closed and barred the gates of the town, while armed groups of citizens took up stations on the walls, facing Richard's men who were camped outside. Other citizens occupied high points within the town and began to prepare for a siege. The soldiers of the crusading

army, seeing this, rushed at the town gates and general fighting erupted at numerous points around the Messina perime-
ter.

Richard seems to have been taken by surprise. He had
not anticipated the outbreak of fighting and in the early hours
of the crisis he attempted to quiet the situation. Mounting
one of his swiftest horses he rode through the army's camp
and tried to persuade his men to fall back from the town walls
and stop the fight. Finding all of them reluctant to give up the
fray, Richard singled out the leaders of the various groups,
rode up to them, and beat them about the ears with a stick.
Even this was not enough to quiet the situation, however,
and sporadic fighting continued.

At this point Richard returned to his lodgings, donned
his armor, and went to King Tancred's palace, where he held
a hasty conference with the Sicilian ruler and King Philip.
With their help, Richard was able to restore an uneasy quiet
to Messina. On the following day, October 4, he met with a
larger group of representatives from the town of Messina and
spokesmen from the crusading army. While Richard was still
discussing matters with the assembled mediators further
trouble broke out. Groups of townsmen assembled and attacked the lodging house of Count Hugh of La Marche, a
member of the crusading army and nephew of the Latin ruler
of Jerusalem, Guy de Lusignan. When the noise of the attacking crowd reached Richard's ears, he was furious. Abruptly
he broke off the negotiations and he returned in rage to his
army's camp. As he seated himself on his portable throne, his
counselors and members of his household silently took their
seats on either side of him. Even his closest friends were terrified by the scowls on the king's face and the roars which he
uttered whenever he thought of the outrageous temerity of
the Sicilian Greeks who had dared to attack his men.

But Richard's rage, real as it may have been, did not
blind him to the strategic problems with which he had to
deal. Quickly he outlined his plan for a punitive operation.

The first essential point was to capture Messina. Then, with the city in his hands, he declared, he would hold it for ransom. He would demand that Tancred turn over all of Joan's dowry, including the legacy of King William. If payment was made fully and promptly, the operation would be closed down at that point. For the immediate operation a select force of 2,000 knights and 1,000 archers on foot would be employed. The operation would be carried out by Richard's own men. The French army was to be left alone, despite rumors that they were secretly sympathetic to the Sicilian Greeks and might even be helping them. Richard was not going to become embroiled at this point in a needless and distracting quarrel with the French. That could wait. First, Messina must be taken.

The orders for the mustering of the select force were quickly carried out. By the afternoon of October 4 the formations were ready to move. Richard took his place in full armor with his troops. His dragon standard was unfurled in the sunlight and carried in front of him. Behind him was the army, the rays of the sun reflected from its golden shields. At the sound of a trumpet, the king's horse began to move forward, followed by the massed troops in good order.

Their opponents took up positions on the walls of Messina and opened fire with arrows as Richard's army approached. Richard's men waited until the bowmen on the ramparts had exhausted their supply of arrows and then began their own attack. Richard's bowmen, who occupied the front ranks of his force, opened up with a fusillade of arrows which drove the defenders to take cover. As soon as the defenders had gone into hiding, seeking what shelter they could find on the city's ramparts, Richard's main force approached the city gates. Bringing up a battering ram they broke down the gates swiftly and the king personally led the forward elements of his army into the city. There they concentrated their efforts in a series of lightning attacks on the fortified buildings within the city and before the afternoon was over resistance had been crushed. It all took less time, according to popular belief, than a priest needs to say matins. The Sicilian fleet was burned in the harbor and totally destroyed. Only King Tancred's palace and King Philip's quarters in the town were spared. All of the other fortified centers were attacked and taken. As each of the defense strongholds was taken, the victors' banners were hoisted upon them and hostages were taken. By the end of the day's fighting, Richard had secured hostages from among the sons of all of the noble families of Messina. He then used his hostages in bargaining for a settlement. His proposition was simple: either the citizens of Messina would give up the entire city to him, or else he would keep his hostages and release them individually, upon payment of a sum to be determined by him in each case.

Faced with Richard's ultimatum, his enemies capitulated quickly. Tancred backed down from the position which he had earlier taken and turned over to Richard an additional 40,000 ounces of gold, beyond the payments he had made previously, as a settlement for Queen Joan's dowry and the legacy left to her by her late husband. Upon receipt of the gold, Richard released his hostages and a peace treaty was agreed to between him and Richard.

Although Richard turned Messina back to the Sicilians as a part of the settlement, he took care to keep his recent victory fresh in their minds. Near the city walls he built a tall, new wooden fortress, garrisoned by his own trusted soldiers. Richard christened this structure the "Greek Killer," as a reminder of what he had done and might do again if the citizens failed to conduct themselves properly.

As a part of the settlement between Richard and Tancred, Richard also agreed that a marriage should be contracted between his three-year-old nephew, Arthur of Brittany, and one of Tancred's daughters. Twenty thousand ounces of gold which he had just received from Tancred were to be settled upon young Arthur's wife at the time of the marriage. In addition, Richard decreed that if he should die without direct heirs, Arthur should succeed to the English kingdom. This stipulation in effect barred John from succeeding to the English throne in the event of Richard's death. It did not rule out the possibility, however, that John might inherit part or all of Richard's French possessions. By the strict laws of inheritance, Arthur, who was the son of Richard's deceased older brother, Geoffrey, probably had a slightly better claim to the succession than did John. The settlement with Tancred was unquestionably a blow to John's prospects and may have helped to drive him into rebellion at home during Richard's crusade.

Once peace had been restored in Messina, Richard was anxious to settle some other matters. On October 8 he met again with Tancred and Philip Augustus. The three rulers jointly drew up a list of regulations to govern the conduct of their armed forces in Sicily. In part the regulations were designed to control the conduct of the troops and to eliminate some of the causes for friction between the different elements in the invading army. The three kings decreed that gambling among the troops must be restrained and agreed on suitable punishments for those who indulged in this vice. Only knights and clerics were allowed to gamble at all and they were limited to bets totaling twenty shillings daily. The kings also prohibited speculation in foodstuffs and established maximum ceilings on profits. No one was to realize more than a 10 percent profit on transactions involving the armies. A maximum price of a penny was established for loaves of bread, while the sale of dough was forbidden altogether, presumably to control the market more stringently. The price of wine was frozen at the rates current when the royal edict was proclaimed. A standard rate of exchange was likewise established, so that one English penny was valued at four Angevin deniers, the local currency. Other regulations sought to stabilize the personnel of the forces by providing that no one could change employers without the consent of the employer whom he left. Knights and clerics, however, were exempt from this restriction. The kings also agreed on a common policy regarding the estates of those who died while serving with the crusading armies. One half of each decedent's estate was to be put into a common fund administered by a committee of trustees. The trustees were charged with disbursing the monies of the common fund in order to help meet the expenses of the crusade. The other half of each decedent's estate could be freely disposed of by will to heirs chosen by the testator. Crusaders who contracted debts after they had set out on their journey were required to satisfy their creditors before returning home. Debts contracted prior to the crusade, however, were not required to be settled until after the crusader's return.

When the documents detailing all of these arrangements had been prepared and endorsed, Richard left Messina for a week's diversion, visiting the country along the coast between Messina and Palermo. By this time the crusaders had agreed that their departure for the Holy Land must be postponed until the spring. By mid-October winter weather had begun to set in throughout the Mediterranean and the shipping lanes to the East were considered closed until March or April of the coming year. Few if any captains of the twelfth century cared to attempt a crossing of the Mediterranean during the winter months, and the transport of a large fleet, carrying thousands of troops in addition to their horses and tons of supplies, was completely out of the question.

The army settled down in tents outside of Messina's walls to wait through the dreary winter months. Among the ranks of tents merchants and vendors from the town plied their wares, while servants struggled through the rain and mud, attempting to maintain clothing and equipment in some kind of regular array. Cooks and provisioners carried on their routines, but for most of the rest of the army, nobles and commoners alike, the greatest problem was boredom. Only a handful of the more eminent noblemen were housed in lodgings and inns within the city walls. The rest had to make do with their tents and temporary shelters, which at best kept out some of the rain and wind and provided a hint of warmth. Chronic discomfort and acute boredom were the army's principal enemies at this point.

For Richard, life during the closing months of 1190 was comparatively peaceful and leisurely. There was a small amount of business to dispatch. He gave his approval, for example, to a charter dealing with royal policy concerning shipwrecks. Hitherto the English kings had claimed the right to confiscate property salvaged and washed ashore from wrecked vessels. Richard's charter renounced this right and guaranteed that the survivors of a wreck and the heirs of those who died in a wreck had the right to claim whatever could be salvaged from such a maritime disaster. What prompted Richard to take this action at this point is not entirely clear. Perhaps his own recent experiences at sea had caused him to turn his thoughts in this direction or possibly the captains of his fleet had suggested to him that such an action would be appropriate.

Other information about his activities between mid-October 1190 and late January 1191 is very scanty. On November 11, Richard wrote to the pope concerning the provisions of his recent treaty with Tancred of Sicily and apparently some minor readjustments in the treaty terms were made at this time.

At some point during the period around Christmas, 1190, Richard faced a crisis in his personal life. To what degree he had previously been an active homosexual, we do not know; but stories and dark hints about his abnormal sexual preferences were widely current. These suspicions were potentially serious in their implications. The Church took an extremely dim view of homosexual behavior and classed it among the most serious types of sexual offence in its catalogue of sins. Even so, homosexuality was by no means rare in medieval society. There are numerous dark hints in sermons and in the writings of moralists which indicate that homosexuality was a particular problem among the theoretically celibate clergy of the Church itself. Moreover, homosexuality was not merely a private moral failing in the eyes of medieval society. The law of the Church made homosexual behavior a serious crime, as well as a sin. Obviously Richard's sexual preferences exposed him to the danger of a major scandal which might seriously undermine his authority as king and also as the leader of a crusade. Some time during his stay at Messina he apparently decided to abjure his preference for male sexual partners. He called the eminent churchmen who were with the army to meet privately with him in the chapel of Reginald de Moyac. There in the presence of his spiritual fathers Richard appeared barefoot, carrying three bundles of branches made up as scourges. Falling to his knees in the chapel, surrounded by his bishops and clerics, Richard confessed his past misbehavior and asked the clergy to assign him a suitable penance for his sins. They pronounced him absolved. One witness declared that "he became a man fearing God and doing good and he did not again return to his vice." This seems to be an overoptimistic report, for Richard did apparently relapse into his earlier habits at a later period of his life.

We know very little about the details of his amorous affairs. The sexual adventures of a monarch are not usually commemorated in charters and contemporary knowledge of a king's sex life is not always retailed by monastic chroniclers. However Richard did apparently make considerable efforts for a time to live up to the commitment he made at Messina and it is surely not coincidental that he was married only a few months after this episode.

The Christmas feast of 1190 offered Richard an occasion to stage a public celebration. He determined that he would keep the Feast of the Nativity at his new castle, Mategrifon, or the "Greek Killer," near Messina and he invited Philip and the more notable members of his army to feast with him. The celebration was characteristically lavish. Only gold and silver goblets and platters were in use that day, many of them elaborately fashioned and studded with gems. Both the eating and the drinking were on a heroic scale and Richard was lavish in ordering costly gifts to be presented to Philip and the rest of those whom he had invited. "Who could count the dishes that were borne in or the rounds of drinks or the lavishly outfitted crowd. . . . There was nothing ordinary or simple there, nothing that was not precious, nothing that was not notable," one witness said in openmouthed admiration. It was a Christmas to remember.

It was also a day to remember among the lower ranks, but for different reasons. On Christmas afternoon some Genoese and Pisan sailors, who had doubtless been helping to drain the wine casks throughout the morning, got into a quarrel with a group of Richard's sailors. The incident degenerated into a fight and then spread to become a general mêlée in the crusaders' camp. By the late afternoon several men had been killed and the situation had become so ugly that Richard was finally informed. Leaving his feast, the king brusquely ordered the rioters to disperse. He was not successful in stopping the brawl, but night fell within a short time and in the darkness the fighting broke up. The next day it resumed when some Pisan sailors ganged up on one of Richard's sailors and stabbed him to death. Again general fighting broke out and again Richard intervened. This time he brought with him King Philip and a party of armed soldiers; between them they were able to put an end to the outbreak.

After the Christmas festival Richard was visited by a colorful and exotic figure, the mystical preacher Joachim of Fiore, who was abbot of a Cistercian monastery in Calabria. Richard was curious to hear about Joachim's prophecies, which were based on his interpretation of the Apocalypse of St. John. He therefore invited Joachim to preach at his court in Messina. Joachim chose for the occasion to deal with the figure of the seven-headed monster described in Revelations

12:1–6. This monster's heads, Joachim said, represented tyrants—Herod, Nero, and Muhammad among them. The sixth head was particularly interesting, since according to Joachim this one represented Saladin, the opponent whom Richard was preparing to fight. Saladin was due for a disastrous loss, according to Joachim's interpretation of the biblical text, and the downfall of the sultan would be brought about by Richard's victory. Saladin, the preacher declared, would be killed in the encounter. Richard was intrigued by all of this. He went on to discuss other matters with Joachim, particularly the subject of the Antichrist. Joachim told the English king that the Antichrist had already been born. He was now fifteen years old, a native of Rome, and would one day become pope. Richard, who was none too fond of the reigning pontiff, interjected bitterly that Clement III must be the Antichrist. More seriously, he then gave his own views about the coming of the Antichrist. He would be born, Richard believed, in Cairo or Antioch, not in Rome, and would be a descendant of the Tribe of Dan. He would reign in Jerusalem for three-and-a-half years, during which he would have a disputation with the biblical prophets Enoch and Elias, whom he would finally murder. Following this, the Antichrist himself would be slain. After the Antichrist's death, Richard continued, God would ordain sixty days of penance, during which those who had been seduced by the Antichrist and his pseudo-prophets would have an opportunity to atone for their sins.

Clearly Richard was neither a theologian nor a mystic. But he obviously had paid attention to the theological speculation of his age and was well enough acquainted with the biblical texts to venture some amateur opinions about them, although he failed to convince Joachim of his views.

After these weighty theological diversions, the new year found Richard dealing with relatively routine matters. The earl of Leicester had died the previous fall and his son, Robert de Breteuil, arrived in Messina to be invested with the sword of his father's earldom. The Mandeville family asked the king to establish by decree a line of descent for the family's lands and Richard issued a charter for this purpose. Too, news had arrived in Sicily of the death of Archbishop Baldwin of Canterbury. The archbishop had joined the crusade, but instead of following Richard's party to Sicily he had sailed directly to Acre. Now he had died and Richard wrote in late January to his brother John and to the prior and monks of Canterbury Cathedral concerning the election of a new archbishop as primate of the Church in England.

At the beginning of February Richard's routine was varied by another celebration. February 2 was a feast day, celebrating the purification of the Virgin Mary in the temple. Richard and his court honored the occasion by holding a mock tournament in which they used reeds instead of the deadly lance as weapons. The game went along playfully until Richard caught a glimpse of William of Barres in the party. Suddenly his mood changed. He had no use for William of Barres, for he had encountered him earlier in real fights and he felt that William had acted unchivalrously by breaking a promise he had made years earlier, when as a young knight he had been captured and held prisoner. William had given his word not to attempt escape and then, at the first opportunity, had fled. When he saw William taking part in the game with the other members of his party, Richard lost his head. He charged at William with his reed, but the tip of his play-lance broke off in the encounter. Then Richard cantered away, turned his mount sharply, and charged back at William, attempting to throw him off of his horse. William was able to stay in the saddle, but Richard's own saddle slipped. He dismounted, commandeered another horse, and charged at William again. The newly created earl of Leicester tried to intervene, but Richard yelled at him to get away and leave them alone. After further attempts to unseat William had failed, the king was exasperated. He turned to William at last and told him to get out and not to return. "Take care," he warned William, "that I do not see you again, for I will consider you and yours as perpetual enemies." William then rode off to King Philip, his overlord, and asked him to intervene with Richard. The next day Philip tried to reason with Richard on the subject, but without success. Richard's mind was set. The day after Philip's futile visit, a delegation of the highest-ranking noblemen of the French kingdom came to Richard's court and pleaded with Richard to forgive William. They even fell on their knees to implore Richard to change his mind, but he was as adamant as ever, and William then had to leave Messina, since no one could protect him against Richard's wrath.

Toward the end of February disturbing reports began to arrive from England. John and the justiciars of the realm were at odds with one another; that much was clear. The sources of the friction and the precise nature of the disagreements between them were far from clear in the reports that Richard received and he must certainly have been puzzled as to what was going on. Richard's chancellor and chief justiciar, William Longchamp, bishop of Ely, was engaged in a power struggle with Richard's brother, John, who had returned with Richard's permission from France to England. Longchamp was in league with King William of Scotland, while John was allying himself with a faction of the English nobility who found Longchamp's regime distasteful and dangerous to their own interests. In order to get a clearer picture of the situation, Richard decided to send the archbishop of Rouen to England to investigate the problems and to report back to him. He also dispatched letters ordering his justiciars—Longchamp, William Marshall, and three royal justices—to admit the archbishop to their councils and to act upon his advice. Hugh du Puiset, bishop of Durham, was no longer a justiciar. Longchamp had eliminated Hugh from the ranks of the justiciars before embarking on his struggle with John.

Just as the archbishop had been sent off on his mission, Richard's mother arrived in Sicily. Eleanor of Aquitaine was sixty-nine years old by this time, but still active and tireless. She crossed the Alps through the Mont-Genèvre pass in January on her way to meet her son. She was accompanied on the journey by Berengaria, daughter of King Sancho VI of Navarre, whom Richard planned to marry. On the way, Eleanor had conferred with the emperor-elect, Henry VI, whose father, Frederick Barbarossa, had died the previous June while on his way to the Holy Land to participate in a crusade. From Lodi, twenty miles south of Milan, where she met Henry VI, Eleanor had made her way slowly down the Italian peninsula and reached Naples late in February. There she was met by ships from Richard's fleet. They had planned to bring her by sea to Messina, but at this point the plans went wrong. King Tancred refused to allow the queen's party to proceed. He told them that there were too many men in the group—apparently Eleanor and Berengaria traveled with a small army of guards—and instead he invited them to go to Brindisi.

Richard learned of Tancred's refusal and went immediately to Catania at the beginning of March. There he met with Tancred and endeavored to persuade him to allow his mother and the Spanish princess to continue on their intended journey. Tancred refused. Richard persisted in his request. Both of the monarchs were on their best behavior. Tancred received Richard as an honored guest, entertained him in his palace, and pressed him to accept a variety of sumptuous gifts. Richard refused, but finally consented to accept a small ring in token of his friendship with Tancred. Richard in turn pressed gifts on Tancred, particularly a sword, which he told his host was none other than Excalibur, the hallowed wonder-working sword of the legendary King Arthur. Tancred, not to be outdone, pressed further gifts on Richard, who ultimately accepted a contribution of four large transport ships and fifteen galleys for the crusaders' fleet.

Underlying all of the diplomatic niceties were some hard political facts. By this time Tancred had allied with

Philip Augustus and was committed to representing Philip's interests. Philip was alarmed by the imminent visit of Berengaria. Berengaria's presence with Eleanor of Aquitaine made it abundantly clear that Richard had finally decided not to marry Philip's sister, Alice, and had made up his mind to marry Berengaria instead. Philip was determined to wring as many concessions as possible from Richard in return for granting him a release from his promise to marry Alice. Tancred was eager to use his position as intermediary to curry favor with Philip Augustus, favor which he could soon exchange for a most useful political alliance, since Tancred's title to the Sicilian throne was insecure. The Emperor Henry VI had a far more legitimate claim in law to the Sicilian throne than did Tancred and Henry's presence in Italy at the moment presaged an attempt to make good that claim and to evict Tancred from his position. Under these circumstances, Tancred needed all of the foreign support he could find, especially from monarchs whose legitimacy was not open to question and whose military potential was rather greater than his own. Undoubtedly Tancred was relying primarily upon Philip Augustus for this support in return for his good offices in negotiating with Richard. But at the same time Tancred was also unwilling to clash openly with Richard, since he still hoped that Richard might be persuaded to assist him in his quarrel with the emperor.

On March 8, 1191, Tancred and Richard went from Catania to Taormina, where Philip Augustus arrived on the same day. At the last moment, during the journey from Catania, Tancred made a bid for Richard's good-will. He told Richard that Philip was plotting against him. Philip, said Tancred, had informed him that Richard planned to take over the Sicilian kingdom. Philip had done this, Tancred said, in order to sow discord between Richard and the Sicilian king. Richard refused to believe Tancred's tale of treachery, until Tancred finally turned over to him some letters of Philip's which bore upon the matter.

When Tancred and Richard arrived at Taormina and found Philip on the scene there, Richard refused to meet with the French king. Tancred offered Philip his hospitality and put him up in his palace, while Richard returned directly to Messina. Philip also returned to Messina on the following day. At this point Count Philip of Flanders stepped in with an offer to mediate the quarrel. For the next three weeks a flurry of negotiations continued, with the count of Flanders playing a major role in resolving the differences between the two kings. By the thirtieth of March agreement had been reached on most of the important issues and the text of a treaty between Philip and Richard was confirmed.

The Treaty of Messina was a crucial document and its provisions continued to play a role in the relations between the French and English kingdoms for the remainder of Richard's lifetime. By this agreement, for one thing, Richard accepted virtually the same territorial concessions which Philip Augustus had wrung from Richard's father, Henry II, in the dark days just before Henry's death. Richard gave up the rights which he had previously claimed to the Auvergne and to the baronies of Issoudun and Graçay. In addition, Richard acknowledged that Philip was the liege lord of the Angevin territories on the Continent and he also made contingent provisions for the succession to his Continental titles in case his forthcoming marriage should produce sons to inherit his lands and powers. Until such time as he had sons of his own to succeed him, Richard had already acknowledged Arthur of Brittany as his heir. If sons were forthcoming from his marriage, Richard agreed that they too should recognize the French king as their liege lord. In return for these concessions on Richard's part, Philip released him from his earlier promise to marry Princess Alice of France and allowed him to retain control of Gisors and the Norman Vexin, which had been a part of Alice's dowry, on condition that he pay Philip 10,000 silver marks of the currency of Troyes. In addition the Treaty of Messina provided that the two kings would share equally in any conquests they might make while on the crusade.

The settlement embodied in the Treaty of Messina cleared the way for Eleanor of Aquitaine to enter Sicily to visit with her son before he sailed to the East. She also delivered to him his new fiancée, Berengaria, "a maiden more prudent than pretty" according to a clear-eyed if uncharitable chronicler. On March 30, Richard escorted Eleanor and Berengaria from Reggio to Messina. That same day, King Philip sailed from Messina to begin the journey to Acre, where other groups of crusaders had landed much earlier and where they were now besieging the city while waiting for the arrival of the main French and English armies from the West. Philip's departure was timed so that he could avoid the embarrassment of having to greet the Spanish princess who had replaced his sister, Alice, as Richard's future wife. Very likely, too, he was anxious to avoid having to acclaim the arrival of Eleanor. She had, after all, been his own father's first wife and her inheritance had created continuing hardships and crises for the French crown. However broadminded and tolerant he may have been—and there is little sign that he was notable for either quality—Philip might have found difficulty in arousing much enthusiasm or good feeling for an encounter with Eleanor. It was more diplomatic and far less difficult to cast off with his fleet from Messina before Eleanor and Berengaria arrived.

Eleanor spent only three days at Messina visiting with her eldest surviving son and bidding him farewell on his expedition to the East. On April 2 she began her return journey to England, sailing from Messina to Salerno and from there to Rome. She was accompanied on her return journey by the archbishop of Rouen and probably arrived at Rome just in time to witness the consecration of a new pope. Clement III, whom Richard so heartily detested, died on April 10 and his successor, Celestine III, was consecrated four days later.

Meanwhile, Richard was completing the final stage of

his preparations for departure. There was one more shake-
down of his army, to eliminate the half-hearted and the unfit,
who were commanded to return home. The returning
soldiers were also required to contribute to the crusading
venture the money and equipment which they had brought
with them to Sicily. Richard dispatched some additional last-
minute instructions to his justiciars and especially to his
brother John, commanding him to be mindful of the promises
he had made and warning him against indulging in any mischief, at least until Richard's return from the crusade. Too,
there were material preparations to be completed. The wooden
tower which he had built at Messina was carefully dismantled and the building materials were loaded into Richard's ships for later use in the Holy Land. There was siege
machinery to be checked for a final time before departure, as
well as the stores of arms, food for the journey, and the load-
ing of horses and men to be supervised. Care had to be taken,
too, for the safe transport of Richard's treasury, which was
divided into small lots and placed under guard in several different ships, so that if one should be wrecked or endangered,
the remainder could be kept safe.

At last on the Wednesday before Easter, April 10,
1191, everything was ready. The wind blew fair. The last letters of counsel and warning had been sent off. Richard's fiancée, Berengaria, had boarded her ship, in company with
Richard's sister, Joan, who was her traveling companion and
guardian. All of the supplies and men had been loaded on all
of the two hundred and nineteen vessels which constituted
Richard's fleet. It was time to cast off lines and commence the
journey. The first to depart was a tiny squadron of three ships,
which included the vessel in which Joan and Berengaria traveled. They were followed by a group of thirteen ships and
after that in order came six further squadrons of ships, each
larger than the preceding one. Richard himself sailed in the
very last squadron, where he could keep track of the ships
ahead of him and where he could come to the aid of any

stragglers who dropped out of their place in the ranks of his flotilla. The individual squadrons sailed abreast and the distance between the ranks of the squadrons was so spaced that trumpet signals could be heard from one rank to the next. This enabled the groups to maintain contact and made it possible for the commanders of the fleet to issue orders for changes in course and to cope with other contingencies as they arose. The order of sailing had to be adjusted from time to time, as the speedier galleys needed to adjust their speed in order to keep in touch with the slower and heavier transport ships.

The fair wind which sped them on their way from Messina soon moderated and then ceased altogether, so that the fleet was becalmed for a time. Then they met contrary winds on Good Friday, April 12, and the ships were blown about in a storm for the greater part of the day. That evening the high winds abated, however, and from the night of April 12 until April 17, when they approached Crete, they made steady progress. Crete marked the halfway point on the journey from Messina to Acre. The fleet put into harbor briefly on the island and Richard made a foray ashore on April 18. As they were docking in Crete, Richard surveyed his fleet and discovered to his dismay that twenty-five of his ships were no longer with the fleet, having been blown off course or sunk during the first stage of the voyage. He quickly reembarked and resumed the journey. The winds began to blow stronger at this point and they made swift progress on the next leg of their journey, which brought them to Rhodes on April 19. Richard and some of his followers landed on the island and they remained on Rhodes for ten days. In part this lengthy stopover was due to the fact that Richard was ill and wished to recuperate before attempting to continue the voyage. In part, too, the layover in Rhodes was extended in order to give the stragglers from the fleet a chance to rejoin the main body of ships and to reorganize their sailing arrangements.

Richard also had a further reason, in all likelihood, for

extending his stay at Rhodes. We know that while he was at Rhodes he made inquiries about the political situation on Cyprus. It is possible that he had already conceived a plan to attack and take that island before continuing on to the Holy Land. There were a great many advantages to be gained from a successful attack on Cyprus. The island lay close to the Palestinian mainland and its possession would give Richard an independent base of operations which might turn out to be extremely useful during his crusade. Then, too, the island was reputed to be quite wealthy and the booty of a successful conquest would do much to replenish Richard's treasury and to finance his further military operations on the crusade. In addition, as he doubtless was told while at Rhodes, Cyprus was plagued by political unrest and the island seemed ripe for a change of government.

Cyprus was ruled at this point by a local despot, Isaac Comnenus, who was extremely unpopular both with the island's population and also with the Byzantine emperors at Constantinople, who had controlled Cyprus for centuries and who had seen it wrested away from them by Isaac. Isaac had first come to Cyprus with letters from Constantinople naming him as governor of the island. Only after he had gained control of the castles and garrisons of Cyprus did it become apparent that his credentials were forged. By then it was too late to evict him except by force. A Byzantine expedition was sent to do this, but was defeated by Isaac's army. Since then Isaac's control of the island had been unchallenged. The Cypriots disliked him because of his greed and his megalomania. He had extorted enormous sums of money from his subjects without conferring any significant benefits in return. More than that, his extravagant expenditures offended his subjects. Further he was supposed to have extremely odd sexual appetites, which he satisfied in various unsavory manners. There were even rumors that he was going to require worship of his image in the churches, a scandalous and hor-

52764

rifying blasphemy which no Cypriot could accept with equanimity.

The Latins in the East were no fonder of Isaac than were the Greeks. Isaac had antagonized them thoroughly by imposing heavy taxes on Latin merchants who visited the island and by openly confiscating the goods of some of them. Since the easternmost point of the island, Cape St. Andreas, was only one day's sail from the Syrian coast, Cyprus had once provided a highly convenient way station for maritime traffic to the Latin states. When Isaac came to power, however, the Latins ceased to visit the island, although they were enviously aware of its presence athwart their trade routes. There was reason to think that Isaac was actively opposed to the crusades and that he deliberately set out to hamper them in every imaginable way. It was rumored that he had gone so far as to murder his only son, primarily because the boy was well disposed toward the crusaders and had sought to better relations with them. There was also some suspicion that Isaac might be in league with Saladin.

Richard had already gained an unflattering impression of the Greeks in south Italy, where they had been his bitterest enemies. In turn, he had done his best to humiliate them when he had gained the upper hand there. Now in the eastern Mediterranean he found another Greek outpost, one which he may have considered to be virtually an enemy base. It is reasonably likely that he set out deliberately to capture it.

If so, his designs were abetted by the weather. Upon sailing from Rhodes on May 1, Richard discovered that some of the ships which had disappeared from his fleet during the earlier storm had foundered on the Cypriot shore. The survivors of the shipwreck had been imprisoned by the Cypriot ruler, while the goods salvaged from the wreck had been confiscated. This was bad enough. Far worse, the ships carrying Richard's sister, Queen Joan, and his fiancée, Berengaria, had been blown toward Cyprus and were now anchored in the harbor of Limassol. Isaac had tried to persuade the noble passengers to come ashore, but they were cautious enough to refuse his offer and remained unmolested on their ships. Still the situation was precarious.

As soon as Richard discovered this situation, he made for the island, arriving there finally on May 6. Directly he demanded that Isaac Comnenus give him immediate satisfaction for the imprisonment of his men and the confiscation of the cargoes of his shipwrecked vessels.

Isaac refused rather rudely to do any such thing, whereupon Richard began at once to disembark his forces. There was a short, sharp fight between Isaac's men and Richard's on the Limassol waterfront, a fight in which Richard triumphed decisively. At dusk Isaac and the remainder of his men withdrew from the city, while Richard landed the rest of his army and deployed his men to occupy the town. The townspeople seem to have welcomed Richard's arrival and to have accepted him as a liberator from Isaac's regime.

After he had occupied Limassol, Richard made contact with Isaac Comnenus once again and initiated peace negotiations with the Cypriot despot. Richard insisted that Isaac must agree to furnish support for the crusade, including a contingent of fighting men to accompany the crusading army to the Holy Land.

While these negotiations were in progress, other events demanded Richard's attention. On May 11 the titular king of Jerusalem, Guy de Lusignan, arrived at Limassol to meet Richard and to urge him to hurry to the Holy Land as quickly as possible. Guy was accompanied by a delegation of other Latin princes, including Prince Bohemond III of Antioch, Count Raymond III of Tripoli, and the brother of the Armenian King Roupen. The leaders of the Latin states in the Holy Land found Richard in a haughty mood. Before he would deal with their requests, Richard insisted that the Latin princes must swear fealty to him, thus placing himself

in the position of their overlord. Reluctantly they agreed to
this demand, since otherwise they feared that they might be
denied the assistance of the military forces which Richard
had brought with him on the crusade. Clearly Richard's purpose in this transaction was to secure an uncontested claim to
be the commander-in-chief of all the Latin forces in the East,
thus placing himself in charge both of the crusading armies
and also of the armies of the Latin settlers who had been living in Palestine and Syria for nearly a century. The fealty
which the Latin princes swore to Richard at Limassol
amounted to a public recognition of his right to command
them and their followers. It thus placed Richard in a domi-
nant position vis-à-vis the rest of the crusading forces before
he even arrived in the Holy Land itself.

King Guy and the Latin princes had arrived in Cyprus
at an opportune moment. On May 12, the day after their initial meeting with Richard, they were invited to witness Richard's marriage to Berengaria of Navarre.

The wedding took place in Limassol. Richard's chap-
lain, Nicholas (afterwards to become bishop of Le Mans) officiated at the ceremony. The marriage rite was followed immediately by a coronation ceremony, in which Berengaria
was crowned as queen of England by Bishop John of Evreux,
assisted by the archbishops of Apamea and Auch and the
bishop of Bayonne. After Berengaria's coronation, Richard
had his clerks draw up a charter settling the terms of his new
wife's dowry. At the feasts and celebrations which marked
this occasion, once the official business had been dispatched,
Richard appeared to be joyous and lighthearted and genuinely happy.

He was in no great hurry to reach the Holy Land. The
celebration of his marriage took several days. Then there was
still the matter of concluding a final settlement with the ruler
of Cyprus. A few days after Richard's wedding, he finally met
in person with Isaac Comnenus and announced to Isaac the

final terms to which he demanded agreement. Isaac temporized and managed to give Richard the impression that he would agree to Richard's demands. Then in the dark of the night Isaac secretly stole away to Famagusta, without having given his formal consent to the peace terms.

Richard was infuriated by Isaac's behavior. The Cypriot ruler had not only dealt dishonestly with him, but after his flight to Famagusta had also had the temerity to order Richard to leave Cyprus at once. Richard began immediately to assemble his troops for battle. One contingent was sent by land to Famagusta under the command of King Guy de Lusignan, Richard's new liege man. Richard himself, with another force, embarked by sea for Famagusta on the island's eastern coast.

When he landed at Famagusta, the town was deserted. Richard quickly discovered that Isaac had taken refuge at Nicosia and he made ready an immediate attack upon the fortress there. Although messengers from Acre sped to Famagusta to try to persuade Richard to end his Cyprus campaign at once and to proceed directly to the Holy Land, Richard simply ignored them. He was on the chase and he sensed that his quarry could not elude him much longer.

Turning a deaf ear to those who tried to dissuade him, Richard moved his army to Nicosia as soon as they had had a brief rest from their journey. The forces spread out in battle formation, anticipating an ambush, and pressed forward in the direction of Nicosia through deserted farms and villages. All at once the Greeks attacked from their prepared positions, but they were unable to scatter Richard's disciplined forces. Then Isaac himself took the field. During the initial stage of the attack, he had remained in hiding. Now he came out openly, offering himself as a lure in the hope of enticing Richard's men to break ranks and pursue him. The ruse failed: the ranks held and then advanced toward the Cypriot ruler. Spotting Richard in the rear of the crusading force, Isaac attempted to shoot him down with two arrows which, according to the English witnesses, were poisoned. Richard was outraged. Spurring his horse forward, he galloped in Isaac's direction, hoping to spear the Cypriot on his lance. Isaac saw him coming, however, and managed to elude Richard's pursuit. Slipping away among the ranks of his own men, Isaac was soon lost to sight. Leaving his forces in the field to fight as best they could, he beat a hasty retreat by back roads and little-used tracks to his stronghold at Kantara.

Richard did not follow up his victory immediately. He was ill and needed a few days to recuperate. Meanwhile, however, King Guy with the part of Richard's forces entrusted to his command was winning other victories against Isaac's supporters. They took two of Isaac's principal defensive positions, the castles of Kyrenia and Didimus. At Didimus they secured an unexpected dividend: Isaac's daughter was among the prisoners taken when the castle was captured and she was now turned over to Richard, who held her for use as a pawn in bargaining with Isaac.

For the Cypriot ruler, the capture of his daughter seems to have been the final straw. His major strong points had already been taken, his remaining followers were few, and even their loyalty to him was uncertain. In these circumstances, Isaac decided to surrender to Richard, rather than to fight the campaign through to the end.

Isaac's surrender came on May 31, 1191. He came down from Kantara a beaten man, doleful and dejected. Kneeling at Richard's feet, Isaac made his formal declaration of surrender. He was ready to give up everything: land, cities, castles, possessions. He was willing, he declared, to become Richard's vassal, at least so long as Richard did not have him put in iron chains.

Richard was delighted. The campaign had been successful beyond expectation. No doubt he had hoped to get a foothold of some kind in Cyprus and a guarantee perhaps that crusaders could land there without molestation; possibly he had anticipated some kind of trade agreement as well and even some men and money to swell his forces. Instead, he now had the whole island in his grasp and a complete surrender from its ruler.

Under the circumstances he could well afford a minor display of generosity toward the defeated Isaac. He had Isaac's daughter brought in and the father and girl enjoyed a brief, tearful reunion. As for Isaac himself, Richard was willing to grant his request. He did not have Isaac manacled in chains of iron. Instead, he put his smiths to work forging silver chains and fettered Isaac in noble metal.

The defeated ruler and his daughter were placed in custody. Isaac was turned over to Richard's chamberlain, Ralph Fitz Godfrey, for safekeeping. The daughter was placed in the care of Richard's sister, Joan, and his new wife, Queen Berengaria. Both Isaac and his daughter were kept in permanent confinement. Isaac was moved about from one set of jailers to another until long after Richard had left the Holy Land. The former Cypriot ruler was finally released only in 1195 and died, possibly of poisoning, shortly thereafter. His daughter accompanied Berengaria and her court throughout the crusade and when the royal party returned to Europe, she went back with them to serve as a pawn in Richard's diplomacy.

Meanwhile, arrangements had to be made quickly for the governance of Cyprus and for reaping the fruits of Richard's campaign there. For the time being two of Richard's confidants, Richard de Canvill and Robert of Turnham, were named as governors of the island. The yield of the Cyprus campaign was exceedingly handsome. Richard laid claim to all of the wealth accumulated by Isaac Comnenus and in addition seized title to one half of the goods of the rest of the Cypriot population. His new subjects had, no doubt, to make their own arrangements to ransom their goods and lands from Richard's governors. The cash yield of this operation is not known, but it was undoubtedly very ample. The Cypriots, in effect, paid a large share of the expenses of Richard's sojourn in the Holy Land. Richard also rewarded his army from the spoils of Cyprus. While he kept all of the gold and silk and jewels for himself, according to one writer, he gave the captured silver and food supplies to the members of his army. Guy de Lusignan, the titular king of Jerusalem, was also handsomely rewarded for his services during the Cyprus campaign.

Beyond simple cash considerations, the possession of Cyprus by the crusaders as a result of Richard's campaign there was the major asset to the Latin forces in the East. It afforded harbor facilities of great usefulness. It was a ready-made source of foodstuffs and other supplies for the crusader states. Beyond these supply and support functions, the island also provided the Latins in the East with a strategic base close to the mainland, one to which they could retire in times of great crisis, one from which they could launch surprise attacks with ease against the whole coastal area of Syria and Palestine.

Richard's first venture on his crusade had brought him money, goods, and glory. He had every reason to be immensely satisfied and pleased with his achievements. Now he could look forward with anticipation and confidence to the next phase of the crusade. Six days after the surrender of Isaac Comnenus, Richard was ready to depart. He had hastily made his arrangements for control of Cyprus, had rewarded his men, given them a brief rest, and then began returning them to their ships. On June 5, 1191, he sailed from Cyprus with his fleet, bound at last directly for the Holy Land.

SIX

✠ —————————————————————————— ✠

The Capture of Acre

The Holy Land, as Richard approached it under sunny skies in June of 1191, was a Muslim province. The Syrian and Palestinian regions which the first crusaders had seized nearly a century earlier were now almost completely in the hands of Saladin, who personified the Muslim foe for Richard and his followers. Saladin's capture of the Holy Land was a recent and sudden development. One lightning campaign in 1187 had delivered it into his control within the space of a few months.

The earlier crusaders, the ones who had taken Jerusalem in 1099, had had to deal with Muslim enemies who were divided against one another, a motley collection of minor states, crippled by internal feuding and hampered by relatively small resources. This situation began to change a generation after the first crusaders had taken control of Palestine and much of Syria and had created their own Latin Kingdom of Jerusalem. Beginning with the rise to power of Zengi, who became governor of Mosul in 1127, the Muslim powers bordering the Latin states in the East had gradually been consolidated. A degree of unity had been imposed upon them, first by Zengi and then, following his death in 1146, by his succes-

sor, Nur ad-Din. Nur ad-Din had slowly added to the territories bequeathed to him by Zengi and had capped his career
by bringing Egypt under his domination in 1169. The acqui-
sition of Egypt rounded out Nur ad-Din's empire and gave
him a commanding position in the Near East. His territories
stretched from the Tigris through Syria, all the way to the
Libyan frontier. His armies surrounded the Latin states and
Nur ad-Din was capable of cutting them off completely from
communication by land with Byzantium and Europe. By the
time he had achieved this, however, Nur ad-Din was already
an old man, tired out from years of fighting and negotiating,
anxious only to prepare himself to face his maker. He died in
1174, five years after acquiring Egypt. At his death, control of
his vast domains fell to Saladin, a Kurdish general, who had
been one of the commanders of the army that captured Egypt
for Nur ad-Din and who had subsequently taken the title of
sultan of Egypt.

Although Saladin was fully aware of the presence of
the Latins along the Palestinian coast, the eradication of the
Latin states was not for him a matter of high priority. The
commercial connections between the Latins and his own territories were an important and valuable asset for Saladin's
domains. The European merchants who came to trade in the
Latin-held coastal cities such as Tyre, Antioch, Acre, and
Jaffa, were eager to buy goods produced within Saladin's empire. The European merchants were important customers for
the textiles, glassware, enamels, and spices which Saladin's
subjects could furnish to them. The best interests of Saladin's
domains were well served not by wiping out the Latin states,
but by maintaining commercial links with them.

Accordingly commercial treaties were negotiated between Saladin's government and the rulers of the Latin states
during the early years of Saladin's rule. The treaties provided
for the conditions necessary to the peaceful exchange of
goods. Saladin's subjects were to be permitted to travel freely
and without harm through the territories of the Latin rulers of

Jerusalem and the other Latin states. Likewise, Latin merchants were guaranteed the right to enter Saladin's empire and to travel and trade there in safety.

The Latin rulers, unfortunately, proved unable to make good their part of the bargain. The Latin king of Jerusalem, Guy de Lusignan, had come to power in 1186, following a long period of internal dissension among the European settlers in the Holy Land. His claim to the throne was shaky and many of his subjects would have rejoiced to see him toppled from power. As a result, he had to rely on the support of a clique of followers whose independence and ambition caused them on occasion to act directly against the best interests of the Latin monarchy. One of Guy's supporters was Reginald of Chatillon, an adventurer who repeatedly disregarded the treaties between Saladin and the Latin kings and attacked caravans of Muslim merchants who were protected by the treaty arrangements. When Saladin called upon Guy de Lusignan to honor his commitments by punishing Reginald, Guy was unable to do so. Reginald was too powerful and, in any event, Guy could not afford to alienate him, since his own position was precarious and he depended on Reginald's support to remain in power.

Saladin, in disgust, concluded that he could not rely upon the Latin king to fulfill his commitments. He decided that at last the time had come to carry through his long-standing plan to wage a holy war against the Latin Christians in the East. Writing to the princes of his empire Saladin outlined his decision and commanded them to ready men and equipment to drive the Latins out of Jerusalem and the other Palestinian cities which they had occupied for three generations.

By April of 1187 Saladin's forces were ready to take the field. After a diversionary attack on the countryside near Acre, they moved on to Tiberias on the Sea of Galilee. The Latin king, meanwhile, had mustered his own army to ward off the invasion. After making a rendezvous at Saffuriyah, the Latin army set out for Tiberias, in the hope of challenging

Saladin's army there. The Latins never arrived at Tiberias. En route from Saffuriyah they were attacked by the Muslims near Hattin, on July 4, 1187. The two armies were closely matched in size, but the Muslim troops were fresh and battle-ready, while the Latins were weary, thirsty, and exhausted after marching in the July heat through arid country, and fighting off harassing attacks. At Hattin the Latins were able to put up only temporary resistance. Although a few escaped, the bulk of the Latin army was killed or captured.

Hattin was a disaster for the Latins. In order to meet Saladin's invasion, they had stripped the garrisons of their towns and castles, leaving behind only token forces. When the field army was wiped out at Hattin, there was no reserve to draw upon to defend the rest of the Latin kingdom. During July and August Saladin plucked off one city and fortress after another and met only nominal resistance. The sole exception was the city of Tyre, which was comparatively well garrisoned and alert, since many of the surviving Latins who had escaped from Hattin had made their way to Tyre. Saladin did not press his attack there, a decision which was to haunt him later. At the end of September Saladin laid siege to Jerusalem and on October 2 the city fell to him. He occupied it peacefully, in contrast to the dreadful slaughter which had marked the Latin conquest of Jerusalem in 1099. A large part of the population was allowed to go free and the greater number of those who escaped capture or who were ransomed after capture fled to Tyre.

There were some further mopping-up operations during the latter part of October and November. By the dawn of the new year, the entire Latin kingdom south of Tripoli, with the sole exception of Tyre, was in Saladin's control. In 1188 he pushed his attack farther to the north, isolating Tripoli and Antioch and capturing virtually all of the rest of the northern Latin states. In the interior of the Latin states only Krak des Chevaliers and a handful of other major fortresses continued to hold out against the Muslim onslaught.

This situation horrified Western Europeans and spurred them to enlist by the thousands in the armies of the Third Crusade. Even before any of the Western armies could arrive on the scene, however, the survivors of Saladin's conquest in the East were preparing their counterattack. Guy de Lusignan, the weak-willed, vacillating, incompetent king who had led the Latins to disaster at Hattin, mustered another army from the ranks of the refugees at Tripoli, where he had taken shelter after Saladin had released him from captivity. With this force he headed south to Tyre, where he hoped to find reinforcements for his army.

At Tyre, however, he received a disappointing reception. Many of the Europeans there blamed him for the disasters which had engulfed the Latin states and they were far from anxious to put themselves again in the hands of the leader whom they held responsible for the fiasco at Hattin. Furthermore, the commander of the garrison at Tyre, Conrad of Montferrat, had ambitions of his own. With the backing of his men, he was preparing to claim the title of king of Jerusalem for himself, on the theory that Guy had forfeited the throne as a result of his defeat at Hattin. Consequently he would not lend any support to Guy's army, nor would he even allow the city gates of Tyre to be opened in order that Guy might enter the town.

While Guy and his forces remained camped outside of Tyre, trying to negotiate an agreement with Conrad of Montferrat, the Latin king had a stroke of luck. A party of Pisan sailors and adventurers who had come to the East in response to the pope's call for the crusade decided to attach themselves to Guy's army. With these reinforcements, Guy and his augmented army set out to the south in August of 1189 and headed toward Acre.

The strategy of Guy de Lusignan in making this move is open to the harshest criticism. On any rational basis, it must be counted a foolhardy step. The city of Acre, alluring as it was, presented no easy problem for a besieging army.

The city was large, well defended, and adequately supplied with provisions to last out a lengthy siege. The garrison within the walls was far larger than the forces Guy brought with him. He was outnumbered by a factor of about two to one at the outset. Furthermore, by investing the city he tied himself and his army to a war of fixed position, in which his enemies enjoyed all of the advantages of mobility, while his own forces were committed to actions within a narrow coastal range. The conclusion seemed obvious: Guy's attack on Acre was doomed to failure from the start. The only excuse for his action is, however, a weighty one—it succeeded.

The success, ultimately, of the siege of Acre was something for which Guy could claim little credit. It was achieved by forces outside of his control, by events which he could not possibly have foreseen when he arrived outside the town on August 28, 1189. Within a few weeks further reinforcements for his army began to trickle in from the West. A fleet of Danish and Frisian sailors arrived in early September and gave much-needed help in blockading Acre from the sea. A contingent of French and Flemish crusaders arrived close on the heels of the Frisians and they were followed by a German group in late September.

Saladin was alarmed by these developments. He was engaged in besieging the castle of Beaufort, about forty miles northeast of Tyre, when he learned of the continuing arrival of Latin forces near Acre. By mid-September he was sufficiently worried to divert a major contingent of his army from the siege in the north and to lead it down to Acre. Once there, he made a preliminary attack on the Latin forces and succeeded in establishing a line of communications with the Acre garrison. Once this was achieved, Saladin settled his men into a permanent camp just to the east of the crusaders' camp and then awaited further developments.

The crusaders recognized clearly enough the danger which they now faced. With the garrison of Acre on one side of them, capable of slipping out from the city gates and making a surprise attack on their camp at will, and with Saladin's forces on the other side, also capable of attacking at any time, their own position was extremely precarious.

In these circumstances the Christian forces decided to take the initiative. They attacked Saladin's position on October 4 and scored a considerable success. They managed to penetrate the enemy camp and even to reach Saladin's tent before a counterattack pushed them back. They retired to their own camp successfully, but with many losses in the engagement.

After this the two armies spent the winter keeping a wary eye on each other. There were a number of small engagements, but no further major battles, and the situation settled into a stalemate.

In the spring and summer of 1190 further reinforcements arrived, bit by bit, including large advance contingents of the French crusading army, who reached the Holy Land well in advance of their monarch. During the spring of 1190 the hopes of the troops at Acre were fastened upon the arrival of a huge, well-disciplined German army under the command of the emperor, Frederick Barbarossa. This army never arrived, however, for the emperor was drowned while making a river crossing in Cilicia. Following Barbarossa's death, the major part of his force returned immediately to the West, leaving only a much reduced contingent headed by Frederick of Swabia to complete the journey to Palestine. This small German force reached Acre in October. While it was a far smaller force than had been hoped for, still the reinforcements were welcome and were a distinct asset in strengthening the army at Acre and buoying up its morale. The arrival of the Germans was followed by the appearance of an advance party of English soldiers, led by Archbishop Baldwin of Canterbury.

The fighting at Acre during the summer of 1190 was sporadic and inconclusive. Neither side was able to gain any significant victory, although there were several sharp exchanges. Saladin's forces at Acre were also augmented during the summer. Once Castle Beaufort had fallen to his armies in July, the sultan was able to transfer additional troops from the north to bolster his southern forces.

The winter of 1190–1191 was severe and the crusading army at Acre suffered from a variety of afflictions during this period. They were chronically short of food and experienced some notable losses, due both to illness and to malnutrition in the camp. Among those who were lost to the army was the leader of the Germans, Duke Frederick of Swabia. His place was taken by Duke Leopold of Austria, Frederick's cousin, but Leopold proved to be a less capable leader than Frederick and he had difficulty in keeping his followers together.

In March of 1191 conditions began to pick up in the crusaders' camp. Supply ships managed to land on the coast, bringing foodstuffs to relieve the hunger of the soldiers. Almost as important, they brought news that the French and English kings were preparing to sail from Sicily. This inspired fresh hope in the ranks that they might soon be able to complete the task they had begun.

On April 20, 1191, the Saturday after Easter, the French king at last made his appearance. He arrived, as he had promised, accompanied by an army of well-equipped and battle-worthy troops and ships full of weapons and other supplies. The weary soldiers at Acre, forgetting for a time the miseries of their long wait and the dreary months during which they had held the positions which the new arrivals now occupied, welcomed them with wild enthusiasm. Philip quickly took charge of the army at Acre and began to reorganize the siege. He had brought with him artificers and material to construct the latest and most sophisticated types of siege machinery and his specialists went at once to work on their tasks. Existing siege weapons were repaired and reinforced, new protective enclosures were built to house them, and the more advanced machines which Philip had brought with him were set up. The whole siege operation took on new life and a brisker, more businesslike pace.

Meanwhile, Richard was engaged in his campaign on Cyprus. Impatience for his arrival mounted in the crusaders' camp and embassies were dispatched to Cyprus to urge him on his way. But Richard would not be hurried. First he had to secure Cyprus. When this was done, he could concentrate on the crusade in Palestine.

Finally, on June 5, he sailed. His fleet headed first for the city of Tyre. Casting anchor in the harbor there, Richard sought to put a party on shore, but the garrison of Tyre refused to allow them to land. They had been ordered, they said, by Philip Augustus and Conrad of Montferrat, not to open the gates and they dared not disobey the orders they had been given. Clearly Philip and Conrad, who was his ally, feared that Richard might act at Tyre in the same way that he had acted on Cyprus: that he might take control of the city and use it as a base for his own operations and for the furtherance of his personal political interests in the Holy Land.

Frustrated and wary of stirring up further trouble at this point, Richard and his army spent the night on board their ships in the harbor of Tyre. The next morning they put to sea again and turned south, toward the Bay of Haifa and the city of Acre.

On its way, Richard's fleet ran across a large transport ship, flying the banner of the French king. The crew, however, appeared to be decidedly un-French. Richard's sailors hailed the vessel to stand to, but they soon discovered that its crew understood neither French nor the signals in use among the Christian fleet. Instead the mystery ship prepared itself for action and showered arrows and Greek fire on Richard's men, who had approached the other ship in a small boat.

Richard then ordered his galleys to make full speed and to try to ram the vessel, which they were now certain was under Muslim command. The attack succeeded. The armored prows of Richard's galleys bit into the enemy ship at a number of different points and the enemy transport was soon on its way to the bottom. The passengers and crew abandoned ship as the attack splintered their vessel. The crews of the galleys slaughtered some of the enemy as they lay in the water, but a few at least were saved and taken prisoner. The ship which had been sunk, Richard's men learned from the survivors, was a troop transport which had been carrying reinforcements to Saladin's army at Acre.

With yet another incidental victory won, then, Richard and his fleet continued on their course for Acre. They finally put into harbor near the camp of the Latin besiegers on Saturday, June 8, and received a tumultuous welcome. Richard's fleet made an enormous impression on both the Christian and Muslim forces at Acre. For their part, the Christian forces rejoiced at his coming, made a great display of joy and exultation, and welcomed Richard's party to the Holy Land with a loud clamor of trumpets and a triumphal procession. Philip Augustus came down to the water's edge to welcome Richard and to congratulate him on his safe arrival after an adventurous voyage.

Muslim observers, looking from afar, found Richard's arrival profoundly depressing. When the celebrating crusaders joyously lit up their camps that night with large bonfires in honor of Richard's arrival, the Muslims in Saladin's camp on the outskirts of Acre, only a short distance from the crusaders' camp, noted glumly that they could see what a vast amount of equipment Richard had brought with him. Even Saladin, although he put on a show of firmness and confidence, found it prudent to renew his pledges to Allah and to ask His assistance in the new phase that was opening in his conflict with the crusading forces.

Most depressed of all were the garrison forces inside the walls of Acre. Although their defenses had not yet been breached, they had become increasingly alarmed as they saw Philip Augustus's new siege engines being set up. Now with the arrival of additional crusading troops and yet more siege machines and supplies in the enemy camp, the besieged troops began to doubt whether they would be able to hold out indefinitely against the augmented forces.

As soon as Richard's tents had been pitched and his household had settled in, he set to the new task at hand. Shortly after his arrival he was approached by representatives both from the Genoese and from the Pisans. Each of these maritime powers was anxious to ally itself with Richard and to share in the conquests which they hoped would be forthcoming under his banner. In short order, Richard decided to join forces with the Pisans, who did homage and fealty to him and pledged their assistance in his campaigns. The Genoese offer he rejected, however, because they had already made agreements with Philip Augustus and Conrad of Montferrat and Richard felt that they would be unlikely to give him whole-hearted cooperation under these circumstances.

Within a few days, Richard was beginning to assume the overall leadership of the crusading forces at Acre. He had a reputation for generosity and for great skill and daring in battle, all of which no doubt made him an attractive leader. More than this, he was quick to demonstrate his ability to take advantage of situations as quickly as they presented themselves. Philip Augustus had made it his policy to pay the men in his service the sum of three gold pieces each month. Richard, immediately after his arrival, announced that he would pay four gold pieces monthly to those who served him and, predictably, this made him extremely popular. The supporters of the French king dwindled almost overnight to a small number of men who were closely bound to Philip Augustus by political ties. The remainder of Philip's army switched its allegiance to the more generous English king. During an early attack upon the crusaders' positions, shortly after Richard's arrival, the effects of the new situation became plain. The Saracen raiders concentrated their attack upon the emplacement of the newly set-up siege machines.

Richard's machines were closely guarded and came through the attack unharmed. Philip's siege weapons were only lightly held and as a result suffered severely and several of them were burnt and put out of action.

Shortly after Richard's arrival at Acre, both he and Philip Augustus fell ill. They suffered from an epidemic disease which the crusading army knew as "Arnaldia." The attack was characterized by a severe fever, in which the hair often fell out. Richard was among those who lost all of their hair temporarily and for some time he was critically ill. He recovered, however, and once again began to immerse himself in military plans and political plots.

On the political side, Richard became embroiled in the divisions over the possession of the throne of Jerusalem. Increasingly he was alienated from Conrad of Montferrat and Philip Augustus and thus found himself drawn into the faction supporting Guy de Lusignan. The quarrels became both more open and more bitter and before Richard had fully recovered from his illness an open rift occurred. Geoffrey de Lusignan, the brother of King Guy, laid a formal complaint against Conrad of Montferrat, accusing him of breach of trust, perjury, and treason against King Guy. Rather than face a trial of the issues, which might have broken up the siege by further inflaming one group in the army against the other, Conrad retired from the crusaders' camp and returned to Tyre.

Philip Augustus's bout with "Arnaldia" was briefer and less critical than Richard's. Within a short time Philip was again up and around, while Richard was still convalescing slowly from his attack. During this period, Philip made a bid to recapture the leadership of the crusading army and to take the military initiative once again. Philip proposed that the crusaders mount an attack against the walls of Acre. Richard, probably because he was not yet well enough to take part in the action himself, refused to sanction Philip's plan and withheld the cooperation of the troops under his command.

Philip went ahead with his plans, despite Richard's refusal, and commenced the attack. In the action, his men were repulsed with serious losses and a Muslim counterattack came perilously close to penetrating the crusaders' own camp. The whole affair was very nearly a complete fiasco and it signaled the end of Philip Augustus's serious chances to resume the leadership of the crusading force. Philip was deeply depressed by the failure of his attack and for some days kept to himself, weeping and mourning his lost chance.

Meanwhile, as the French king was sorrowing over his reverses, Richard was slowly recovering his strength. He was never a patient invalid and he was anxious to get back to the business of capturing Acre. Even before he was fully recovered, he began giving orders and making preparations for a new attack. He had erected a new machine of the catapult type surrounded by a latticework shed to protect it from attempts to set it afire. This machine he now ordered installed in a trench near the walls of Acre and, when he had sent his most skillful and experienced technicians there to operate it, he had himself carried to the machine on July 6. He traveled in a silken litter to watch the work of the new weapon and, no doubt, he also calculated that the enemy might be awed and unnerved by his presence. He may also have calculated that the sight of him, even on a litter, would be enough to lay to rest any rumors about his death or incapacitation which may have been circulating among the enemy forces. Under Richard's direction, his machine began firing missiles at the city walls with gratifying results, since it inflicted a sizable number of casualties on the enemy troops manning the walls.

At the same time, Richard put another group of his troops to work as sappers. They dug a mine from their protected position outside of the walls down toward the foundation of the city's defenses and were able to hack out part of the foundations of one of the towers. As their work proceeded, the sappers propped up the walls of their mine with timber supports and, when they judged that they had penetrated far enough, they evacuated the mine and set fire to the supporting timbers. At the same time, Richard ordered his men on the surface to step up their bombardment of the walls with heavy rocks. The repeated hits of the stone missiles finally knocked the tower, which was the focus of the attack, to bits.

Although his attack had succeeded in reducing a portion of the city's defenses to rubble, the enemy still held the breached area with strong forces and the broken-up terrain immediately in front of the breach made it impossible for Richard to launch a mass attack through the gap in the enemy's defenses.

Pondering the results of the day's action, Richard concluded that a successful assault on the city would depend on devising some means to widen the breach in the walls. By doing this, it would be possible for significant numbers of men to attack along the flanks of the breached area and to penetrate directly into the city without being held back under fire by the impassable terrain directly in front of the tower he had smashed that day.

In order to widen the breach, however, he could not depend on using his machines to batter down the adjoining sections of the walls, since that would simply widen the impassable area and would not leave the necessary access paths for the attackers. Richard therefore announced that he would offer a reward of one gold piece to anyone who could creep up to the walls, loosen a stone, and bring it back. The reward would be paid for each stone brought back to the camp and the offer attracted a number of takers. There were not enough men, however, who were sufficiently foolhardy to risk the excellent chance of being killed by the enemy sentries stationed on the walls and at the breach for the price of one gold piece. Consequently Richard raised the reward, first to two gold pieces per stone, then to three, and then finally to four. This latter figure was too attractive an offer to pass up. A great many brave and greedy young men in the crusaders' camp found the offer attractive enough to brave the dangers and a significant part of the wall was torn down, stone by stone, by the hands of foolhardy volunteers.

Still, it was disappointing to find that the wall was even thicker and more massive than was originally believed and although large numbers of stones were brought back to the crusaders' camp, the breach was still not great enough to admit the kind of attack that Richard had planned. At the same time, the casualties suffered in the course of this project were severe and the army could not sustain such a casualty rate indefinitely without being badly crippled. Accordingly, Richard and his advisers began planning for an all-out assault which would bring the siege to a crisis and which might be able to sap the strength of the defenders at last.

Meanwhile, Saladin was observing these events with growing alarm. The defending forces, he knew, were under tremendous pressure. They could see the defenses crumbling and the very foundations and structure of their city weakening, bit by bit, as the siege engines continued to catapult heavy rocks against the walls and into the adjacent areas of the town. Seeing that the chances of the town holding out indefinitely were slim, Saladin began to take practical steps to prepare for the possibility that it might be taken by his enemies. On July 8, he sent a detachment of his men to the city of Haifa, at the other end of the bay on which Acre was situated. If Acre fell into the hands of the crusaders, Haifa's situation would become untenable very quickly and Saladin decided not to attempt to hold on to it. He ordered his men to evacuate the city and then to burn and destroy the town, so that it would not offer another strong point for the crusaders to occupy. During the next two days, following the destruction of Haifa, Saladin's troops applied the torch to the villages and the crops standing in the fields in the vicinity of Acre, so as to make it difficult for the crusaders to maintain their control of the region even if they did manage to take the city.

Even amid the fighting on both sides, there were gracious interludes. Saladin felt no personal animus against the kings of France and England and the rigors of the siege were lightened by the gifts of plums from Damascus, pears, and other delicacies which he sent to his fellow monarchs, even while his armies were devastating the whole region roundabout and making it uninhabitable for their forces. Doubtless Saladin had some hope that he could reach a compromise agreement with the kings from overseas and that he might be able to settle upon some partition of the Holy Land which would save their honor and yet leave him in actual control of the region. At this point, however, neither Philip nor Richard was disposed to negotiate seriously with the sultan and, although they accepted his gifts, they refused to bargain with him.

Meanwhile, the garrison in Acre was growing desperate. They had been under siege for almost two years. The recent attacks had far surpassed in their ferocity anything that the garrison had previously experienced and the signs that an all-out assault was being prepared daily became clearer. As early as July 4, the authorities in the city sent messengers to the crusaders' camp, intimating that they were considering surrender and proposing terms to the leaders of the crusade. Richard and Philip agreed in rejecting the proposals which were made to them and declared that while they might consider allowing the populace of Acre to go free, they must receive in return a cession of all of the territory captured by Saladin from the Latin states, as well as the return of all the prisoners held by him and other concessions in addition. The representatives of the Acre garrison could not have met these terms even if they had wished to do so. They had not been empowered by Saladin to negotiate on his behalf and, indeed, he was as yet unaware that they had made any peace feelers toward the crusading forces.

On July 5, the leaders of the crusade leaked the news of the peace proposals from Acre to the sultan. Saladin was shocked to learn that his garrison had been negotiating without first informing him of their intentions, but he also sympathized with the position in which they found themselves. He promised the defenders that he would do his best to help them, but in fact there was little he could do. After the crusaders attacked in force with their machines and sappers on July 6, Saladin could only agree with the commanders of his garrison that surrender might be the best solution for the city.

The siege dragged on several days longer. On July 11 the garrison made a last effort to drive off the crusading army, but without any significant success. On the following day, July 12, the defenders of Acre agreed to surrender to the crusaders. They did so with Saladin's reluctant permission. The garrison had sent a swimmer to contact him. He had agreed that they should bargain for the best terms they could get and the messenger returned with this news to the city.

Armed with Saladin's permission to surrender, the commanders of the Muslim garrison at Acre then turned to complete their negotiations with the crusaders. They offered to turn over the city entirely to the Latins and to vacate their own citizens. In addition, they promised that, if they were allowed to leave the city without hindrance, they would turn over the relics of the Holy Cross, which Saladin had captured at the battle of Hattin, together with 200 Christian prisoners whom they held.

The crusading leaders pronounced these terms unacceptable and declared that they must have further concessions. The Muslim negotiators then tried to improve their offer. In addition to the points specified in their earlier offer, they stated their willingness to turn over additional Christian captives, to a total of 2,500 in all, and to give the crusaders the sum of 200,000 dinars. Further they specified that their surrender of the city would include all of the equipment, weapons, supplies, ships and other goods in the town. The citizens would leave the city, taking with them nothing but the clothes in which they stood. Beyond this, the Muslim negotiators promised an additional payment of 400 dinars to Conrad of Montferrat, who acted as the representative of the Latin forces in the surrender negotiations.

Conrad duly reported the new terms to King Richard, King Philip, and the other Latin leaders. The two kings, in turn, consulted with their own advisers and quickly reached a consensus that they ought to accept the new terms. They stipulated that the surrender terms must be put in writing and that the leading citizens of Acre together with the chief officers of the town's garrison must be taken into Latin custody and held as hostages to insure the performance of the surrender agreement in good faith.

While the final statement of the surrender terms was being drawn up, the Acre garrison's leaders reported the agreement to Saladin. He was shocked at the harshness of the terms and was inclined to advise the garrison not to agree to them. While he was still making up his mind as to whether or not he should require the garrison to bargain further, Saladin looked out at the walls of Acre and saw the crusaders raising their banners and putting up crosses on the city walls, while shouts of rejoicing were lifted in the crusaders' camp. It was noon on Friday, July 12, and the surrender of Acre was an accomplished fact. There was nothing more that Saladin could do to save the city and its population.

As Saladin sat in his tent, somber and dispirited over the loss of Acre, the crusaders were busily taking control of the city. Conrad of Montferrat bore the standards of Richard and Philip Augustus into the town and raised one to the pinnacle of the citadel, the other to the top of the minaret of the Great Mosque, while other standards were fluttering from buildings and walls within the town. Duke Leopold of Austria, as one of the early besiegers of the city, had his own banner unfurled and carried solemnly into Acre, just following Richard's banner. Richard was grossly offended by this, for Leopold by this symbolic action appeared to be claiming a share in the glory of capturing Acre equal to his own. Richard's men, interpreting his haughty disapproval of Leopold's action, seized the Austrian duke's banner, threw it to the ground, and trampled it into the dirt. Leopold, incensed at this insult, withdrew from Acre and left the vicinity that same night, accompanied by his own followers. He returned as quickly as possible to Austria, still nursing resentment and hostility toward Richard.

Meanwhile Richard and Philip ordered public criers to circulate among the crusaders and to proclaim new regulations for the conduct of the victors toward the vanquished. The crusaders were not to curse or revile the men whom they had defeated. There was to be no ill-treatment of them. The crusaders were strictly forbidden to throw stones or other missiles at the defeated Muslims and they were ordered to maintain decorum and order in their own ranks.

When they describe the evacuation of the city by the Muslims, the Christian writers who were present show, for once, a strangely respectful attitude and a real admiration for their defeated foes:

On this critical day, one of them wrote, the probity of these Turks was admirable, as was their great bravery, for they were most vigorous in military enterprises, distinguished in their magnificence. Now, as they crossed over their high walls on their way out of the city, they were regarded by the deeply curious eyes of the Christians, who admired them especially as soldiers and who recalled their memories. Their appearance, as they emerged almost empty-handed from the city was, nonetheless, amazing in its gracefulness and dignity. They were unconquered by their adversities.*

As the Muslims left, the crusaders formed up for their mass entrance into the deserted city. The gates were opened

---

* *Itinerarium regis Ricardi*, 3.18, ed. W. Stubbs, p. 233.

and the victors crowded in, dancing, shouting, and giving vent to their gratitude and relief that the long siege was successfully over. The city was partitioned between Richard and Philip Augustus. King Philip took possession of the former palace of the Knights Templars and settled his household and attendants there, while Richard took over the royal palace, where he established his wife and sister together with the royal servants and other members of his immediate retinue. The rest of the army was scattered throughout the city in the houses just vacated by the Muslim population. The soldiery roamed through the streets, snatching up the goods and furniture left behind by the evacuation of the Muslim population and searching for more valuable treasure caches everywhere. It was a time for rejoicing, of relaxation, and thanksgiving in the Christian ranks.

Saladin observed all of this in gloomy silence. On July 13 he ordered most of his forces to pull back a short distance from the positions they had occupied during the siege of Acre. He himself remained at his original post, accompanied by a small retinue, in order to keep a close watch on developments at Acre. He had the troop movement carried out at night, hoping against hope that when the Latins saw the next morning what had happened they would try to attack his outpost and thus give him a chance to surprise them with an attack from the rear. Richard and the other commanders of the crusading army, however, refused to play into Saladin's hands and concerned themselves instead with the problems of administering Acre.

There were plenty of problems to cope with. For one thing a system for guarding the hostages turned over to them by the enemy had to be set up. The hostages were divided between Richard and Philip Augustus and each assumed responsibility for the safety of his own share of the captives. There were problems concerning the return of property in Acre which had belonged to members of the Latin army before Saladin's capture of the city and of ensuring an equitable settlement of their interests now that the city had passed again into Latin hands. Problems also arose concerning the property rights of the conquerors, who had partitioned the city, but had left some areas in dispute. The detailed solution of individual complaints and petitions was left for the most part in the hands of Hugh de Gournai, whom Richard appointed the governor for the portion of the city under his jurisdiction, and of Drogo de Mello, who was appointed by Philip Augustus to govern his part of the town.

On July 16, there were lengthy religious services, presided over by Cardinal Alard of Verona, the pope's representative, to purify the churches which had been put to other uses during the Saracen occupation and to restore them to the service of Christianity. Besides, Richard was busy with new diplomatic negotiations. Saladin had already sent presents to him; now Richard was obliged to observe the niceties of relationships between monarchs by returning the favor. Moreover, on the same day there arrived ambassadors from another Muslim potentate, the sultan of Muscat. This ruler was worried by Saladin's ascendancy in the Muslim world, for he feared that the growth of Saladin's power might diminish his own position and that Saladin might even attack his domains. He therefore dispatched an embassy to Richard, proposing that he and Richard combine their interests and their forces to make war upon Saladin. Saladin, learning of this, made counter-proposals of his own. He was interested not only in preventing Richard from joining with the sultan of Muscat, but also in achieving, if possible, a settlement which would forestall any further campaigning in Palestine by Richard and the crusading army. Ultimately, however, Richard rejected the terms offered by both of his would-be Muslim allies.

During the next several days, Richard and Philip dealt with a variety of further demands. The bankers and merchants from the Italian cities, who had long-standing commercial interests in the Holy Land, demanded that part of Acre be set aside for their businesses and that they be awarded the right to create within the commercial quarters of the city self-governing enclaves of their townsmen. These merchant quarters were to be treated as extraterritorial extensions of the home cities of the businessmen who settled in them. The negotiation of detailed treaties concerning these settlements was a time-consuming and wearying business, but it was also vitally important for the economic health of Acre under its new Latin overlords. The nobles who served in the army which had captured the city also demanded that they be rewarded with concessions within the town and dealing with their demands was also a tiresome but essential matter for the two kings. The nobles who were dissatisfied with the concessions allotted to them threatened to quit the crusade and to return immediately to the West and a number of them did precisely that then they found that further concessions would not be forthcoming. Settlement of these claims in a satisfactory fashion was thus essential to the continuation of the crusade itself.

On July 22, Philip Augustus revealed that he, too, proposed to return to Europe and to abandon the crusade at this point. The furor in the crusaders' camp as a result of this announcement was enormous, yet the sentiment itself cannot have come as a great surprise either to Richard or to the other leaders of the crusade. Philip had never been an enthusiastic crusader in the way that Richard was. He took no delight in warfare and considered the whole business simply as one means among many for achieving what he wanted. Whereas Richard genuinely loved to match his strength and wits against others on the field of battle, Philip was more calculating and, in a sense, more modern in his attitude. The crusade held no great attraction for Philip, but it did serve his policy to participate in it, up to a point at least. By serving as a crusader, Philip put the Church permanently under an obligation to himself. And the Church constituted a major power within the French kingdom; ecclesiastical support was essential for a successful king. Philip calculated, quite rightly, that not only the pope and the Roman curia, but also the French hierarchy throughout his kingdom would find it difficult to oppose the policies of a crusader-king. This had been one of his major reasons for going on crusade, but by now he had invested sufficient time and money in the crusade to establish his identity as a crusader beyond any question. If he prolonged his participation in the crusade, that would not significantly increase the good which he could expect to extract from his status as a crusader. Accordingly, now that Acre was in the crusaders' hands and the crusade had achieved a solid success, Philip felt that he had done his part. No further purpose, from his viewpoint, would be served by staying longer in the Holy Land.

There were other considerations, too. Philip was certainly a sufficiently acute judge of persons to have concluded that Richard would disagree with him about the desirability of returning to Europe at this point. He could count on Richard to stay in the East, at least for a few months, possibly for an even longer term. Thus if Philip returned home at this point he could count on having a relatively free hand for perhaps half a year or more, while Richard remained in Palestine. This would give Philip opportunities in plenty to raise havoc with the Angevin lands and feudatories in France. Perhaps Philip foresaw even more fertile chances for disrupting the Angevins. We simply do not know what he thought, but we have every reason to believe that his thoughts had taken some such line as this, for such plans are entirely consistent with everything that we know about his character, his actions, and his way of proceeding in political affairs.

When Philip informed Richard, through the bishop of Beauvais and other intermediaries, of his intention to leave the Holy Land forthwith, Richard's reaction was equivocal. He was to some degree disappointed to see his overlord and peer withdraw from the crusade while its business was, from his own point of view, only partially completed. On the other hand, Richard recognized that if Philip were to leave, then there would be no other Christian prince in the East to challenge his authority or to compete with him for power there. Philip's departure would leave Richard a free hand to conduct the remainder of the crusade as he saw fit, and this prospect delighted him.

Richard's official answer to the French king's message reflected his equivocal attitude: "It will be a shame and a disgrace for my lord if he goes away without having completed the business on which he came here. But still, if he finds himself ailing, or in bad health, and is afraid lest he should die here, his will be done."

Philip was perfectly satisfied with this response. Richard had offered him a reasonable way out and he took it. He had, indeed, been plagued with a series of illnesses since he arrived in the Holy Land and there was nothing dishonorable about yielding to the demands of bodily infirmity. He could leave with a clear conscience, or at least with a reasonable excuse for his actions, together with the half-reluctant blessing of his principal comrade in arms. Moreover, he was willing to leave behind such of his own men as wished to continue campaigning in the Holy Land. The French army need not return with their king and the choice was left to each individual to make for himself. The duke of Burgundy was appointed as Philip's representative on the crusade to guard his interests after his departure, but in point of fact Richard of England became the universally accepted commander-in-chief of the crusading forces.

Once the decision had been made that Philip was to leave, there were some important issues to be settled immediately. Of capital importance was an agreement between Richard and Philip on French affairs. Richard was not naive, to say the least, and he recognized that Philip had both the motive and the opportunity to damage his interests in Europe so long as Richard remained out of the way in Palestine. Richard wanted assurance that Philip would not attack his subjects and allies in France, at least until Richard was in a position to defend himself. He also demanded that Philip agree to some equitable procedure for settling any quarrels or crises which might arise during the period between Philip's return to France and Richard's later arrival in his own realm. Philip agreed, with some reluctance, to give assurances that he would not harm Richard's French domains until the English king's return and that, should any crisis arise within those lands during Richard's absence, he would not intervene until a forty-day cooling-off period had elapsed. This was the most that Richard could secure by way of reassurance and with it he had to be content.

The other outstanding issue of great importance which needed settlement at this juncture was the question of the possession of the throne of Jerusalem and of the succession to that office. On this matter, a compromise was eventually reached after some discussion and negotiation between Richard and Philip. Conrad of Montferrat laid formal claim to the title of king of Jerusalem on the basis of his contention that Guy de Lusignan had forfeited the title by his defeat at Hattin. Richard was not willing to allow Guy, whose family were allied to his own, to be thus rudely dispossessed. Philip, on the other hand, stood behind Conrad's claim. There was a considerable bandying of words over the conflicting claims, but eventually a settlement was reached. By the terms of the compromise, Guy was to retain the title of king of Jerusalem for the remainder of his lifetime, provided that his heirs and descendants were to forfeit any rights of succession to the royal office. His tenure of office was thus reduced to a personal title for life. Further it was agreed that Conrad of Montferrat and his wife, Isabella, were to succeed to the Jerusalem throne upon Guy's death and that their children should have an hereditary claim to the succession after the deaths of Conrad and Isabella. For the immediate future, so long as Guy lived, the revenues of the crown were to be split between Guy and Conrad, each receiving half. At Guy's death, the entire income of the crown was to revert to Conrad and his wife. Moreover, Conrad was to have possession of Tyre, Beirut, and Sidon even during Guy's lifetime, while King Guy and his brother, Geoffrey de Lusignan, retained control of the remaining territories of the Latin kingdom, which at this point meant principally the city of Acre, plus Jaffa and Caesarea, which Geoffrey controlled.

Agreement on this settlement was reached on July 28. There were few other issues to be discussed. Philip declared, as he had done before, that by terms of the agreement between himself and Richard at Messina, the spoils of Richard's conquest in Cyprus should be considered part of the spoils of the crusade and thus that he should receive one half of Richard's booty there. Richard denied this interpretation of the Messina agreement. Further, he pointed out that the count of Flanders had just recently died and that Philip laid claim to his inheritance. If Philip was going to consider the Cypriot conquest as part of the spoils of the crusade and claim half of them, then Richard declared that for his part he would consider the legacy of the count of Flanders as spoils of the crusade and would lay claim to one half of that inheritance. Neither king was willing to concede the other's rights in either of these cases, and the question was left unsettled.

At last, on July 31, Philip departed from the camp of the crusading army and made his way to Tyre. He was accompanied by Conrad of Montferrat, who was not eager to remain at Acre or to serve in the army under Richard's command. Three days later, after a brief stopover in Tyre, Philip embarked with a small fleet carrying his household and a few followers and set sail for Brindisi.

The departure of Philip left Richard in control of the crusade and he entered immediately into further negotiations with Saladin. The earlier surrender agreement concerning the delivery of Acre to the crusaders had been concluded with the sultan's subordinates; Richard wanted assurance from Saladin himself that he was prepared to fulfill the commitments made by the Acre garrison. Saladin, in reply, assured Richard that he had every intention of honoring the commitments and that he was working to implement the delivery of money and prisoners which had been conditions of the surrender terms. The sultan's messengers intimated, however, that Saladin would prefer to turn over both the prisoners and the money payments in three installments, separated by a month between each delivery. Richard agreed to this, in part because he was having difficulty in laying his own hands upon the Muslim prisoners who were supposed to be exchanged in the bargain. The Muslim hostages were physically in the hands of Conrad of Montferrat at Tyre and it required some further negotiation, undertaken in the first instance by Hubert Walter, bishop of Salisbury, and at a later stage by the duke of Burgundy and other envoys, to secure their transfer to Richard's possession. After much persuasive argument, Conrad gave up the hostages to Richard's representatives, but he refused to return to Acre himself.

Meanwhile, the date set for the payment of the first installment of the ransom money was approaching. When the envoys from Richard's camp met with Saladin's representatives on August 11 to superintend the transfer of men and money, there was a dispute. The crusaders claimed that, although the number of men whom they received was right, their instructions specified that certain named individuals were to have been among those exchanged and that these individuals were missing. Saladin's representatives denied this, claiming that the agreement under which they were operating had not specified the names of individuals to be exchanged on the three dates which were stipulated. Neither side would agree to the other's version of the matter, and accordingly both groups of envoys returned to their camps with poor reports of the cooperation from the other group.

Richard was dissatisfied and impatient, restless to be on the move again. Further negotiations with the Muslims seemed likely to hold little hope of a speedy resolution of the disagreement. In his impatience, Richard ordered his tents set up outside of Acre's walls and on August 14 he moved from his quarters in the palace in Acre to his tents in the field outside, where he remained for the following week. Presumably he was waiting with increasing testiness for Saladin to give way and to come round to fulfilling their agreement in the way that Richard interpreted it. As the days passed, Richard's fury increased proportionally. When the twentieth of August arrived and still no concessions had been made by his antagonists, Richard's fury burst its bounds. He would wait for the enemy no longer. On the afternoon of that day he ordered his forces to move down to the wells near Tell al'Ayadiyya and to occupy the plains between that point and Tell Kaisan.

When the infantry and cavalry units had encircled the indicated site, Richard had the Muslim hostages brought out, some two thousand seven hundred men chained together. When they had been prodded into position, Richard gave the signal for his troops to fall on the chained prisoners and murder them. They did so, we are told, with eagerness and thanked God for the opportunity furnished them by Him and Richard to take revenge for their comrades who had fallen during the siege of Acre.

It was cold-blooded butchery, flagrantly in violation of the laws of warfare as they were then understood and clearly at odds with the standards of that chivalrous conduct upon which Richard so prided himself. The murder of his Muslim prisoners at Acre reveals the worst side of Richard's character: he could not endure being thwarted and when he was opposed strongly enough to frustrate his designs, there was no depth to which he would not sink in order to relieve his frustration. His prisoners at Acre had become an embarrassment. Richard was eager to get on with his campaign and he preferred not to be bothered with a cargo of men who were useless to him. When he found that he could not quickly exchange them, he had them slaughtered. It was as simple as that. Richard's apologists, both among his contemporaries and later, have found this action difficult to reconcile with an idealized picture of Richard as a chivalrous gentleman, as well they might. That he thought that he had a perfect right to deal with his prisoners in this way is no doubt true, but it is also true that he consistently expected others to live up to a stricter standard of honor than he did. He would have denounced most sternly a similar action by his opponents, but was not overly scrupulous in accounting for his own actions.

The crusaders, after beheading their prisoners, proceeded to mutilate their bodies. They slit open the bellies of the slaughtered men and drew out their viscera, in order to recover the gold coins which some of the condemned men had swallowed.

The Muslims, who watched the beginnings of the massacre in horror, took the field too late to save any of the prisoners from their fate. Although Saladin's men attacked Richard's forces soon after they realized what was going on, they were unable to break through the lines and rescue their compatriots. Although this rescue attempt failed, Latin prisoners subsequently taken by the Muslims were to pay with their lives for Richard's atrocity at Acre.

On the following day, the Muslims reoccupied the killing ground and collected the mutilated bodies of their compatriots and co-religionists. While they were busy with their grisly task, Richard and his army were preparing to leave Acre. Richard decided to leave his wife and sister, together with the daughter of Isaac of Cyprus, whom he still held as hostage, in Acre. He appointed Bertram of Verdun and Stephan Longchamp as his agents to look after his interests in Acre during his absence from the city.

On August 22 Richard led his forces out of Acre and headed south along the coastal road, while the ships of the crusaders' fleet paralleled his march just offshore.

SEVEN

Richard's Crusade: The Final Phase

Richard was determined to press on with his crusade as soon as possible after the departure of Philip Augustus from the Holy Land and the settlement of the pressing questions which were raised by his leaving. From all indications, however, Richard's army was not nearly so eager to hurry onward as was their leader. The army had found Acre delightful. The weather was fair and the climate was almost as seductive as the native women who swarmed into the city and delighted the men with their appearance and their talents. The wine of Acre was delightful, too, and the rank-and-file of the army in a few short weeks had come to accept Acre as a reasonable approximation of paradise. It was a wrench to tear themselves away from the city and from the pleasant life it held. But Richard insisted and few were so foolhardy or so careless of their health as to disobey Richard's direct order.

They set out from Acre on August 22, marching under the summer sun in a curious kind of lockstep with their opponents. For as Richard's army moved southward, with its ships at sea paralleling the line of march, so also the Muslim army under Saladin followed their movements and pursued another closely parallel course farther inland. Their progress was slow. They did not reach Haifa, the next town of importance, until August 26. They spent a full day there, replenishing supplies, and marched to the River of Crocodiles on August 29. The name by which they knew the river was not merely an imaginative nickname: two soldiers from the army were devoured by the beasts, who swarmed along the river's banks. Two days later they were at Caesarea, and they camped at the River of the Dead on the first day of September. Throughout the march Richard led the van of the army, accompanied by the Norman banner, which was carried by a knight specially chosen for this honor. The standard was used as a signal flag, both to mark the position of the king and also to direct troop movements. Behind the Norman banner marched the English, while the French troops in the army brought up the rear, under the command of Duke Hugh of Burgundy.

The heat was a constant burden to the men. Considerable numbers fainted daily from heat exhaustion and several of them died from the exertion of struggling on through the summer days. When possible, those who suffered most severely from the heat were transferred to the galleys of the fleet, so that they might not hold back the progress of the army.

On September 3, the forces left their camp at the River of the Dead and marched to the Salt River, where they camped for the two following nights. They rested there and feasted on the bodies of the horses that had died on the journey. The meat supplies of the army were inadequate and Richard made a special point of regulating the distribution of the horse meat so as to prevent hoarding. Properly seasoned, one of his companions noted, it was delicious and their stay at the Salt River was a memorable occasion for the men.

Leaving this camp, they resumed their march on September 5. On this leg of their journey they were marching through wooded country in the forest of Arsuf and that night they reached the Nahr Falek, a river the crusaders knew as Rochetaille. By this point the situation of the crusaders and their opponents was coming to a crisis. Saladin could not follow the crusading army down the coast indefinitely without attempting to halt their march and defeat them. There had been some preliminary attempts at discussion between emissaries of the leaders on September 5, but these were inconclusive and the talks had been broken off. Now Saladin chose his ground for battle. His disposed his men so as to block the passage of Richard's army across the plains which separated the city of Arsuf from the forest.

Richard sensed that the crisis was imminent and began disposing his troops to deal with the situation as it developed. He decided to let Saladin make the initial attack, rather than to try to forestall his enemy by attacking first. The animals bearing the army's baggage were sent to the coast and spread out in a string along the seashore, where they and the infantry assigned to guard them acted as an anchor for the crusaders' battle formation. In a line in front of the baggage train the mounted knights in full armor were disposed. Surrounding them, in turn, and forming a wall in the front ranks of the whole army were the archers on foot, kneeling behind their shields, which presented a solid front to their attackers. In the center of the line of knights was King Richard, with his English and Norman troops on either side of him. Beyond them on the right, to the south of the Anglo-Normans, were the Bretons, the Angevins, and the troops of Guienne, while the Templars held the end of the line and the right flank. To Richard's left were the Flemings and the Latins of the Holy Land, together with the French forces. The northern end of the line and the left flank were manned by the Hospitalers.

The troop dispositions were in order and the men had taken up their assigned places in the early morning. They stood to their places in the morning sun until almost nine o'clock, when the enemy opened an attack against their lines. The initial attack was made by lightly armed infantrymen, using bows and light spears. The first wave of attackers were Turks; they were followed by a contingent of Negro troops, then by Bedouin Arabs on foot. The whole visible area on the plains, between the forest and the front ranks of the crusaders' army was covered, it seemed, by screaming Muslim attackers, who shot their arrows at a high trajectory to bring them down into the ranks of the Latin infantry, while others attempted to break bodily through the infantry screen and to penetrate to the second-line defenses where the knights stood their ground. In the fiercely pressed attack the Latin infantry lines gave way at several points, pushed back by the weight of numbers and by the heavy rain of arrows and missiles falling on their ranks. Some of the Latin infantrymen, terrified by the seemingly endless waves of attackers, threw down their bows and took to their heels, seeking refuge from the torrent of enemies who hurled themselves repeatedly against the shield-wall of the Latins' front line. Even where the enemy was able to penetrate the front line, however, they were unable to make a dent in the ranks of the heavily armored knights.

Richard's plan was to keep his troops in place and to wait until the enemy attack had worn itself out before launching his countermove. Throughout the morning he rode up and down the lines of his men, encouraging them to hold their places and to keep orderly ranks. He needed to lure the main enemy forces closer to his own ranks before counterattacking if he was to succeed in his battle plan.

Suddenly the massed waves of the enemy infantry opened their lines and a further wave of attackers charged through. These were Turkish light cavalry, armed with swords and battle axes. The enemy cavalry concentrated their strike against the left flank of Richard's battle line, bringing the heaviest pressure to bear on the Hospitalers, the Flemings, and the Latins of the Holy Land. As the Turkish cavalry attacked, retired, and attacked again, impatience flooded the ranks of the Latin knights. The master of the

Hospitalers sent messengers to Richard, begging permission to break ranks and charge the enemy. Richard refused and ordered the ranks to hold. Twice more the request was made and twice more Richard refused to allow his men to counter the attack, as successive Turkish charges halted and turned back when they were unable to break through the crusaders' lines.

Still Richard held to his tactical plan: no forward moves until the enemy had committed his reserves irrevocably to the battle. The Hospitalers in particular felt that they were being pressed beyond tolerable limits. They burned with eagerness to charge at the enemy, certain that the weight of their forces would run the Muslims literally into the ground; but still Richard commanded them to hold back. It was a tribute to the strict discipline of the military orders that the master and their officers were able to keep their men in line as long as they did in the face of overwhelming temptation to strike back at the foe.

Suddenly, two men broke ranks. They were the marshal of the Hospitalers and Baldwin Carew. Defying Richard's orders, these two took matters into their own hands. Spurring their horses, they charged at the enemy lines. Seeing their move, other knights in the line, thinking that the order to attack must finally have been given, started out after them. Soon the whole cavalry line was in motion.

The direction of attack was not clear, since it was unplanned and uncoordinated. The planned order of battle was reversed because the men who precipitated the counterattack were from units that were supposed to bring up the army's rear guard. Richard, seeing what was happening, decided instantly that he must make the best of the situation. To call back his charging knights was clearly impossible, for that would give the enemy the initiative and his knights would be extremely vulnerable if they attempted to retreat to their earlier positions and reform their lines. Richard accordingly rode into the mêlée to take command of the attack that he had not planned. Bringing some order into the chaos of milling men and horses, he rallied his forces and directed their attack at what he thought was the weakest point of the enemy's line. Richard himself was in the middle of the shock of combat. Swinging his sword with all his might, he smashed it down on the enemy soldiers and split the body of one of them cleanly in two. With a scything motion, Richard hit out right and left, cleaving a path through the enemy forces like a field hand at the harvest. As the tempo of the fighting increased, clouds of dust were kicked up by the swirling hooves of the horses, so that the combatants themselves had a hard time telling friend from foe and sometimes were uncertain just who it was they were fighting. Through the clouds of dust they could intermittently make out a confused panorama of banners and pennants of all colors and shapes. The swords of the dead and wounded littered the field underfoot, interspersed with Turkish bows and the teeth of hideously grinning corpses whose faces had been slashed into ribbons by the wheeling and clashing swords. The horses of the slain wandered through the clouds of dust on the field, nuzzling curiously at the severed heads of bearded Turks, looking for their lost masters.

In the face of the initial shock of the crusaders' attack, the enemy forces fell back temporarily and seemed to lose their initiative. As the lines of the Latin army reformed, however, their enemies got a second wind and renewed their own attack. Richard, seeing the tide of battle beginning to turn against him, withdrew momentarily from the middle of the fighting. Quickly detaching a small company of selected knights from his main force, Richard wheeled around with his companions and speedily made his way to the right flank, then wheeled again and attacked the enemy from the side, while his main forces were still engaged in the center and on the left flank. This final attack ultimately won the day. The enemy, finding himself threatened from still another quarter, was thrown into confusion. Muslim troops began to break ranks and to flee from the field of battle. Although Saladin personally plunged in to rally his troops and to lead another charge against the crusaders, it came too late. By sundown the enemy had retired from the field of battle, leaving it in the weary, blood-spattered hands of Richard and his army.

As they began clearing their way through the debris and carnage of the battlefield, the dimensions of Richard's victory slowly began to appear. The piles of enemy dead were impressive: one of the men estimated that there were seven thousand bodies on the field, among them thirty-two emirs. Although Richard had failed to gain a decisive victory which would put the enemy out of action permanently, he had certainly achieved a significant success. No longer was there any thought that the Christians in the Holy Land had lost their fighting spirit. Moreover, the aura of success that Saladin had enjoyed was at least temporarily shattered. Richard had proved that it was possible to beat him on the field of battle and to weaken his army seriously. Coming soon upon the heels of the capture of Acre, the Battle of Arsuf made many feel that the tide of Muslim victory had been turned at last. There was new hope in the ranks of the crusaders. Perhaps after all the reconquest of Jerusalem was possible, now that the Christian forces had a leader of Richard's stature, who could stand up to the best men that Saladin could put into the field and could overcome them.

Richard's reputation was unequaled at this point among the princes of Christendom. Although he had not been able to hold his men in check long enough to sweep the enemy entirely off the battlefield, he had shown astonishing capacity as a commander at Arsuf. Rallying his men in the heat of battle, taking advantage of a situation which had developed unpredictably and devising new battle plans while personally locked with the enemy in savage combat: these were feats no ordinary commander could bring off. Tired as he must have been, Richard never looked better than he did that evening among the noisome smells and hideous piles of corpses which testified to his victory at Arsuf. True, he did not—probably could not—follow through his victory and exploit the situation to its fullest. Had he been able to rally his forces yet again at the end of the day and to pursue the enemy further than he did, he might have increased the magnitude of his triumph. But as it was, the day was clearly his and his army in all likelihood could not have been spurred on any further than it was.

For Saladin, the situation was becoming serious. He had not been able to save Acre. He had made the fatal mistake of waiting too long and allowing his foes to build up forces which he could not overcome. That in itself was a failure of serious dimensions. Now, on top of that, he had suffered a major defeat on the field of battle itself, in a straightforward contest with his Christian enemies. A battle lost was one thing, and the damage could be repaired without undue delay. But Saladin was on the verge of losing more than just a battle. The prestige he had accumulated, the aura of unbroken success which he had earned—these were valuable assets and Richard's victories at Acre and at Arsuf were eroding those assets quickly.

On the day following the Battle of Arsuf, Richard was busy. James d'Avesnes, one of the stalwarts of the crusading forces, had been slain at Arsuf after fighting heroically and killing great numbers of the enemy. His body was recovered and brought into the city of Arsuf where, with great solemnity, a funeral Mass was held at the Church of St. Mary. King Richard, accompanied by King Guy de Lusignan, attended the ceremony, together with a great crowd of knights and notables from the ranks of the crusading army. Following the burial of James and the interment of the other dead, Richard reorganized his forces for further action.

On September 9, the day after the funeral services, Richard led his forces out of Arsuf and headed in the direction of Jaffa, where they arrived on September 10. There they settled in for almost a month. Saladin, meanwhile, after following the crusaders to Jaffa, moved his own army to Ascalon, where he evacuated the population and had his men dismantle the fortifications. Clearly he feared that the crusaders might successfully attack Ascalon and make it into another strong point on the Mediterranean shore. Rather than allow this to happen, he was willing to destroy the city and resettle its populace elsewhere. Once Ascalon had been dismantled, Saladin moved on to Ramla. There he dismantled the castle, for the same reasons that he had leveled Ascalon, and then in late September he went to Jerusalem to superintend the strengthening of the walls and defensive works there. Clearly Saladin was preparing to concentrate his maximum defensive strength at a few essential points, while allowing Richard and his army to move comparatively freely through the rest of the region.

At Jaffa, the crusaders were also engaged in construction work. The city was an important coastal town with a relatively good harbor and had for centuries served as the port city for Jerusalem. Richard's strategy called for the preparation of a strong base at Jaffa, where he could stockpile supplies and men safely in preparation for an attack on Jerusalem itself. Hence Jaffa's fortifications now required repair and strengthening to fit the city for its role in Richard's plans. Richard was engaged during most of September and the opening days of October in supervising the construction and repair work there and also in laying in supplies in preparation for the next stage in his projected campaign. While this work was proceeding, Richard also sent a small force of scouts farther down the coast to reconnoiter the situation there and to report back on the conditions at Ascalon. His interest in this region presumably meant that he was considering further plans for occupying one or more strategic sites in the south which could serve to cut Saladin off from direct communication by land with his base in Egypt.

September 29, the Feast of St. Michael the Archangel, was a festive day in the English camp and Richard took advantage of the break to make a hunting trip. Accompanied by a handful of companions, Richard went out with his hawks into the country to enjoy a day's respite from his cares. The chase and the thrill of working with his hawks had always been one of Richard's joys and at this point it provided him with badly needed diversion. As the party followed the birds, they kept their attention fixed on the action in the air and paid scant attention to their own security arrangements. Suddenly a force of Turkish soldiers appeared, seemingly out of nowhere. The Turks swept down upon the little hunting party and attacked them. Richard, who was standing as he worked his falcon, was scarcely able to mount his horse before the attackers reached him. At once he spurred his horse to put some distance between himself and the enemy and then drew his sword to defend himself against the onslaught. At one point in the fray Richard was completely surrounded by enemies and seemed about to be taken prisoner by them, when one of his companions, William de Préaux, realizing the seriousness of the situation, created a diversion. William knew some Arabic and he began shouting so that the enemy could hear him, saying that he himself was the king. Immediately the group of Turks around Richard broke up and set off after William, whom they captured and quickly took away. Meanwhile, Richard and the rest of his hunting companions were defending themselves as best they could against the other Turks. Four of Richard's party were killed in action during the mêlée, but the rest of the group was able to get back to Jaffa without serious damage.

Richard's narrow escape caused a furor among his followers. Several of his closest friends took the chance to try to persuade him to take better care of himself and to be more cautious of his personal safety in the future. Richard, however, paid little attention to their advice and continued to be as reckless of his own person as he was cautious for the safety of those who followed him.

A few days later, Richard opened a new diplomatic offensive by dispatching a messenger to Saladin's camp offering to begin talks about peace terms. Obviously Richard was not entirely happy at this point about the prospects for a clear-cut military victory in the Holy Land. Moreover, he had other problems to consider. The situation on Cyprus was troublesome, for one thing. One of Richard's governors on the island had died and the remaining governor, Robert of Thornham, had been faced by a revolt of the Cypriot population. He was able to quell the uprising, but the situation of Richard's garrison forces on the island was precarious. Rather than continue to be distracted by the cares of governing Cyprus, Richard decided to dispose of the island. He approached the Templars and was able to strike a bargain with them whereby he would turn the control of Cyprus over to them in return for a cash settlement, of which a down payment of 40,000 dinars was turned over to him immediately. The Templars promised, in addition, to pay him a further 60,000 dinars in installments as they collected revenues from the island. Meanwhile the down payment relieved Richard's immediate financial worries and provided a useful supply of ready cash. Although the Cyprus problem was soon disposed of, at least temporarily, other problems could not be so quickly dispatched. Richard's army found Jaffa a pleasant city, if not quite so pleasant as Acre had been, and, as the men discovered diversions in the town, the army's discipline and fighting readiness perceptibly decreased. Instead of keeping themselves fit with exercises and maintaining their fighting form by readying their weapons for combat, the men found it more amusing to divert themselves with the ladies of the town and to enjoy the luxury of supplies brought to them from the fleet. Some of the troops drifted back to Acre and after Richard had sent Guy de Lusignan in vain to bring them back to Jaffa, he found it necessary to make the trip himself early in October. Richard spent a week in Acre. In part he had to organize the members of his army whom he found there and arrange their transport back to Jaffa. In addition, he had to negotiate with the Genoese, for by this time he recognized that he must secure their help, as well as that of the Pisans, to secure his communications with Europe and to assure his army of a constant flow of supplies from the West.

When Richard returned to Jaffa on October 13, he resumed his diplomatic contacts with Saladin. The negotiations were carried on, in the main, by Richard dealing directly with Saladin's brother, Saif ad-Din al-Adil. At a meeting on October 17, Richard made a concrete set of proposals for a peace settlement. There were three points at issue, he told Saladin's representative: the relic of the true cross, the city of Jerusalem, and the disposition of the land between the sea and the Jordan River. The first two points, Richard indicated, were not open to negotiation. The crusaders must have the relic of the true cross, which in any case was of no value to the Muslims, since for them it was simply a piece of wood. The city of Jerusalem, likewise, must be returned to Christian hands if there were to be any agreement on peace between them, since it, too, was an object of veneration for the Christians. As for the land, the Christians wanted control of the territory up to, or even beyond, the Jordan River as a part of any settlement to which they might agree.

Saladin found these terms entirely unacceptable. In a message to Richard he rejected all three proposals. Jerusalem, he said, was just as holy to the Muslims as it was to the Christians, and while the relic of the cross was not important to the Muslims, they would not give it back without receiving substantial concessions in return.

It was Richard's turn to try again. Within the next two days he worked out another plan which he transmitted to Saif ad-Din. In essence, Richard now proposed that there should be an alliance between them. Saif ad-Din should marry Richard's sister, Queen Joan of Sicily. Joan would then take up residence in Jerusalem and Richard would turn over to her his claims to the portions of Palestine which he controlled— Acre, Jaffa, and the other territories where he currently had troops. Simultaneously, Saladin was to turn over to Saif ad-Din all of his own holdings in Palestine, as well as the relics of the true cross. Thus the possessions of both the crusaders and Saladin in Palestine were to be reunited, vested in Saif ad-Din and Joan as joint rulers, and presumably entailed to their offspring as a perpetual inheritance. In addition all prisoners held by the two sides were to be released to their respective monarchs. When all of this was done, Richard promised, he would return by sea to the West, leaving the Palestine question, as he saw it, permanently solved.

Saif ad-Din, who first received the terms of this remarkable proposal, decided that they might contain the basis of a workable agreement and on this assumption he transmitted them to Saladin. The sultan at once approved the terms, although he was convinced as soon as he heard them that Richard was not really serious and that the proposal was, in fact, an elaborate practical joke. Still he affirmed his willingness to agree to the terms as a basis for bargaining and sent word of his agreement back to Richard.

At this point Richard raised new problems. His sister Joan, he announced, had been beside herself with indignation when he had told her that he proposed to see her married off to Saif ad-Din, a Muslim. Joan, he added, would agree to the marriage only if Saif ad-Din would consent to give up his own religion and would become a Christian. This, Richard was told in reply, was quite impossible and at this point negotiations lapsed for several days.

Meanwhile, there was further action on the battlefield, although only on a minor scale. A skirmish outside of Jaffa resulted in a minor victory for the crusaders, when a Muslim raiding party was beaten off. Similarly, on November 6, there was a fight between the Templars and Saladin's troops at ibn-Ibrak, about two miles from Yazur, when a large force of Saracens surprised a foraging party from the crusaders' camp. News of the fray soon reached Jaffa, whereupon Richard took the field in person, together with Andrew de

Chauveny, the earl of Leicester, and Count William of St. Pol. The fight was brief but vicious and Richard, despite the urgings of his companions, threw himself like a madman into the midst of it. He emerged unscathed, having accounted for several of the foe, and the enemy forces were driven off successfully.

During the next several days the parties reverted to diplomacy. Secretly and unbeknown to Richard, Conrad of Montferrat had begun making overtures to Saladin, proposing that the sultan and he should form an alliance. Meanwhile, Richard was entertaining Saif ad-Din at Yazur and attempting to find some way to continue negotiations on the basis of his plan to marry Joan off to Saif ad-Din. One difficulty, as Richard explained it, was that the pope was inclined to be difficult over such matters as marriages between Christians and Muslims. Richard proposed that Saif ad-Din should give him six months in which to arrange matters with His Holiness so as to secure papal consent to the marriage. In the meantime, Richard added, he would like to meet personally with Saladin in order to work out further details of the proposal. He asked Saif ad-Din to arrange such a conference, but this Saif ad-Din refused to do, despite the apparently genuine admiration and even affection he was coming to feel for Richard.

Conrad of Montferrat, in the meantime, was dealing directly with Saladin, who was intrigued by Conrad's offer to ally with the Sultan. From Saladin's viewpoint, this offer might provide a splendid opportunity to disrupt the crusading army by creating a division within its ranks. He made it quite clear in his discussions with Conrad that he expected Conrad to break openly with Richard and that if he did so, Conrad could expect military assistance from Saladin's camp.

At the same time that Saladin was conferring secretly with Conrad, he continued to receive reports of the negotiations with Richard and on November 9 he received Humphrey of Toron, Richard's ambassador, in open audience. The message which Humphrey brought from Richard was a straightforward political appeal: "I told you that I would give these regions of Palestine to your brother," Richard's message said, "and I want you to be the judge between us in the division of the land. But we absolutely must have a foothold in Jerusalem. I want you to make a division that will not bring down on you the wrath of the Muslims, or on me the wrath of the Franks."

Saladin, his secretary tells us, was impressed by this message. He respected Richard's pragmatic political realism and he apparently entertained cautious hopes that some kind of settlement could be reached. Still, at heart, he was pessimistic. "When we have made peace with them," he said in a private conversation with his secretary at about this time, "there will be nothing to prevent their attacking us treacherously. If I should die the Muslims would no longer be able to muster an army like this and the Franks would have the upper hand. It is better to carry on the Holy War until we have expelled them from Palestine, or death overtakes us."

Despite his personal pessimism about the matter, Saladin took steps to carry the negotiations further. He now had two offers of alliance in hand: one from Richard, the other from Conrad of Montferrat. On November 11 he summoned his advisers to meet with him to discuss the offers and to decide what policy they should adopt. After explaining the terms proposed by the two Christian leaders, Saladin asked his counselors to speak their minds. In the discussion his advisers agreed that they should opt for the offer made by Richard for, they reasoned, it was not likely that Christians and Muslims would be able to operate successfully as allies in the fashion proposed by Conrad. Evidently Saladin's advisers were impressed, as the Sultan himself had been, with the frankness and realism of Richard's proposal and saw in this a possible basis for settlement.

Following his lengthy deliberations with his advisers, which took four days to complete, Saladin took action to implement their suggestions. He dismissed Conrad of Montferrat's representatives, telling them that the agreement which they had proposed was unacceptable, and he continued negotiations with Richard through intermediaries.

The essential point which required elaborate discussion was the problem of the marriage of Richard's sister, Joan, to Saif ad-Din. Richard had difficulties on this point. The idea outraged Joan, for one thing, and although she might be talked into accepting the proposal, it was not an easy task. Nor was the proposed marriage popular with Richard's advisers and followers, many of whom viewed the whole idea as an infuriating concession to the Muslims. There was also the question of the attitude of the pope and the hierarchy, who were sure to be dubious, at the very least, of the project. Richard finally had to ask Saladin to be patient and to consent to at least a three-month delay in further negotiations while he sent messengers to Rome to try to convince the pope that the proposed marriage had merit. If his emissaries could not succeed in securing papal consent to the arrangement, Richard added in his message to Saladin, he would be willing to offer his niece, Eleanor of Brittany, as a wife for Saif ad-Din. Richard was Eleanor's guardian and, in view of this, assured Saladin that he would not require the pope's consent to arrange her marriage, even to a sultan's brother.

Meanwhile sporadic and desultory fighting continued between the two armies. Saladin had retired to Jerusalem in mid-November and planned to remain there during the winter. Richard set up his winter headquarters at Ramla on December 8, although in fact he spent only a few weeks there. On December 20 there was an outbreak of fighting at Blanche-Gard, where Richard narrowly escaped being captured when he was surprised by a small Muslim force. In another skirmish, the earl of Leicester and some of his companions were actually taken prisoner by a detachment of Saladin's army, but the prisoners were rescued by Andrew de Chauveny and two other knights, who pursued the raid-

ing party and retrieved the prisoners before they could be
taken back to the Muslim camp.

Just before Christmas Richard moved his own quarters from Ramla to Latrun, about halfway between Jaffa and
Jerusalem. There he spent the holiday season. He had with
him his wife, Berengaria, and his sister, Queen Joan, as well
as the daughter of Isaac of Cyprus, whom he was still keeping as a hostage. The ladies had come down from Acre a
few weeks earlier to join him and Guy de Lusignan was also
included in the party. The holidays passed quietly, as the
king and his entourage rested from the strenuous campaigns
of the preceding year. The weather did little to encourage
jollity, for it was cold, rainy and stormy throughout the holidays. Richard and his court were content to keep dry and
warm, while the wind and rain spent their fury outside, as
they celebrated their quiet Christmas in the Holy Land.

Two days after Christmas Richard ordered his forces
to break camp and to move toward Jerusalem. An advance
party, composed of members of the Knights Templars and
Knights Hospitalers, made a reconnaissance patrol into the
hills above the Holy City itself, to spy out the disposition of
the enemy forces and report back on the situation around
Jerusalem. In the closing days of 1191 and the first days of the
new year hope sprang up in the crusading army that an attack
on Jerusalem was imminent and that soon they might begin
to storm the Holy City itself. Anticipation of the coming
struggle sharpened day by day, but Richard was beginning to
have second thoughts. On January 10 he returned to Jaffa and
called upon his principal advisers to meet with him to decide
on the strategy to be followed. There was considerable pressure, especially from the rank-and-file of the common folk in
the army, to commence an attack immediately upon Jerusalem. The representatives of the military orders, the Hospitalers and the Templars, however, thought differently and in
the meetings of Richard's council it was they who carried the
day. The council decided that before Jerusalem could be

taken it would first be necessary to secure the southern flank of the crusading army by seizing and rebuilding Ascalon, which Saladin had destroyed during the previous autumn.

Once this decision had been made, Richard returned to inform the troops that they were to retire from the positions which they had taken and that they were to prepare to march down the coast to Ascalon. The reaction of the army was one of intense disappointment. The French troops, in particular, were bitterly unhappy that they were not going to proceed immediately against Jerusalem and a large part of the army's French contingent forthwith deserted from Richard's command. The French deserters soon made their way independently to Tyre, where they attached themselves to Conrad of Montferrat's party.

Richard and his forces meanwhile fell back, first from Beit Nuba to Ramla and then to Yavna. From there they marched to Ascalon, arriving on January 20. The journey was miserable, as the army plodded on under leaden skies, alternately bathed by cold rains and blinded by flurries of sleet and snow. Richard was constantly in attendance on his men, riding up and down the lines of march, encouraging them, urging them forward, and comforting those who were ready to succumb to their miseries and give up. When at last they arrived at Ascalon, the men were worn out, tired, exasperated, cursing the day they were born. The sight of Ascalon itself further dampened their gloomy spirits. The city was in ruins. With great efforts they managed to force their way through the ruins of the gate, which was nearly blocked by fallen stone, only to find virtually every house in the town likewise in ruins. Dejectedly the army camped amid the rubble of the city and tried to rest and regain its strength.

For the next four months Richard was almost continuously at Ascalon, planning and superintending the reconstruction of the fortress-city. Soon after the army's arrival there, Richard called upon the French soldiers at Tyre to rejoin him and to continue with their crusade. The leaders of the French contingent gave a qualified assent to the invitation. They would come to Ascalon, they said, and would remain there until Easter. When they arrived, sometime after the beginning of February, the work of reconstruction moved forward at a swifter pace. Everyone joined in the labor, knights and noblemen, squires and servants, clerics and laymen alike. Richard not only provided the money to meet three quarters of the expense of reconstructing the city, but also put in stints of physical labor himself, helping to shift stones and assisting the masons whom he employed to rebuild the walls and the fifty-two towers of the city.

When he took a break from his work on the rebuilding of Ascalon, Richard spent some of his free time reconnoitering the countryside. In part he was concerned to familiarize himself with the region in case his army should be attacked before they had completed their work at Ascalon; and in part he was presumably preparing for future military engagements to be undertaken once the reconstruction was completed. On one of these patrols during February, 1192, Richard and a small company of soldiers came by chance across a group of Christian prisoners, who were being held by their Muslim captors in a church at Deir al-Bela. As the banners carried by Richard's companions came in sight, the Muslim guards fled to the nearby fort, leaving their captives and their horses at the church. Richard and his followers swooped down upon the settlement, released the prisoners, whom they took away with them, and also herded off the horses, which they brought back to replace the mounts that had perished in earlier fighting.

While the work on Ascalon was still proceeding, Richard also sought to unify the available forces, with a view to resuming active hostilities once the winter had passed. With this in mind he attempted to make peace with Conrad of Montferrat. While Conrad refused to come down to Ascalon to discuss matters with Richard, he did agree to meet with him at Casal Imbert. The meeting proved, however, to be fruitless and Richard was unable to secure Conrad's promise of cooperation in future military actions. There was also trouble with the French. They were running short of funds and Richard, who had earlier assisted them financially, felt that he could no longer continue to support the French army as well as his own. As a result, the duke of Burgundy and many of the French troops went back to Acre. At Acre there was further trouble: the Pisans and the Genoese were at each other's throats and there was open fighting between the two groups in the streets of the city. When the duke of Burgundy and his disgruntled French followers arrived, they agreed to support the Genoese party in the struggle. The result of this was that the conflict worsened. The Pisans at this point appealed to Richard to intervene. Leaving the work in progress at Ascalon, Richard hurried to Acre, arriving there on February 20. He peremptorily commanded the two sides to patch up a truce with each other and to cease their squabbling. Once a precarious peace had been established, Richard lingered on at Acre until the end of March. For part of this time he was engaged in further negotiations with Saladin's envoys, especially Saif ad-Din. Indeed on Palm Sunday, March 29, 1192, Richard took the singular step of conferring knighthood upon Saif ad-Din's son and in the course of the ceremony presented the boy with a magnificent military belt, one of the principal emblems of knightly status among the Christians.

On March 31 Richard returned to Ascalon. Relationships between him and the French troops meanwhile had not improved. The day after Richard's arrival in Ascalon he finally agreed to allow the French contingent to separate from his army and to march to Tyre, where they wished to join Conrad of Montferrat. The remainder of the army was pained to witness the departure of their French comrades on Holy Thursday. Saladin, who soon learned of these developments, rejoiced at the dissensions within the crusaders' camp and began to make preparations for his spring offensive. Just as the Christian army was weakened in strength and diminished in numbers by the defection of the French contingent, so Saladin's forces were also somewhat weaker and somewhat smaller in numbers than they had been during the previous year's campaign. The reverses of 1191 had made his feudatory princes more cautious, his subjects more wary of committing all of the manpower and money at their disposal to the sultan's holy war. Nonetheless, the army which Saladin assembled was still a potent one and even Richard could not have helped feeling some uneasiness at the thought of renewing the struggle.

He was also uneasy and mildly alarmed at the prospects of the immediate future for other reasons. On April 15 Prior Robert of Hereford arrived at Ascalon, bringing letters and oral messages from England. The news was disquieting. The letters from Bishop William of Ely, Richard's chancellor, were filled with complaints about Richard's brother John, who was said to be usurping the chancellor's powers and attempting to take over the administration of the realm for himself. There was no money left in the treasury, the chancellor reported, and, moreover, the barons of the kingdom were hatching seditious and treasonable plots against the government. Although royal administration and the arts of peaceful government had never been matters that particularly interested Richard, it was plain that the situation in England was approaching a crisis and required his immediate attention. In addition, Prior Robert may have passed on rumors which were current when he left England in February to the effect that Philip Augustus, after arriving safely in France, had made overtures to Count John with a view to concluding an alliance with him against Richard. Moreover, the French monarch was openly making ready to renew his struggles against Richard's lands and subjects on the Continent. Philip had begun to strengthen his fortresses along the frontiers between his territories and Richard's lands. He had also placed large orders for new weapons and Richard's representatives in France were busily preparing to meet a new onslaught from the French king.

On April 16, the day after Prior Robert's arrival, Richard summoned all of the leaders of the crusading army to meet with him. To them he explained the situation, laying particular emphasis on the seriousness of the disturbances in England, and announced that in the light of what he had just learned he might find it necessary to go back to England in short order. Even if he had to leave quickly, he added, he would undertake to meet the expenses of a force of three hundred knights and two thousand foot-soldiers whom he would leave behind him in the Holy Land. In view of his own possible departure, he added, it was essential that the question of the succession to the crown of Jerusalem be settled definitely and immediately. The interim solution which had been adopted earlier would no longer do, for if Richard were to leave, there must be someone in a position of authority to take his place as the universally acknowledged leader of the crusaders' forces. Hence, he went on, he must insist that a decision be made here and now about the leadership. There were only two possible choices open: King Guy de Lusignan and Conrad of Montferrat. The council members, Richard stated, must now make an unequivocal choice between them.

Richard had made it amply plain in the preceding months which of the two candidates he preferred: Guy had been his protégé throughout his crusade and he had never gotten on well with Conrad, who was allied to Richard's perennial enemy, Philip Augustus. Richard must surely have hoped that the barons assembled in council would follow his wishes and cast their votes for Guy. It was a painful shock, therefore, when in the discussion which followed his announcement, no one spoke up to support Guy's candidacy. Instead the whole assembly unanimously turned to Conrad and made him their choice. Faced with such unanimous opposition, Richard's only option was to give way as gracefully as he could. He indicated that he would accept the will of the assembly and immediately designated a party of ambassadors, whom he commissioned to proceed at once to Tyre to announce the results of the meeting to Conrad. Richard designated his nephew, Count Henry of Champagne, as chief spokesman of the group. They set out at once on their mission and the news which they bore was joyfully received, both by Conrad, as one might have expected, and also by his followers in the city of Tyre. Arrangements for Conrad's coronation began immediately, while Richard's ambassadors, having discharged their mission, proceeded at once to Acre, where the coronation was to take place. They arrived about the twentieth of April. They brought back Conrad's assurance that he would come down to Ascalon in short order and would at last rejoin the crusading army. There was a general expectation that now, at last, the business of the crusade could be dispatched under a united leadership and that the quarrels and dissensions of the past could be forgotten.

Richard and the crusaders were soon shocked out of this optimistic hopefulness by a tragic event. On April 28, Conrad was at dinner with bishop of Beauvais, alone and in good spirits. The two men were celebrating Conrad's recent election as king and his imminent coronation. After dinner, Conrad mounted his horse to ride back to his palace, where his wife was expecting him. As he turned a corner on his return journey, two men jumped out armed with daggers. They rushed at Conrad, knocked him from his horse, and attacked him with their weapons, wounding the king-elect fatally. Conrad died within a few minutes of the attack. The two attackers then attempted to flee. Both of them were apprehended almost immediately. One was killed on the spot. The other was able to take sanctuary in a nearby church, but was soon seized and hauled out to answer for his crime. This assailant was roughly interrogated and told his captors that he and his companions were members of the Assassin sect. They had been sent, he said, by the Old Man of the Mountain, the leader of their sect, with instructions to murder Conrad of Montferrat. One version of their confession states that their orders had originated with King Richard. As soon as they had extracted a confession from the second assassin, his captors executed him by dragging him through the streets of Tyre, bludgeoning him to death slowly as they went.

Did Richard procure two assassins to murder Conrad of Montferrat? It seems unlikely, on the whole, that he did so. Certainly Richard had ample reason to dislike Conrad and, if the assassination had taken place a month or two earlier, Richard would have been a prime suspect. But in fact he had just accepted, however reluctantly, Conrad's election as king of Jerusalem and such evidence as is available indicates that he did so in the genuine belief that the election of Conrad would provide a solution to the political dissensions which had rent the crusade. It is wholly improbable that, having taken this step, he would then procure Conrad's assassination. Numerous others have been suspected as the masterminds behind the assassination—Saladin, Guy de Lusignan, Humphrey of Toron, and the master of the Assassins. A recent writer has suggested that Henry of Champagne, Richard's nephew, may have been the culprit, while other possible candidates might well seem to have had motives, even if their means of securing the assassination are either unknown or difficult to reconstruct. There were, in fact, many more people who were pleased to see Conrad dead than was entirely seemly.

The death of Conrad completely upset the political settlement that had just been achieved. From Richard's point of view, whatever may have been his complicity in the murder and his feelings upon learning of it, the most important consideration was to reestablish a political equilibrium in the Holy Land, preferably by securing as Conrad's successor a candidate for the throne of Jerusalem who was personally more acceptable to him than Conrad had been.

Such a candidate was, in fact, immediately at hand. He

was Count Henry of Campagne. As soon as he learned of Conrad's death, Henry came at once to Tyre. Within two days he was engaged to marry Conrad's widow, Isabella, and was sending messengers to ask Richard's consent both to the marriage and to his candidacy for the crown of the kingdom of Jerusalem. When Richard finally received the message—he was out in the field and had been fighting a minor action against a Saracen patrol force—he gave his consent at once to both proposals. On May 5, after one week of widowhood, Isabella was married to Henry of Champagne, who had formally been elected as king of Jerusalem three days previously.

At the same time, Richard took care to provide for Guy de Lusignan. When it had become clear that Guy was no longer to enjoy the crown of Jerusalem, Richard had set in motion a scheme to transfer to him the island of Cyprus, which the Templars then held. The Templars were not anxious to retain possession of the island, for they had found, as Richard had earlier, that control of Cyprus involved a continuing problem of restraining the population from revolt. The knights had come to regret the agreement they had made to purchase the island from Richard. Richard now sought to solve two problems at the same time: to satisfy the Templars by relieving them of the obligation to pay him the 60,000 dinars which they still owed him for Cyprus and also to provide for Guy de Lusignan by transferring ownership of the island from the Templars to him. Guy was able to find backers who would put up 40,000 dinars as a down payment on the island. This money was given to the Templars, who then resigned their rights to Cyprus. Richard subsequently transferred ownership of the island to Guy, who moved immediately to take possession of it, assisted by a band of followers who had remained faithful to him through all the vicissitudes of the previous five years. Guy also assumed the responsibility for paying Richard the balance of 60,000 dinars still outstanding from the original bargain for the sale of the island, although in fact he never fully paid off this debt. Still, Guy was soon in physical possession of the island. He found there a situation with which he could deal adequately and his rule on Cyprus was comparatively successful.

Meanwhile there was a military campaign to carry on. As soon as possible after settling the succession of Henry of Champagne and the transfer of Cyprus to Guy de Lusignan, Richard, who had been away from the city on a minor raid, returned to Ascalon. He had urged Henry of Champagne and the duke of Burgundy with their respective forces to join him as soon as possible at Ascalon, so that they could jointly mount a spring offensive against Saladin. While he was waiting, Richard heard that Saladin's position was being menaced by a revolt in the eastern regions of his empire, in Mesopotamia. Richard regarded this as a splendid opportunity to commence operations, since if his major enemy was preoccupied with serious internal troubles elsewhere, he might find it necessary to reserve a part of his army to deal with the internal threat. Accordingly, without waiting further for Henry and the duke of Burgundy, Richard set off for the fortress of Darum, on the coast, about twenty-five miles south of Ascalon. Darum was controlled by one of Saladin's Turkish lieutenants. Richard arrived there on May 17 and at once launched an attack. The fortress was impressive and formidable. Its thick, heavy walls were punctuated by seventeen towers and surrounded by a ditch, which made an attack directly upon the walls almost impossible. Richard brought up his siege engines, which had proved their usefulness so dramatically at Acre. When transport difficulties arose, Richard himself, together with some of his noblemen, shouldered the weapons and carried them up from the seacoast, where the ships had landed them, to the army's camp. According to an astonished witness, Richard carried one of the machines for almost a mile without even sweating. As soon as the siege engines had been set in place, Richard ordered them to begin a nonstop bombardment of the walls of Darum, thudding chunks of rock and other missiles day and night against the battlements. Other machines kept up a steady fire of heavy, pointed rods and other missiles, while at sea Richard's ships blockaded the port and prevented delivery of any supplies or reinforcements to the besieged. After five days of this the garrison of Darum was ready to surrender. They offered to give up their city on condition that they be allowed to leave freely with their lives. Richard, however, refused to accept this condition. Instead he ordered his forces to step up the pace of their attack and simultaneously set a party of sappers to work at undermining one of the towers in the city walls. The sapping operation was a total success. When the miners had completed their work, a barrage of stones from the siege machines cracked into the undermined tower and it slowly subsided and crashed to the ground with ear-rending force. Richard's troops made their way into the city through the holes which they had knocked in the walls, while the remnant of the garrison scrambled to safety in the largest of the remaining towers. Once the crusaders occupied the rest of the city's defenses and began to penetrate this last stronghold, the defenders at last surrendered unconditionally. The survivors were badly treated, even by the rough and ready standards of twelfth-century warfare. Some of them were flung down from the battlements of the town and lay broken and crushed outside of the walls until the victors found time and inclination to finish them off. Others, more mercifully, were beheaded or had their throats slit, while the remainder were shackled and taken away as slaves.

By crushing Darum, Richard had made a clean sweep of Saladin's major holdings on the coast of Palestine. In a real sense, his victory there marks the climax of his crusading campaign. From this point onward he was more concerned with holding what he had got than with attempting to ingest further conquests, for what he had succeeded in doing was to secure a territorial basis once more for the struggling Latin kingdom of Jerusalem. True, the conquered territories were confined to a very narrow strip of land along the coast. There was no conquest in depth to give the crusaders any significant penetration into the center of the country. But Richard was at last in a position to control the coastal region and his conquests furnished the Latins in the East with a chain of maritime cities from which they could carry on their commerce with the West, while tapping the trade routes of the Near East for goods which could profitably be exported to European markets.

There was still one major problem to be faced: the problem of Jerusalem. The whole aim of Richard's crusade involved securing possession of the Holy City. For reasons both emotional and ideological, the taking of Jerusalem was vital to the crusade. Strategically, however, it was an open question whether the city could be taken and it was even more questionable whether, if once taken, it could be permanently held. Richard apparently had doubts about the feasibility of conquering Jerusalem on both of these counts and during the coming weeks he was tormented by the need to make a decision about the matter.

The forces of Henry of Champagne and the French troops of the duke of Burgundy, meanwhile, had been making a leisurely progress toward Darum. They finally arrived only after the fighting was over and the campaign had been won. Despite their late arrival, however, they enjoyed the fruits of victory, for Richard immediately turned Darum over to Henry of Champagne and then prepared to set out for Ascalon. On the way he prepared to take another objective, the so-called Castle of Figs, but found that it had been deserted by its Muslim garrison, who had been terrified by what had happened to their compatriots at Darum.

While Richard was still on his way up the coast to Ascalon he was met by a party of messengers, led by the archdeacon John of Alençon. The messengers brought more bad news: John was creating turmoil and confusion in England; Richard's mother, Eleanor of Aquitaine, had attempted to re-

strain him, but had failed; John was believed to have concluded an agreement with Philip Augustus with the aim of
depriving Richard of the English throne.

Richard's reaction was indecisive: he felt that he
ought to return immediately to England to salvage the situation there. Yet he also felt that he must cap his campaign in
Palestine with an assault on Jerusalem, if possible; and in any
event, whatever happened with regard to the Holy City, he
must conclude a stable peace with Saladin before he left. In
perplexity and despair, he turned his counselors with their
conflicting advice out of his tent and took to his bed. Meanwhile rumors buzzed through the ranks of the army. Some
said that the king had made up his mind to return and was
going to leave at once; others that had had no intention of
leaving until Jerusalem was taken. The feeling of most of the
men was that Jerusalem must be captured and there were
those who promised that they would stay to capture the Holy
City no matter what decision Richard might reach.

At length Richard roused himself from his tent and announced that the army would proceed to Ascalon. They arrived there on June 4 and on the following day Richard let it
be known that he had made up his mind to remain in the
Holy Land until Easter of 1193 and that meanwhile he would
besiege Jerusalem and take the Holy City if it were possible
to do so. He commanded that preparations were to commence for a march to Jerusalem.

The army left Ascalon with Richard at its head on June
7, bound for Jerusalem. That night they stopped at Tel es-
Safi, where they remained for two days. On June 9 they made
another march, this time to a position north of Latrun, where
they waited for the siege machines to be brought to them.
They resumed marching on the following day, camping for
the night at Castle Arnold, and on June 11 they reached Beit
Nuba, just thirteen miles from Jerusalem. Here they made
camp and remained for a month. Richard dispatched Henry
of Champagne from the camp to Acre, where he was in-

structed to rout out all of the deserters from the crusading army and any other fighting men he could lay hands on. Henry was to bring them to Beit Nuba to reinforce the Christian army for the assault on Jerusalem. On June 12 Richard learned that there were bands of Turkish troops in the hill country near his camp and set out with a small patrol to try to intercept them before they could stage a raid on his position. He managed to locate a small group of the enemy near the springs of Emmaus. Leading the attack upon the Turks, Richard and his companions managed to kill twenty of them, while the others scattered and disappeared into the distant hills. The action produced a satisfying quantity of loot: three camels, together with horses, mules, and some handsome prisoners, as well as quantities of spices and other valuable goods which had obviously been destined for Saladin in Jerusalem. Climbing farther up in the hills, Richard came to a spot where he could look out and see the walls and turrets of Jerusalem in the distance. At once, we are told, he brought up his shield to cover his face, for if he could not capture Jerusalem, he did not wish to glimpse the Holy City.

A week later a spy brought in news of a large caravan which was making its way from Egypt toward Jerusalem. The caravan was bringing munitions and supplies for Saladin's forces in anticipation of a coming attack upon Jerusalem. Richard made up his mind to intercept the caravan. He sent scouts back to shadow the enemy's movements and meanwhile gathered a sizable raiding party to mount the ambush. On June 21 the scouts returned with further reports: the caravan was nearing the "Round Cistern." Richard set out with his men. On June 23 the caravan and its armed escorts, unaware of Richard's presence in the vicinity, camped at Kuwaifa. At dawn the following morning Richard and his men attacked. They achieved a complete tactical surprise and although their opponents were able to form a hasty defensive line, they had no time to dig into position before Richard's men were on top of them. The fighting was fierce but quickly over. Richard as usual was in the thick of it, but he emerged without harm and quickly set his men to pack up the loot which they had taken. The spoils were enormous in quantity and highly varied in kind: thousands of horses, camels, mules, spices, precious metals and fabrics, weapons, tents, biscuits, bread, flour, drugs, chess boards, pepper, cinnamon, sugar, wax, and money of all kinds in large amounts. By the afternoon Richard and his men were on their way back, driving their new captives, who were laden with booty, in front of them.

They were back at their camp at Beit Nuba by June 29 and were received there with rejoicing. The return of the victorious raiding party seemed to many of the men in the crusading army to signal that it was time to press on toward Jerusalem. With their newly won supplies, they were in a better position to undertake the campaign than they had ever been before. But Richard was not convinced. He consulted his advisers again and they counseled him that he should be prudent. It would not be wise to start an attack on Jerusalem in midsummer when there were no certain sources of water supply in the vicinity. There was also the still-unsettled problem of what to do with Jerusalem if it were taken. Where could the men be found to hold the city indefinitely? How could it be supplied and how could the strategically exposed corridor between Jerusalem and Jaffa be secured and protected from attack?

To these questions Richard could find no answers. Reluctantly he decided to abandon his plans for an attack upon the Holy City. As soon as his decision was announced, there were bitter reactions within the army. The French soldiers began to sing scurrilous songs about Richard's cowardice, songs full of vulgar references to his personal habits. Richard replied by composing some songs of his own, celebrating the cowardice of the French soldiery and their leaders. The texts of these ballads have not survived, but those who heard them agreed that they were both obscenely witty and well founded. Amid the jeers and insults, Richard kept his temper remarkably well. With outward calm, he began making preparations to pull back. On July 2 a group of men from the army made a quick dash into the hills above Jerusalem, where they paraded about ostentatiously, making sure that they were seen by the Muslims down below. Then they retired.

Saladin was sure that an attack was about to be launched against his positions in Jerusalem and he began to prepare for the worst. In fact, the crusaders were commencing to break camp and to retreat. On July 4 they abandoned their positions at Beit Nuba and fell back to Ramla and by July 6 they had arrived at Yazur. From there Richard reopened negotiations with Saladin.

At this point Richard seems to have revised his planning again. Having given up the notion of attacking Jerusalem, his aim now was to strike as good a bargain as could be had with Saladin and to return to England as soon as an acceptable treaty could be worked out. In the early stages of the new round of negotiations a basic agreement was reached: Richard should retain the coastal areas he had conquered, while Saladin would retain the interior of Palestine. The border areas between the two regions were to be partitioned between them. There was difficulty in reaching agreement over the southern part of the coastal region. Saladin was anxious that Ascalon and Darum should be dismantled, since the existence of strong, fortified bases in Christian hands there threatened his land communication lines with Egypt. Richard was equally anxious that these fortresses remain under Christian control. Saladin offered to make over to Richard the Church of the Resurrection in Jerusalem if Richard in turn would agree to the evacuation of the southern strongholds. Richard insisted on keeping them. Saladin countered with an offer to turn Lydda over to Richard if he would give up Ascalon and Darum in return. Richard then ordered his forces to evacuate and destroy Darum, but he also sent orders to strengthen the fortifications at Ascalon. On July 11 he moved his forces to Ascalon and informed Saladin that the city must remain in the hands of his troops. Two weeks later he returned to Acre and was considering further plans to force Saladin's hand.

Saladin meanwhile had also been busy. Even before Richard began his return march from Ascalon to Acre, Saladin had moved his headquarters and a sizable part of his army out of Jerusalem and in the direction of Jaffa. On July 28 he commenced an assault on Jaffa. On the following day, Richard learned of his enemy's move. Immediately he went into action. He and a select company of knights embarked at once on ships and put out to sea, headed for Jaffa. The major part of his army, meanwhile, was commanded to set out by land for the city.

Meanwhile Saladin had poured every effort into the siege. Three days of ferocious bombardment had breached the city's walls and Saladin's troops poured through the breach into the town. The garrison retreated to the citadel, but when it was surrounded by enemy forces, it soon became evident that they would have to surrender and on July 31 they began truce talks with Saladin. Richard's ships meanwhile had been delayed by contrary winds. Late in the afternoon, just as the truce parley was about to conclude, Richard's ships appeared in the harbor. The Jaffa garrison at once broke off negotiations and the battle resumed while Richard's forces were beaching their boats and struggling through the water into the city, with Richard himself in the lead. Saladin was caught off guard. He was still talking in his tent with some representatives of the Jaffa garrison when an aide brought in the news that the fighting had resumed and that relief forces, led by the English king, were pouring into the streets of the city. Saladin was scarcely able to believe his ears, but the sight of his men fleeing before the surprise attack convinced him. After struggling briefly to rally his men, Saladin was finally forced to order a retreat and was only able to restore order among the survivors of his force after fleeing five miles outside of the town.

Richard, meanwhile, accompanied by a mere eighty knights and four hundred archers, assisted by a small contingent of Italian sailors, was fighting like a madman in the streets of Jaffa. Swinging his sword left and right, he scattered his enemies with vicious blows and on occasion cut men squarely in two with a single swipe of his weapon. By sunset the town was again in the hands of the crusading forces.

The next morning, while the troops were still clearing away the bodies of the slain and picking their way through the rubble in the streets, the peace talks were renewed. The problem of the southern cities, however, remained unchanged and neither side was willing to give way to accommodate the other on this point. After some fruitless exchanges of messages, the discussions were broken off.

Meanwhile the main part of the crusading army finally arrived at Jaffa and the men were set to work cleaning up the city and rebuilding the sections of the walls that had been breached or badly damaged during the recent siege. The Muslims, at the same time, were becoming desperate. At midnight on August 4 an enormous raiding party of some seven thousand Mamelukes and Kurds broke into the crusaders' camp and made for Richard's tent. Their mission was to capture him and thus break the resistance of the crusading army. Fortunately for Richard an alert Genoese sentry spotted them in time to raise the alarm. Richard scrambled out of bed, seized his sword and helmet, and began setting up his defenses with the help of ten light-sleeping companions who were the first to awake at the sentry's alarm. The enemy forces were divided into seven groups who planned to distract Richard and the defenders so that they could not coordinate their resistance. Richard, however, kept his men under control and, at a signal, they launched a concerted attack at the center of the enemy forces. The Muslims, who had expected at most to face a passive defense, were taken completely by surprise when Richard's men charged and they were unprepared to meet the blow. Richard's force was able to penetrate the enemy battle line and throw them into utter confusion. Saladin, who had come up to watch the action, was both distressed and amazed at Richard's incredible ability to recover and fight back. At one point in the battle, when Richard's horse had fallen and the king was thrown to the ground, Saladin sent a groom with two fine Arab mounts to give to Richard. Richard, although surprised, accepted them gratefully, leaped into the saddle, and resumed the fight. The struggle continued on through the day, but by sundown the crusaders had won the day and Saladin pulled back with his entire army to Jerusalem.

The situation was stalemated. Neither side was anxious to continue the struggle, but neither could afford to back off and modify the terms on which it would make peace. In the middle of August, about two weeks after the abortive Muslim attempt to capture him at Jaffa, Richard fell ill. He was weak and feverish and for weeks on end was unable to leave his sickbed. In part he was simply worn out by his exertions and, in part too, he seems to have been troubled by the increasingly bad news which kept arriving from his domains in Europe.

Illness and anxiety finally broke down Richard's resolve to secure a peace settlement on his own terms. On August 28 he recommenced negotiations, using as his intermediary Bishop Hubert Walter of Salisbury. After five days of strenuous bargaining an agreement was finally reached.

The terms of the treaty provided that Ascalon, which Richard had been so determined to keep, would be given up, its population evacuated, its defenses demolished. Further, Richard agreed that he would not attempt to rebuild the city for three years. The other coastal cities, as far south as Jaffa, were conceded by Saladin to the Christians. The Christians, moreover, were guaranteed free access to the city of Jerusalem and each side undertook to allow merchants and travelers to journey freely through their territories. Peace between the parties was to be guaranteed by both sides for three years.

Richard recognized, however reluctantly, that these were the best terms he could get. The agreement was reduced to writing and read to him, whereupon he gave his formal assent to it on September 2, 1192.

A week later Richard's health was sufficiently improved that he could undertake a journey to Haifa, whose climate was thought to be particularly salubrious. There he handed over the command of the army to Henry of Champagne. After resting and further recovering his health, Richard journeyed back to Acre to make the final arrangements for his return to the West. The French forces had already left. Many of Richard's followers were occupied in making pilgrimages to Jerusalem, where they prayed at the sacred shrines and satisfied the formal obligations of their crusading vows. Richard, however, refused to make the journey to Jerusalem himself. Instead he sent a message to Saladin warning him that he did not consider his crusade completed and that he intended to return to the Holy Land at a later date to complete the conquest which he had this time only begun. Saladin replied gallantly that if he was going to lose Palestine, there was no prince to whom he would rather lose it.

Meanwhile there were other matters which must be attended to. Richard had debts to pay and he attempted to discharge all of them before he left Palestine. He also tried, with less success, to collect the sums owed to him by various persons to whom he had advanced money during the crusade. There were also logistical preparations to oversee: provisions had to be bought and loaded on the ships, passage space had to be allocated, and plans for the return journey agreed upon.

On September 29, Queen Berengaria and Richard's sister, Queen Joan, who had so narrowly escaped marriage to Saladin's brother, embarked on their ships and began the journey back to Europe with an advance party of the fleet. Berengaria enjoyed a leisurely and placid voyage homeward. She landed at Brindisi in November and subsequently spent several months at Rome. She then made an extensive journey through northern Italy before crossing the Alps into France. Clearly she and Richard were estranged, presumably because of personal differences. They did not meet again until April, 1195.

Richard stayed on in the East for ten more days after Berengaria's departure, in order to complete the process of handing over the government of the reestablished Latin kingdom to Henry of Champagne. At last, on October 9, Richard reluctantly boarded ship to sail from Acre, where he had landed sixteen months before. He had concluded the greatest and most satisfying adventure of his life.

EIGHT

✠───✠

Captivity and Ransom: Richard in Germany

When Richard sailed from Acre, it was apparently his intention to return to his domains in Europe by the most direct route. This would involve sailing to Marseille, where he could disembark and reach his French domains overland on horseback within a matter of a few days. At some point during the westward voyage he changed his plans: where this happened and, still more puzzling, why it happened as it did is difficult to say. Presumably the change in plans occurred during the days just before Richard's planned arrival at Marseille, for the evidence seems to indicate that a significant change in course took place off of the Tunisian coast. The reported reason for the change in plans was that Richard learned during his journey—possibly from news brought by passing ships, possibly from reports picked up in the harbors where the fleet stopped along the way—that the count of Toulouse planned to seize him if he were to land, as he had originally intended, at Marseille. There was reason to fear that these reports might be true. Although Count Raymond V of Toulouse was nominally Richard's vassal, relations between them had been strained since 1186, when Richard had first invaded Raymond's territories, and there was every reason to believe that Raymond might not be restrained by his feudal obligations to Richard if he saw a chance to exact revenge for the humiliations which he felt he had suffered at Richard's hands. Moreover, Raymond was almost certainly in league with Philip Augustus, who wished to delay Richard's return as long as possible.

Clearly there was some risk involved in adhering to the original route by which Richard had proposed to return home. The obvious alternative was to continue by sea through the Strait of Gibraltar and to land either in friendly territory on the western coast of France, or else to remain on board ship until the fleet reached England. Why Richard did not elect one of these relatively safe alternatives is not clear. It may be that, like Philip Augustus, he was prone to seasickness and wished to spend a minimum of time at sea. The fact is, however, that he did not choose the obvious course of action. Instead he ordered his fleet to alter course and to make for the island of Corfu off the Greek coast. The crusaders' fleet arrived at Corfu on November 11. While they were in the harbor there, Richard spotted three pirate galleys lying offshore. Embarking from his ship in a small boat, Richard hailed the galleys, which immediately hove to and commenced to attack Richard's small craft. Amid some confusion, Richard managed to get the message across to the captains of the galleys that he wanted to make a proposition to them, whereupon they ceased the attack and pulled alongside to learn what was wanted. Richard's proposition was simple: he would pay the pirate captains two hundred silver marks if they would take him and a few companions farther up the coast to Ragusa. After some bargaining the captains agreed and they all sailed back, accordingly, to Richard's ship. There Richard gathered up some personal effects and chose twenty men to accompany him. Together they transferred their gear to the three galleys and pushed off, leaving the remainder of the fleet to make its way back home independently.

Richard's voyage through the Adriatic turned out to be more hazardous than he had bargained for. Although he was no stranger to the sea and its perils, Richard was frightened half out of his wits by the way in which his newly hired pirate galleys navigated the rock-strewn Dalmatian coast. In his terror, he made a vow that when, or if, he reached solid land again he would donate generously to the nearest monastery, or found a new monastery if need be, in thanksgiving for his deliverance from the perils of this journey. His pirate friends put him and his companions ashore near Ragusa which was then an independent city-state under Byzantine protection. There he spent some days with his companions, all of them disguised as a group of pilgrims returning from the Holy Land. Richard was anxious not to be recognized lest the Byzantines be tempted to take him prisoner. As the conqueror of the island of Cyprus, after all, Richard was responsible for taking and keeping territory that the Byzantines claimed was rightfully theirs. If he fell into Byzantine hands, Richard could reasonably expect to be despoiled of his Cypriot claims, in addition to whatever other indignities might befall him. His disguise, however, was not convincing. He cultivated a beard and tried to blend into the scenery by affecting the type of clothing which was worn locally, but both his height and his commanding manner made him stand out as a strange and exotic visitor in twelfth-century Dalmatia. Moreover, Richard spent far too much money and lived in much too lavish a style to fool anyone with his pretense of being a simple pilgrim on his way home from a pious visit to the shrines of the Holy Land. Even a one-eyed Dalmatian peassant could see at a glance that Richard was something other than what he pretended to be.

The shallowness of Richard's disguise was further demonstrated by his lavish gifts, in fulfillment of his vow while at sea, toward the building of Ragusa's new cathedral. At last it dawned, even upon Richard, that if he stayed very long in Ragusa the Byzantine imperial authorities were almost certain to get wind of his presence and arrest him.

Again he took ship—whether on the same galleys or not we do not know—and sailed farther north along the Dalmatian coast with his companions. Somewhere in Istria, at the headwaters of the Adriatic, between Aquileia and Venice, Richard's ships were wrecked. The king and his surviving followers floundered ashore—exactly where, we again do not know—about December 10 and, after drying out, tried to decide what course they should take.

Their situation was obviously touchy and potentially very dangerous indeed. Richard decided to try once again to pass unnoticed. This time he adopted the guise of a traveling merchant named Hugh, who, according to the story Richard tried to put about, was accompanying Baldwin of Béthune home from the crusade. Baldwin was, in fact, among the companions whom Richard had with him and the king's intention was to convince the authorities that Baldwin was the leader of the group, while Richard posed as a relatively insignificant attendant of the great man.

The deception was as futile now as it had earlier been at Ragusa. By the time the rumor was abroad that the English king was traveling in disguise on the Continent and it was natural to suspect that he might hide himself with parties of crusaders returning home from the East. In a vain effort to carry off the masquerade, Richard sent a messenger to the chief nobleman of the region, the count of Goritz, asking his permission for Baldwin of Béthune's party to pass through the count's territories. The count, in turn, suspected that Richard might be among Baldwin's companions and sent word of his suspicions to Frederick of Betesov, a local worthy at Friesach in Carinthia, where Baldwin's party was heading. By the time that they arrived at Friesach, about 120 miles from the point where Richard's group had landed, the local authorities were waiting for them. A Norman knight, Roger de Argentan, had been appointed by the count of Goritz to find out where Richard was staying. The count apparently hoped to take Richard prisoner and to hold him for ransom. Roger discovered the king's hiding place without difficulty, but he decided not to obey the orders he had been given. Despite the fact that he had been living for many years in Carinthia and was married to the niece of the count of Goritz, Roger apparently still felt strong ties of loyalty to Richard, as duke of his ancestral home in Normandy. Instead of handing Richard over to the count of Goritz, therefore, Roger warned Richard that his disguise had been penetrated and that his presence was known. In order to gain time, Richard passed a large sum of money to Baldwin of Béthune and ordered him to stay at Friesach for the next four days and to make a point of spending money liberally. Richard's hope was that attention would be fastened upon Baldwin and that while the local authorities were investigating Baldwin's story and verifying whether or not he was the English king, Richard himself would have time to get away and to put so much distance between himself and Friesach that the count and others would have difficulty in picking up his trail.

Roger de Argentan agreed to cooperate with this proposal. He went further and loaned Richard one of his own speedy horses and then returned to the count of Goritz to report that the whole story that Richard was in the vicinity was a fabrication. Baldwin of Béthune, he told the count, was simply a noble crusader with lots of money and lavish tastes, on his way back home from the Holy Land.

Richard, meanwhile, accompanied only by William de l'Estang and a German-speaking servant boy, was making for Vienna as quickly as he could, hoping that the confusion he had sown at Friesach would convince the locals to call off the search for him. In this calculation he was entirely mistaken. The count of Goritz continued to be suspicious and soon had Baldwin of Béthune and the rest of the party arrested. Under questioning he discovered the truth, or something approximating it, and the search for Richard was intensified.

By the time that the count's interrogation of the unfortunate Baldwin and his men was completed, Richard and his two companions, having ridden continuously for three days and three nights, had covered 145 miles and had gone to ground in a Vienna suburb. They were exhausted and needed time to sleep and recuperate.

In the meantime the count of Goritz had informed Duke Leopold of Austria that Richard was loose in his dominions and that he was thought to be heading for Vienna. The authorities there were on the lookout for suspicious strangers and when, after three days, Richard's German-speaking servant lad showed up in Vienna with a supply of Byzantine gold coins which he was attempting to exchange for local currency, he was immediately picked up and questioned. The boy made the best of a bad situation. He was employed, he told his captors, by a rich merchant who had come into possession of the Byzantine money in the course of one of his transactions. The boy added that his master was not presently at home, but would return in three days and would confirm his story when he arrived. With this the authorities were momentarily satisfied and they let the servant boy go.

He returned to Richard's lodging as soon as he was released and warned Richard that he should flee at once. Richard was still recovering from his earlier escape, however, and decided to risk staying another day or two in his temporary hiding place. On December 20, he again sent his servant boy to market to buy some food and other provisions. This time the boy made the mistake of tucking a pair of Richard's gloves into his belt as he left. When he appeared in the market with the handsomely adorned gloves in his possession, the suspicions of the authorities were again aroused. The gloves were unlike anything that a merchant, no matter how well traveled or wealthy, would be likely to give to a casual servant. Again the boy was detained and this time he was beaten and interrogated with more vigor than finesse.

Under rough questioning he confessed that his master was indeed at home and that he was no traveling merchant, but the king of England.

Leopold of Austria was at once informed and ordered his troops to surround the lodging house where Richard was concealed. The king, aroused by the arrival of the troops, realized at last that he was well and truly taken. Rather than try to fight his way out of a trap in which he was overwhelmingly outnumbered, he offered to surrender, but demanded, with a touch of his usual arrogance even in this situation, that Duke Leopold must come in person to accept his surrender. Leopold duly put in his appearance and Richard gave himself up, if not gracefully, at least without a fight.

Leopold, for his part, was delighted and triumphant. Ever since his humiliation by Richard at Acre he had cherished his resentment against the English king and had dreamed, without perhaps a great deal of hope, that he would someday be in a position to take his revenge for the humiliation he had suffered at Richard's hands. Now, by a special dispensation of providence, as it must have seemed, Richard had been delivered squarely into his hands. To make things even better, Richard had effectively put himself into Leopold's control, so that his own good fortune was caused by his enemy's folly.

Richard surrendered his sword to Leopold on December 20, 1192. Two days later, he was taken from Vienna to Dürenstein, a remote castle in the hills above the Danube, about forty-five miles from Vienna, where Leopold presumably felt he could keep his prisoner safely and where the possibilities of a successful rescue or escape would be minimal. Richard was placed under strict confinement at Dürenstein, constantly watched by guards who were with him day and night and who had instructions to keep their swords drawn and ready for action at all times.

Leopold presumably hoped that he would be able to hold Richard for ransom and thus profit financially from Richard's captivity. In this he was only partially successful, for there were others, more powerful than he, who stood ready to take advantage of the situation.

Leopold was perhaps unlucky in view of the fact that his cousin and overlord, the Emperor Henry VI, intervened within a few days. For the emperor, as for Duke Leopold, Richard's capture was a godsend. The emperor's own position was critical: his enemies in Germany, particularly the Welfs, were stirring up grave trouble for him and even his possession of the crown was endangered by their plots. The emperor's interest in securing control of the English king, now that he was in captivity, was clear and obvious. By December 28, Henry was already busily involving himself in the affair and on that day he dispatched a letter to Philip Augustus in which he announced the joyful news that Richard had been taken prisoner. Henry had no doubt that Philip would be delighted by this turn of events, and expressed his own pleasure at what had occurred. Henry was determined to capitalize on Richard's captivity and, like Leopold, he felt that he had abundant reason to dislike Richard and ample justification for making the most out of the situation.

Henry was a man of large ambitions, combined with an unusual fund of energy and imagination. He had designs to become the master both of the Mediterranean world and of Central Europe. In his view, Richard had already made himself a nuisance and a threat to the achievement of those goals. One of Henry's immediate objectives was to secure control of south Italy and Sicily, where his chief opponent was Tancred of Sicily, with whom Richard was allied. This itself was a good enough reason for Henry to see Richard's capture as a golden opportunity. But in addition, Henry's chief political opponents in Germany, Henry the Lion and the members of the Welf family, were also Richard's allies, while the emperor had already formed a close alliance in the West with Philip Augustus, who entertained no fondness for the English king. From every point of view, Henry stood to profit by securing control over Richard. As soon as he learned that Leopold had taken Richard prisoner, Henry was determined that Richard must be put into his own hands at the earliest possible opportunity.

Early in the new year, within ten days of the time when Henry learned of Richard's capture, he had Leopold bring Richard to the imperial court at Regensburg. Leopold and Henry immediately began to bargain over the terms under which Richard would be turned over to the emperor. The initial negotiations proved to be unsatisfactory to Leopold and he quickly returned Richard to Dürenstein, while the bargaining between himself and the emperor continued over the next six weeks. A formal agreement was signed at Würzburg on St. Valentine's day 1193. Under the terms of the agreement, Duke Leopold undertook to deliver Richard into the emperor's custody. It was agreed between them— Richard was not present—that Richard would be required to pay 100,000 marks to Henry. Henry, in turn, guaranteed that half of this sum would be paid to Leopold, who would use the money as a dowry settlement for the marriage of one of his sons to the Princess Eleanor of Brittany, daughter of Richard's brother, Geoffrey. The marriage was to take place on the following September 29, the Feast of St. Michael. The money was to be paid on February 23, 1194, and was to be divided half-and-half between the emperor, Henry, and Duke Leopold. Beyond this, Leopold and Henry agreed that they would require Richard to furnish the emperor with a fleet of fifty galleys, completely outfitted with all necessary equipment, and a force of one hundred knights. The fleet and the hundred knights were to be used by the emperor in his campaign against Richard's ally, Tancred of Sicily. Further, Henry would demand that Richard participate in the campaign against Tancred and that Richard bring with him an additional one hundred knights to serve in the campaign under his own command. Moreover, they agreed that they would require Richard to furnish two hundred hostages. They would be held prisoner by the emperor until Richard had fulfilled his obligations under this agreement and until Richard had also persuaded the pope to revoke any penalties which the pontiff might invoke against Leopold for having violated the Church's law by capturing Richard while he was returning from his crusade and while he was, therefore, under the pope's protection. Beyond this, Henry and Leopold agreed that they would require Richard to release the tyrant Isaac of Cyprus and his daughter. If Richard failed to fulfill any of the conditions before the terminal date of February 23, 1194, which they had imposed upon him, Henry and Leopold further agreed that he should be returned to Leopold's custody.

The terms of the agreement were both harsh and humiliating. They were designed, in all probability, as a statement of a bargaining position, rather than as a realistic statement of what Leopold and Henry expected to get from their captive. Certainly there was little possibility that, as things then stood, Richard could have been induced to agree to the stipulations of their joint agreement.

On the other hand, the two signatories of the agreement were also aware that they had powerful support from other quarters for exacting the harshest possible settlement in return for allowing Richard to regain his freedom. Philip Augustus had written to both Leopold of Austria and the Emperor Henry during the previous month and had made it exquisitely clear that he was prepared to go to almost any lengths to prevent Richard from securing his freedom. Philip Augustus had assured Henry, in particular, that if he would keep Richard permanently out of circulation, the French king would be willing to pay a sum equal to or greater than any sum which Richard might offer as a condition of regaining his freedom. Given this kind of guarantee, Leopold and Henry may well have calculated that the terms of their agreement outlined a settlement which would appeal to Philip Augustus and which they, together with Philip, might be able to coerce Richard into accepting.

At the same time that Philip wrote to Leopold and to Henry, he also dispatched messengers to Richard. These emissaries, in accordance with their instructions, informed Richard that Philip no longer considered Richard to be his vassal and that, accordingly, Philip no longer felt himself bound to honor the agreements which had earlier been concluded between them. Moreover, the emissaries presented Richard with a formal declaration of war against him by Philip Augustus. This meant, in effect, that Philip was now absolved of any constraints either in allying himself with John or in attacking Richard's possessions in France. In short order Philip in fact launched an attack upon the Duchy of Normandy.

On February 28 the justiciars, Richard's chief lieutenants in England, met at Oxford to discuss what measures they should take to secure Richard's release. Rumors had been circulating widely concerning the king's captivity and the justiciars were concerned in the first place to establish just what the situation was. A copy of the emperor's letter to Philip Augustus had come into their hands, so that they had a reasonable idea of the kinds of negotiations that were going on among the king's enemies. The justiciars directed that Richard's vassals and other subjects should renew their oaths of allegiance to Richard. They concluded, after discussing various possibilities for further action, that they must make direct contact with the imperial court and with Richard before taking any formal decisions. The bishop of Bath, Saveric de Bohun, who was related to the emperor, Henry, had already established communications with his kinsman on this matter and had met with Henry to discuss the conditions under which Richard might be freed.

The justiciars now sought to establish direct contact with Richard, through two deputies who would be sent to Germany for this purpose. The men chosen were the abbot of Boxley and the abbot of Robertsbridge. The two churchmen went directly to Germany, but had great difficulty in discovering where Richard was being kept. They finally located

him at Ochsenfurt on the Main River, about ten miles south-
east of Würzburg, and visited him there about March 20.
They found Richard in comparatively good spirits. The king
inquired anxiously about conditions in England and Scotland
and complained bitterly about the activities of his brother
John. Richard was aware of John's open alliance with Philip
Augustus and while he feared the damage that might result
from the alliance, he was inclined to discount John's ability
to lead an effective rebellion against his own authority. "My
brother John," Richard told the two abbots, "is not the man to
subjugate a country, if there is a person able to make the
slightest resistance to his attempts."

On the day following his meeting with the two abbots,
Richard was given an audience with the emperor. Henry presented Richard with a list of the demands which he and Leopold had agreed upon earlier. At this meeting Richard had no
opportunity to respond to the conditions which Henry laid
down, but he reported to the abbots that he would not agree
to what was proposed even if his refusal were to cost him his
life.

The following day, March 22, saw another meeting between Richard and the emperor. Henry again sought to domi-
nate the discussion and began by setting forth a bill of partic-
ulars itemizing his grievances against Richard. In this list of
accusations, Henry bore down heavily upon charges that
Richard had in effect treacherously betrayed the cause of the
Latins by making peace with Saladin. He also accused Richard of complicity in the murder of Conrad of Montferrat.
These charges apparently were based upon stories about
Richard's conduct during the crusade which Bishop Philip of
Beauvais was circulating among Richard's enemies. The
bishop had ambitions of his own: he was greedy to secure
control of some of Richard's Continental domains for himself.
In addition, Philip of Beauvais was a confidant of Philip
Augustus, who also helped to publicize these rumors in an at-
tempt to blacken Richard's reputation.

Richard had an opportunity to reply to the charges laid against him. He defended his actions in the East and pointed out forcefully to Henry that his treaty with Saladin had been no surrender, but rather a negotiated settlement that included terms that made it possible for the Latin kingdom of Jerusalem to survive. As to his part in the murder of Conrad, Richard denied the charges vigorously and apparently convinced Henry of his innocence in that affair.

Their discussion then turned to the conditions for Richard's release. Categorically Richard refused to accept the conditions laid down by Henry on the previous day. He would, however, consent to pay a ransom, the sum of 100,000 silver marks that had been agreed upon. Richard demanded, and Henry agreed, that the emperor must also, in return for his money, pacify Philip Augustus. Henry undertook to arrange a peace between the French and English kings and promised that if he could not induce Philip to agree to a peace, he would allow Richard to return home to England without paying any ransom at all.

Under the circumstances, Richard had struck a good bargain. He went to work immediately to set the wheels in motion to raise the ransom money. On March 26, by which time he had been transported from Ochsenfurt to Speyer, Richard wrote to the prior of Christ Church, Canterbury. He told the prior what had happened, how he had fallen into the emperor's hands and how he and Henry had just agreed upon the ransom terms. Would it be possible, he asked the prior, for the Church of Canterbury to lend him from the Church's wealth the 100,000 marks necessary to secure his freedom?

As it turned out, the prior of Christ Church could not oblige the king in this matter: although the See of Canterbury was by any ordinary standards a wealthy one, liquid capital in such large amounts was difficult for Canterbury or any other ecclesiastical body to secure and Richard had to seek other means of finding the needed sum.

During the closing days of March, Richard was busy

with other correspondence. In a long letter to his mother, Eleanor, Richard dwelt at length on the problem of defending the kingdom and maintaining its unity in the face of attacks both from Philip Augustus and also from John. He thanked Eleanor for all that she had done thus far to keep his heritage intact and begged her to continue her efforts. He also commended to his mother's attention Bishop Hubert Walter of Salisbury. Hubert had joined Richard in Germany a short time before, having learned about his monarch's capture while he was on his way back to England from the crusade. Richard urged Eleanor to promote Hubert's candidacy for election to the See of Canterbury. At the same time Richard was also urging Hubert's election upon other correspondents, including the justiciars of the realm. On about the first of April, Hubert and the two abbots set out on their return journey to England, while Richard was shifted to Trifels and then to Hagenau, near Strasbourg. In mid-April Richard, who was then at Hagenau, wrote again to his mother to bring her up-to-date on recent developments. Since coming to Hagenau, he told her, he had had further meetings with Henry in order to clarify some details of their agreement. The emperor had now agreed that Richard would be released as soon as he had paid in 70,000 marks out of the total of 100,000 for which he was obligated. In the meantime, William Longchamp, bishop of Ely and chancellor of England, had visited him, had assisted in the negotiations with the emperor, and would soon return to England. Queen Eleanor and the justiciars, Richard directed, were to begin taking steps to secure the ransom money and the hostages whom the emperor required as a surety for the settlement. Eleanor was to be in charge of the money raised for the ransom and was empowered to choose whatever assistants she needed for keeping and safeguarding the treasure. Richard directed particularly that the queen mother and justiciars should send him a list of all of his nobles and should make a note of how much money was contributed toward the ransom by each of them.

In addition, the justiciars were to seek out and take all of the gold and silver vessels and ornaments of the churches. For each vessel taken they were to give a pledge that the value of the vessel would be repaid when the king was freed. Henry, Richard added, would send an official, formal letter to the prelates and barons of England, setting forth the conditions for Richard's release and the terms of the agreement reached between them.

This letter reached England early in May. The emperor, in the meantime, was busy trying to raise the stakes for Richard's release above what had been agreed upon. For this purpose he arranged to meet with Philip Augustus between Vaucouleurs and Toul on June 25. Richard, when he learned of this, was alarmed. He suspected that Henry might not only bargain with Philip to secure a counter-offer which would enable him to raise the ransom price, but that he might also even contemplate turning the English king over to Philip as a part of the bargain. Richard was well aware that if once he was put in Philip's hands, his chances of ever securing his freedom were virtually nil.

With this in mind, Richard set to work to try to prevent the scheduled meeting. Fortunately for him, he found a situation ready-made for his purposes. In the previous November, Albert of Louvain, bishop of Liége, had been murdered in circumstances that led many of the bishop's powerful relatives and allies to believe that the emperor Henry had instigated the assassination. Accordingly a coalition of German bishops and the noble relatives of the late Bishop Albert was preparing to attack the emperor to seek revenge for Albert's death. Richard now sought to bring together the leaders of the move against Henry and to induce them to give up their plans for revenge. In this enterprise he was successful. He persuaded Henry to meet with the dissident faction and the emperor took an oath in their presence, swearing that he had had nothing to do with the murder of Albert. In addition, Henry promised to restore to the members of the opposition party the lands and castles which he had confiscated from them and their relatives. For their part, the dissidents agreed to give up their plans for an attack upon the emperor and accept his assurances of innocence in Albert's assassination.

Richard had thus been instrumental in averting a civil war in the empire. In recompense for Richard's role in this affair, Henry agreed to give up his projected meeting with Philip Augustus and he agreed further to leave the ransom terms as they then stood.

In England, meanwhile, efforts to raise Richard's ransom money were proceeding at a hectic pace. The kingdom had been drained of money four years earlier in order to finance Richard's crusade. During his absence in the Holy Land, the justiciars had been hard put to it to meet the ordinary expenses of the government. Now a further extraordinary outlay was demanded and the resources for meeting the demand were difficult to envision. The sum of 100,000 marks was roughly equal to the surplus which had been left in the treasury at the time of Henry II's death. All of that money, of course, plus a great deal more had already been spent during the four years of Richard's reign. To meet the new demand, a form of direct taxation must be resorted to. The justiciars decreed that all of Richard's subjects, including the clergy, must pay one fourth of their annual revenues for the year into the Exchequer. In addition, the gold and silver vessels of the churches, as Richard had personally directed, were to be confiscated and added to the ransom fund. Beyond this, each knight's fief was assessed the sum of twenty shillings, while the monasteries of the Cistercian and Gilbertine orders, which had no gold or silver ornaments to contribute to the ransom, were to pay in the receipts from their crops of wool for the year.

By June 1, when the royal council met at St. Albans, the receipts from these taxes were already beginning to be hauled down to London from the county towns, where the sheriffs were collecting the money from the laity, while the bishops supervised the collection of the clergy's share. The council appointed a committee to assume direct responsibility for safeguarding the ransom funds and accounting for them. The members of this committee included Hubert Walter, who had just recently been elected archbishop of Canterbury at Richard's request, as well as the earls of Arundel and Warenne and the mayor of London. Queen Eleanor, Richard's mother, assumed the overall supervision of the ransom funds and the committee was responsible directly to her. The money was laid down in large locked chests in St. Paul's Cathedral, each chest being sealed up as it was filled under the queen mother's seal.

Before the council meeting broke up, Longchamp, the chancellor, summoned a group of notables, including the bishops of Rochester and Chichester, the abbot of Peterborough, Richard de Clare, Earl of Hertford, and others, to accompany him when he returned to Richard in Germany. The chancellor also announced that he had orders to bring with him a company of noblemen's sons, who were later to be placed in the custody of the emperor Henry as hostages for the fulfillment of the ransom terms. To this demand, however, there was resistance, even from Queen Eleanor. The reluctance of the magnates to entrust their sons to the chancellor derived in part from his notorious reputation as a homosexual: "We will put our daughters in his care, but never our sons," they are reported to have said. In the event, Longchamp had to return to Germany without the youthful hostages whom he had promised to deliver.

Longchamp was in Germany with Richard by June 25, at which time there was another meeting between the English king and his captor, this time at Worms. The meeting at Worms resulted in a written agreement, stipulating the terms of the ransom in greater detail. The 100,000 marks were to be assayed as pure silver and were to be weighed following the system used at Cologne. When the money had been received, assayed, and weighed at London in the presence of witnesses appointed for this purpose by both Richard and the emperor, the money chests were to be sealed in the presence of the emperor's agents and were to be transported through Richard's territory at Richard's risk, under the care of guards appointed by him. When the money chests reached the imperial frontiers they were to be transferred to the care of the emperor's men and their further transport was at the emperor's risk. One half of the total sum was to be paid to the emperor and the duke of Austria jointly: 30,000 marks to Henry, 20,000 to Leopold. A fresh attempt was to be made to secure the hostages whom Longchamp had been unable to raise. These hostages were to be given to each of the two recipients as surety for the payment of the balance owed to them. When the final installment of 50,000 marks was paid, the king was to be liberated. In addition this version of the ransom agreement stipulated that Richard was to use his good offices to make peace between the former duke of Saxony, Henry the Lion, and the emperor. If he succeeded in this effort, payment of a part of the ransom money was to be forgiven. In addition Richard was bound to give his niece to one of Leopold's sons in marriage. Further it was specified that when Richard was released he was to be escorted to the imperial frontiers by guards supplied by the emperor.

News of this final settlement of the terms for Richard's release was profoundly depressing to Richard's enemies. Philip Augustus wrote to John upon hearing of the agreement that he should take care of himself, "for," he said, "the devil is now let loose."

Philip was quick to take his own advice. On July 9 he met with Richard's representatives, Longchamp the chancellor, John de Préaux, and William Briwerre, at Mantes to settle peace terms between himself and the English king. The terms were extraordinarily favorable to Philip, who received in the end a concession by which Richard's representatives granted him the right to retain as much as he wished of the land he had conquered from Richard. In addition, John's possession of the lands that he held both in England and France at the time when Richard departed on crusade was guaranteed. There were allegations abroad that John had been going about collecting money, allegedly for Richard's ransom, which he was keeping for his own uses. John was to be required either to prove his innocence of the charge or else to return the money he had secured under false pretenses. A number of Richard's other enemies in France also demanded and secured reassurances that Richard would respect their landholdings and would not take vengeance upon them when he was released. Moreover, Richard was bound by the terms of the treaty to do service to Philip for the fiefs which he held from the French crown and to pay him 20,000 silver marks, Troy weight. As security for this payment, Richard was to hand over to Philip his castles at Loches and Châtillon-sur-Indre. Two other castles were to be delivered to the archbishop of Reims, to be returned to Richard when he paid Philip the sum of money agreed upon.

Harsh as the settlement was, it was a necessary preliminary to the conclusion of the arrangements for Richard's release. If he had failed to satisfy Philip Augustus, the chances were very great that the latter would have contrived to put pressure upon the emperor to retain Richard in captivity. Richard had little choice at this point but to make such concessions as were demanded of him.

During the summer and fall of 1193 the work of collecting Richard's ransom occupied his government in England almost to the exclusion of everything else. The details of the collection process are little known, since the money did not pass through the Exchequer and thus the records of that office furnish no details of what happened. It is clear enough, however, that the handling of the collections was somewhat haphazard. No one had any very clear notion of just how much money the levy of one fourth of the income of Richard's subjects ought to bring in and, at least in some areas, the tax collectors apparently made repeated assessments until they arrived at what they felt was a suitable sum. There was apparently a considerable amount of pilfering and thievery in the process and the collectors were widely suspected of having pocketed a goodly share of the proceeds for themselves.

Little by little the chests stored in St. Paul's were filled up with the proceeds of the tax collection, however, and by October or November there was enough on hand for the emperor's agents to come to London to begin the process of weighing and checking the totals. The money was then consigned to armed guards for transport to Germany. On December 20 the emperor wrote from Gelnhausen to inform Richard's subjects that he proposed to release Richard on January 17. The release, he said, was to take place either at Speyer or at Worms and on the following Monday, January 24, Henry proposed to crown Richard as king of Provence. This coronation was important as a symbolic ceremony only, since the kingdom of Provence was not in fact in the emperor's possession, nor did Richard ever claim it. The meaning of the ceremony was simply that it would technically make Richard a subject of the empire and thus create a formal bond of allegiance between him and Henry.

By the time that this letter was dispatched, Queen Eleanor and the archbishop of Rouen were already on their way to Speyer, where they joined Richard and spent the Christmas of 1193 with him. At the same time, Richard appointed Archbishop Hubert Walter as justiciar of England, replacing the archbishop of Rouen, Walter of Coutances, who had been serving as a justiciar since 1191. Once the new year had arrived, hopes for Richard's speedy release grew.

Richard's release had been scheduled for January 17, and when the day came, a large assembly of notables convened at Speyer. As the formal preparations for Richard's release were commencing, emissaries arrived representing John and Philip Augustus, with a counter-offer for Henry's consideration. The affair was postponed for two more weeks, until the last formalities could be ironed out. Then on February 2 at Mainz another meeting was held. Richard and Eleanor were there, together with the emperor, the duke of Austria, and a formidable group of high-ranking churchmen and lay magnates from both Germany and England. Henry was still tempted by the thought that he might somehow be able to collect ransom from both the English and the French, but Richard's supporters insisted firmly that the emperor was bound to honor his earlier commitment to release Richard upon the receipt of the ransom money which he had already collected. At length the emperor gave in and agreed to release Richard as he had promised. Then the matter of the hostages who were to be delivered to the emperor had to be settled. All of this took time and it was not until Feburary 4, 1194, that the final details were completed. In a formal ceremony at Mainz, Henry at last turned Richard over to Queen Eleanor, his mother, and released him from the imperial control. Once he had been released, Richard then divested himself of the English kingdom and turned a cap, symbolizing his English crown, over to the emperor. Henry, as previously agreed, then reinvested Richard with the English crown to be held as a fief of the empire, on condition that Richard should henceforth pay to the emperor the annual sum of 5,000 pounds sterling as a token of his homage to the emperor. The regalia of the English kings was also turned over to Henry, so that he might henceforth be able to invest future English kings with the symbols of their royal office. The opportunity to do this was, in fact, never forthcoming. When Henry died in 1198 the claim to imperial suzerainty lapsed and his successor, Otto of Brunswick, restored the regalia.

The ceremonies connected with Richard's liberation continued on the following day. On February 5 Richard received the homage of a number of German nobles and in return he granted annual pensions to each of them. Following this, Richard together with the emperor and his assembled magnates dispatched letters informing Philip Augustus and

John of Richard's release and demanding that they restore to Richard the castles, towns, lands, and other possessions rightfully belonging to him which they had seized. The emperor and his men threatened that if Philip and John did not comply with this demand, they would join forces with Richard to aid him in recovering the possessions which he had lost. Richard also dispatched letters of his own, informing Henry of Champagne, the nominal king of Jerusalem, that he intended to return to Palestine as previously arranged in order to complete the work which he had begun there.

After completing the ceremonies for his release, Richard set out on a leisurely journey toward England, accompanied by his mother and his chancellor, William Longchamp. The party journeyed down the Rhine valley, armed with imperial letters of safe-conduct. They spent three days at Cologne, where they were guests of Archbishop Adolf. From there they passed through the lands of the duke of Louvain, on to Brussels and finally to Antwerp, where Richard was met by ships belonging to his own fleet. The party boarded ship at Antwerp on March 4 and sailed to Swine, which they reached on March 7. At Swine they had a delay, while they waited for favorable winds. At length, when the winds were right, they sailed for England and landed at Sandwich on March 13.

Returned at long last to his birthplace, Richard headed directly for Canterbury, where he offered thanks for his safe homecoming at the shrine of St. Thomas the Martyr. Then he began his journey to London, meeting Archbishop Hubert Walter at Rochester on the way. His formal entrance into London was celebrated with universal rejoicing on March 16. The crusading chapter in Richard's career was finished. Although he firmly intended to return to the Holy Land, he was never able to do so. For the rest of his life he was engaged in trying to recover from the losses which his crusade had cost him and to secure a firm control over the possessions which his father had left to him.

NINE

✣————————————————————————✣

Richard's Last Years
(1194 – 1199)

Richard's return to England in 1194 marked the beginning of a new and, as it turned out, a final phase of his life. Although he hoped to return one day to the Latin East to complete his crusade, which he regarded as still unfinished so long as Jerusalem remained in Muslim hands, Richard was never in fact to realize this dream. As the years passed, he may even have begun to realize reluctantly that the prospect of a new crusade was for him a chimera.

The last five years of his reign were played out for the most part in France and throughout those last years his rivalry with Philip Augustus was at the forefront of Richard's concerns. But before he could successfully deal with his Continental problems, Richard needed to make sure of his hold over his base of operations in England. In addition, he had to raise money in England to finance his ventures in France, for England was the prime source of the ready cash which supported Angevin campaigns on the Continent.

In England, Richard faced problems of reestablishing order that, to be sure, were of some seriousness, but that were not nearly so complex and so difficult to settle as were the problems of his Continental domains. His brother John had, indeed, tried to begin a civil war in England during Richard's absence. With the backing of a small band of mercenaries John had seized a number of castles, but on the whole he had been able to do only minor mischief. Still, John's supporters remained in control of the two castles of Tickhill and Nottingham at the time of Richard's return and these fortresses had to be retaken in short order. There were in addition some lesser centers of resistance to the reimposition of Richard's rule, but these could readily be reduced. Richard's mere presence in England was enough to discourage all but a handful of the rebels. Indeed, the news of his release from captivity was such a powerful shock to the rebellious constable of St. Michael's Mount that he dropped dead of fright upon learning of Richard's return to the realm.

On the Continent, Richard faced a far more dangerous and competent antagonist than he did in England. Philip Augustus was determined to make himself master of the lands held by Richard both in Normandy and in the south. Philip had begun to harass the Angevin frontiers in France as soon as he returned home from the crusade in 1191. Richard's capture had furnished him with a golden opportunity to broaden these attacks and to increase both their scope and their intensity. In 1193 Philip had not only occupied the Norman Vexin and taken Gisors, but had besieged Rouen itself. Although he had to withdraw from the siege without taking Rouen, he had still made dangerous inroads upon the Norman domain. In addition, he enjoyed the active cooperation of Count John, Richard's brother. John had done homage to Philip in Paris and in return had received formal investiture with the Norman duchy, which meant in effect that the French king recognized him as the rightful ruler of the Norman duchy. In return for John's cooperation in Normandy, Philip had promised to give John lands that he had recently acquired in Flanders. These Flemish possessions were to stand as dowry for Philip's sister Alice, whom John had once promised to marry. Philip himself had also made an alliance with the Danes and had married a Danish princess, Ingeborg, as a part of a further scheme to launch an invasion of England with Danish support. Philip cast John as his nominee for the English crown if his invasion plans were successful. Beyond this, Philip had also made inroads upon Richard's possessions and authority in Aquitaine and the Touraine. Although Richard's father-in-law and brother-in-law, Sancho VI and Sancho VII of Navarre, had done their best to safeguard Richard's interests in the south, Philip had gained a large number of allies among the rebellious and chronically discontented nobility of that region. And there, too, John fell in with Philip's plans. Almost on the eve of Richard's liberation, John turned over to the French king a whole series of strategically vital points commanding the principal defenses of the Loire, Cher, and Indre river valleys. At the same time, he also surrendered to Philip all of the Norman frontier territory which Philip so badly wanted. In consequence of this, Philip was in a highly advantageous position to push home his attacks almost at every point where the hereditary lands of the Angevins touched the domains of the French monarchy. John apparently saw all of these transactions as preliminary to a general assault by himself and the French king on all of Richard's Continental possessions. John seems throughout to have been motivated partly by greed and partly by an almost pathological jealousy of Richard.

Even before he was freed from captivity in Germany, Richard had learned piecemeal of the achievements of his enemies and the encroachments they had made upon his territories. When at last he returned to England, he had already conceived some plans for regaining what he had lost and for putting the situation right. Once he was back in England, he wasted little time. He reached London on March 16, 1194, and was received with universal relief and rejoicing. The city was in holiday spirits. Houses were decorated, bright banners fluttered from every prominence, and the citizens thronged the streets to cheer the king's return and to welcome him once again to his capital. The clergy of London turned out en masse to assist in the homecoming ritual for a returned crusader and at St. Paul's the ceremonial reunion of the king and his realm was duly celebrated.

The occasion was the sort that Richard dearly loved and under other circumstances no doubt he would have done his best to draw out the celebration and prolong the festivities. But there was work to be done and for once Richard was impatient to be about his royal business. The welcoming ceremonies in London and the civic celebration, therefore, were limited to one day only. As soon as he decently could, Richard took his leave of London and pushed off to the north. He first visited the shrine of St. Edmund at Bury and then set out for Nottingham, where he arrived on March 25. The rebel forces which he came to meet consisted in the main of discontented nobles who had accepted John as their leader. The dissatisfactions of the rebel party were due largely to the heavy taxes imposed upon them by Richard's government, taxes that were raised in order to underwrite Richard's foreign ventures. In part, too, the rebels were motivated by discontent with the government of the justiciars whom Richard had appointed as his representatives in England during the crusade. The rebellion was not so much an expression of confidence in John as it was a protest against Richard's policies and the officers who executed those policies. By the time that Richard arrived at Nottingham, the other centers of resistance had been extinguished and a formidable army had already gathered to reduce the castle of Nottingham. The garrison of the castle refused at first to believe that Richard had come in person to take charge of the operations against them. They were soon convinced. Once Richard with his own eyes saw the rebels killing men who had pledged their allegiance to him, his formidable fury was aroused. Using the latest technical wrinkles in siege warfare that he had learned and experimented with in the East, Richard took charge of the operation in earnest. His first order was to his carpenters. He directed them to build gallows in clear view of the castle's walls. If there were any doubts that the threat implied by this gesture would be carried through, Richard was determined to lay them at rest. Accordingly he had a number of John's adherents who had been captured in earlier encounters brought forward. The unlucky wretches were then promptly hanged and left to dangle from the gallows' ropes, as a reminder to the castle garrison of what their fate was going to be.

It took only two days for the lesson to be learned. On March 27 emissaries from the besieged castle nervously approached Richard while he was at dinner with Archbishop Hubert Walter, who had just come to join the royal army in camp. The emissaries wanted to verify that it was indeed King Richard who had taken command of the siege. Once they were convinced, they surrendered, placing themselves at the mercy of the king. The surrender of the rest of the garrison followed shortly and Nottingham was once again under royal control. Tickhill followed suit, thus breaking the back of the rebel forces in England. The capitulation of Tickhill left the remaining members of the opposition no viable base for further resistance.

With the rebellion crushed, Richard took a day's leave from business to visit Sherwood Forest, which he had never previously seen. Following this visit, he returned to Nottingham to take counsel with a group of trusted advisers. The business at hand concerned the reshaping of a vital part of the English administration. The sheriffs of all but seven of the counties of England were removed and replaced by men who were considered trustworthy—and who were also willing to pay handsome premiums for receiving their new offices. Richard consulted his advisers about the measures to be taken against John. They also discussed the imposition of new taxes to pay for the redemption of the hostages who were still held by the emperor and to meet the anticipated expenses of new wars in France against Philip Augustus and his allies on the Continent.

The meeting of the royal council was no sooner concluded than Richard set out for Southwell, where he met with
King William of Scotland. The Scottish monarch was anxious
to secure territorial concessions in the north of England. The
territories which he had his eyes on were regions that at
various times in the past had been a part of the Scottish realm
and which King William claimed should be restored to him.
Richard was unwilling to grant the concessions the Scots demanded, but at the same time he was anxious to avoid giving
the Scottish king any cause for future quarrels with England.
Since Richard confidently expected to be involved in territorial struggles on the Continent in a short time, he could not
afford to risk the chance that the Scots might attack England
while he and his troops were fully committed in France.
After several days of deliberation, Richard finally made a
counter-proposal, which King William accepted. Instead of
giving William the lands which he claimed, Richard offered
monetary compensations to him, which the Scottish king was
finally prevailed upon to accept.

After concluding his negotiations with King William,
Richard moved to the south, to Winchester, where he arrived
on April 15. Two days later, on Sunday, April 17, he was
crowned for a second time as king of England, this time in
Winchester Cathedral. The purpose of the second coronation
was in part to symbolize Richard's reunion with the realm following his crusade and imprisonment. There was some feeling that Richard's separation from his kingdom and especially the fact that, in order to secure his liberation, he had
been invested with the English crown by the emperor, might
have cast some cloud upon his title to the throne. The second
coronation was designed to cure this defect. To witness the
coronation and to sanctify the ceremony by their presence,
Richard had the cream of the British hierarchy turn out for
the occasion. Hubert Walter, the archbishop of Canterbury,
was naturally the chief officiating prelate, assisted by the
archbishop of Dublin and eleven other bishops as well. As at

his first coronation, Richard arranged for this coronation ceremony to be conducted with sumptuous display. The Scottish king was in attendance, as were a multitude of earls, barons, knights, and commoners, who packed every available inch of the cathedral and the surrounding area outside the church. Queen Eleanor, Richard's mother, together with the noble ladies of her court occupied the northern part of the sanctuary, while Richard and his attendants filled the south side. Richard's wife, Queen Berengaria, significantly, was not in attendance. Richard and Berengaria had been separated for much of the time that he was in the Holy Land and had not met, even formally, for more than a year and a half. There is reason to suspect that Richard had in the meantime reverted to the homosexual relationships which he had solemnly renounced prior to his departure on the crusade.

The second coronation was, in some respects, not quite so solemn an occasion as the first one had been. In actual fact, the king donned his crown prior to the ceremony itself and, although many of the prayers and ceremonies of the first coronation were repeated, the ritual anointing and conferring of the crown were not repeated. The king wore his crown throughout the ceremony, which in effect was rather more on the order of a renewal of the original coronation than it was a coronation properly speaking.

Following the solemn ecclesiastical ceremonies which reunited the king with his kingdom, there was a splendid banquet in celebration of the event. This feast took place in the refectory of the monastery attached to Winchester Cathedral and was marked by a great display of rejoicing over the king's return.

By this time Richard was fretting to take leave of England once again and to get on with his business in France. The three weeks following the second coronation ceremony were a hectic round of preparations for his imminent departure. There were any number of pressing last-minute arrangements to be made and settlements to be concluded.

Each day the scribes and officials of the court were busy, engrossing charters to be approved and sealed, finalizing the texts of agreements, drafting and dispatching letters, supervising the collection of accounts, and submitting documents for Richard's inspection.

On April 24 Richard and his court moved to Portsmouth, where his army was assembling and making ready to cross the Channel to France. Richard's impatience to depart grew every day, particularly as each fresh messenger from France brought further information about the inroads that Philip Augustus was making on Richard's possessions there. The weather turned hostile and the crossing had to be delayed, one day after another. By May 2, Richard's patience was exhausted. Despite continuing storms on the Channel he was determined to make the crossing at once. The fleet accordingly put to sea, despite the advice of Richard's naval aides. They ran immediately into a violent storm. After tossing about on the waves for a day and a night, Richard was finally convinced and returned to Portsmouth harbor. Eight days later the weather finally cleared. Richard reembarked, together with Queen Eleanor and the army, and sailed without mishap this time to Barfleur where he arrived on May 12. His fleet numbered a hundred ships and he was fully prepared for a strenuous campaign.

As soon as they reached the Norman coast, Richard proceeded via Bayeux to Caen and thence to Lisieux. At Lisieux he met at last with his brother John. Queen Eleanor was instrumental in bringing her two sons together and in mediating the differences and hard feelings between them. She succeeded ultimately in convincing Richard to forgive John for his decidedly dubious conduct during Richard's absence. When John was at length shown in to face his brother, Richard was uncommonly gentle and understanding. "Don't be afraid, John," he told him. "You are a child. You have had bad companions and your counselors shall pay." Then he had a fresh salmon cooked and offered it to John, comforting him like a little boy who has been amply scolded for his mischief. But even the queen mother could not convince Richard to restore John's lands and castles to him immediately.

Once peace of a sort had been made between himself and his brother, Richard turned to deal with Philip Augustus. Philip had been besieging Richard's city of Verneuil at the time of the English king's arrival in Normandy and he continued the siege while Richard was patching up his relationship with John. As soon as Richard was free to turn to other matters, Philip abandoned the siege of Verneuil, rightly calculating that Richard would love nothing more than to catch him and his army dug into a position there where they could easily be attacked from two different quarters simultaneously. Richard hastened to Verneuil, but arrived too late to find either Philip or his forces. They had departed on the previous day.

From Verneuil, Richard hastened to Montmirail, which was under siege, but again the siege had ended before he arrived on the scene. He pushed on into Touraine, where troops belonging to his brother-in-law, Sancho the Strong of Navarre, were besieging Loches, which surrendered to them on June 13. Sancho had brought an army of eight hundred knights north into Aquitaine as early as 1192 and since then had campaigned intermittently around Toulouse in support of Richard's interests. Now he was again in Aquitaine with another force in order to harry Richard's enemies. Sancho's cooperation with Richard was based upon the terms of the alliance between them which dated from the time of Richard's betrothal to Berengaria. Despite the apparent failure of that marriage, the alliance was still intact and it was, indeed, an essential factor in Richard's Continental strategy. Presumably Sancho saw the alliance as an opportunity to gain loot and possibly also politically useful support from Richard. These considerations transcended any personal resentment he may have felt over Richard's unchivalrous treatment of Berengaria.

Philip Augustus, meanwhile, continued hostilities elsewhere. On June 14 the town of Fontaine, near Rouen, fell to his forces. After this success, Philip retired into his own territories.

During the first part of June representatives of both the English and the French kings had been negotiating with each other in an attempt to arrange a truce between the two monarchs. The negotiators were finally successful in reaching an agreement on June 17. When Richard learned from his representatives, however, that the proposed truce would involve his granting amnesty to the Poitevin barons who had switched their allegiance and had done homage to Philip Augustus as their overlord, he rejected the proposal and refused to agree to the truce unless this provision was deleted from the agreement. The fighting therefore continued.

Philip, for his part, made a devastating raid on Evreux in Normandy and then headed south into the County of Blois, which was safely outside of Richard's domains, and made camp near Châteaudun. He calculated, apparently, that from this position he would be able to move quickly into Normandy, Maine, or Touraine, as circumstances decreed, and that Richard would be hard put to it to anticipate the direction from which the next attack might be launched.

Richard, meanwhile, departed from Loches, crossed the Loire, and on July 6 camped in the unfortified little town of Vendôme, at the same time that Philip was moving into a new camp at Fréteval, about ten miles away. Scouts and patrol parties from the two armies brought each side news of the shifting locations of the other party and both sides prepared for a confrontation. After a day of waiting, Philip changed his mind and began pulling his army back. Richard, who had been keeping the French forces under close surveillance, decided that the time was ripe for an attack and hastily mustered a light force which fell upon the rear of the French army as it was retreating. The French forces made no attempt to hold their position, but tried rather to elude the attack with as few losses as possible. The surprise attack, although it did no appreciable harm to the bulk of the French army, was immensely gratifying to Richard. It was the first time that he had tasted the enemy's blood and the occasion gave him a small measure of revenge for the indignities which the French king had heaped upon him in the past three years. In addition, although most of Philip's men escaped unharmed from the attack, Richard did manage to capture the baggage train of the French forces, including part of Philip's treasury. Richard also acquired a very satisfying bundle of parchment documents, which included the charters issued by Philip to those noblemen in Normandy who had renounced their allegiance to Richard and had pledged their support to the French king.

As the troops who accompanied him concentrated their attack on the baggage train of the French army, Richard hurried forward in search of Philip himself, breathing threats as he rode along, anticipating the satisfaction he would feel if only he could manage to take Philip prisoner and hold him for ransom, just as Richard himself had been held. Stopping momentarily on his quest, he asked a Flemish soldier where the French king had gone and was told in reply that he was some distance ahead. Richard mounted a fresh horse and spurred off in pursuit. He failed to find Philip, however, for the very good reason that the French monarch had taken the precaution of hiding himself in a church along the way and was piously hearing Mass, while Richard rode wildly about in a fruitless chase. At length Richard gave up the chase and returned to his own lines, while Philip, having finished his devotions, rejoined his army and retreated back into safe territory.

Giving up, for the moment, his attempt to force a confrontation with Philip, Richard now turned his attention to his domains in the south. Aquitaine had been left in the special care of the queen mother, Eleanor, at the time of Richard's departure on the crusade. She had taken as her chief assistant for the management of affairs there the seneschal of

Poitou, Peter Bertin. The seneschal, in cooperation with Sancho of Navarre, had made a valiant attempt to quell the rivalries of the Aquitainian nobles and to safeguard Richard's interests in the region, but he was unable to prevent Philip Augustus from making trouble there as he was also doing in the north. Geoffrey of Rancogne in the county of Angoulême was a willing ally of Philip's and had, indeed, been a thorn in the side of the Angevin kings for nearly thirty years. Following Geoffrey's lead, a number of the other Aquitainian nobles declared their open allegiance to Philip and renounced the homage they had done to Richard. The indispensable Sancho of Navarre had come forward to assist Peter Bertin in putting down the rebels and between the two of them they had buffeted Richard's opponents severely even before Richard appeared upon the scene. The result of all of this was that when Richard made his re-entry into his southern domains he found only nominal resistance. In a swiftly moving campaign he won a series of quick successes at every point along the line. Writing to Archbishop Hubert Walter on July 22, Richard gave a proud and probably inflated account of his swift succession of victories:

> Know that, by the grace of God, who in all things has consideration for the right, we have taken Taillebourg and Marsillac, and all the castles and the whole of the territories of Geoffrey of Rancogne, as well as the city of Angoulême, and Châteauneuf, Montignac, La Chese, and all the other castles, and the whole of the territories of the Count of Angoulême, with all things thereunto appendant and appurtenant. The city of Angoulême and the suburb we took in a single evening; while on the lands which we have captured in these parts, we have taken fully three hundred knights and forty thousand armed men.*

* Roger of Howden, *Annals*, s.a. 1194, trans. H. T. Riley, p. 328.

This engagement was followed immediately by a resumption of negotiations with Philip Augustus with a view to reaching a truce agreement. On July 23 representatives of the two monarchs met at a place between Verneuil and Tillières, where they were able to settle upon the terms of a truce which they agreed should last from the time of its ratification by the two kings until the first of November, 1195. The truce agreement provided that Philip Augustus was to be left in possession of the territories which he held at the moment and that he could do with them as he pleased for the period of the truce. Richard likewise was permitted to fortify or destroy the fortresses which he held, but he was forbidden by the agreement to rebuild any of the fortified sites that Philip had already razed, save for four places which were specified in the truce terms. Each of the kings was to regard certain named subjects of his rival as covered by the terms of the truce and these persons were to be unmolested so long as the truce agreement lasted. Provision was also made for the appointment by each king of two mediators, who were given the title of "dictators." These dictators were to decide whether subsequent actions of the parties constituted an infringement of the terms of the truce and the dictators were empowered to assess damages against those who broke the agreement.

The detailed provisions of the Treaty of Tillières were drawn in a fashion that was on the whole very favorable to the interests of Philip Augustus. Both Philip and Richard apparently ratified the treaty and expressed their willingness to abide by its terms. Richard, however, was not entirely serious in giving his consent to the treaty's provisions, for as soon as he returned to Normandy in August he repudiated the agreement and declared that he would not consider himself bound by it. It seems that his motive in agreeing to the Treaty of Tillières was to buy a few weeks' time, and thus to prevent Philip from regrouping his forces and attacking Normandy once again. Richard waited until Philip's forces were safely dispersed before renouncing the truce agreement. Richard sought to blame his chancellor, William Longchamp, for his own dishonorable behavior in repudiating the agreement which he had made. Richard tried to give the impression that Longchamp had exceeded his authority and had used the great seal to ratify the Treaty of Tillières without the king's express consent to do so. Almost certainly this was a ruse on Richard's part to evade responsibility for his own actions and to escape as best he could from the onus of going back on his word. If he relieved Longchamp of his office as chancellor at this point, as one writer asserts, he quickly restored him to favor and there seems to have been no real interruption in Longchamp's management of the royal chancery. All of this was simply a smoke screen put up by Richard to hide his own reprehensible evasion of responsibility.

How seriously Philip Augustus took Richard's repudiation of the treaty of Tillières it is not possible to say. Certainly Philip did not attempt to launch an attack during the period of the truce or to take any other steps to avenge himself on Richard for revoking the agreement. Both sides acted, in fact, as if the treaty remained in effect and it is possible that the repudiation of it by Richard was simply an angry outburst of the vicious temper for which he and other members of his family were widely known.

After these episodes, the remainder of the year was a quiet period in Richard's life. As usual his court followed the king's progress from one stronghold to another, although his pace was slower than usual during these months. For weeks at a time Richard stayed put. He spent most of August at Ville l'Évêque, then moved on in turn to Argentan, Alençon, Chinon, and Rouen. At each step he transacted some business, but apparently he found ample time for his favorite diversions, especially hunting with falcons and behind his dogs. His companions were for the most part comfortable old friends. Baldwin of Béthune, his companion on his return from the Holy Land, spent weeks at Richard's court. There, too, were Longchamp, his chancellor; Geoffrey, his half-brother; and lesser men of the court, men whom Richard trusted but who played only minor roles in his administration, men such as William de l'Estang, Warin Fitz Gerold, and Robert de Wancy. They spent the evenings, after the day's sport, sitting in the hall of one after another of Richard's castles and manor houses, warming themselves by the fire, drinking, talking, listening to singers, amusing themselves at chess, or applauding the dancers and tumblers who frequented the court.

When Richard returned to Normandy in August, he was busy once more with routine administrative matters, at least in part concerned with raising money from the English kingdom. Late in August he wrote to Archbishop Hubert Walter outlining one of his more imaginative money-raising schemes. In the letter he granted the archbishop the right to allow tournaments to be held in England at certain places, under the condition that each entrant in the tournaments should pay to the king's account a sum of money which bought him, in effect, a royal license to participate in the tourney. Tournaments had previously been entirely forbidden in England, as indeed they theoretically were throughout the Christian world. The pope had, in fact, just recently reissued legislation prohibiting Christians from participating in these mock-battles, but this decretal, like its predecessors, was widely ignored. Richard himself had often participated in these combats in the south of France, where they were a favorite noble sport, and there is every reason to believe that he enjoyed them thoroughly. His motive in permitting tournaments to be held in England, however, was fiscal rather than sporting. The popularity of tournaments on the Continent ensured that when they were allowed in England they would be well patronized. The tariffs to be charged participants, as outlined in Richard's letter to the archbishop, would create an ample source of additional royal revenue, which Richard badly needed.

We have no information at all about what Richard was

doing during September and October of 1194. Presumably he was still in Normandy and presumably he was enjoying a respite from his recent exertions. His activities during the last two months of the year have left only modest traces in the historical record. A considerable amount of Richard's attention at this period was probably given to the problem of redeeming the hostages who were still being held in Germany and Austria under the terms of the agreement by which Richard had been freed. Leopold of Austria was being unusually nasty, even for him. He threatened to put the hostages to death unless Richard complied speedily with Leopold's interpretation of the further satisfaction due from Richard on the ransom agreement. It must certainly have been with considerable relief and gratification that Richard finally learned of Leopold's death at the end of the year. The Austrian duke was in spiritual difficulty, too, which probably increased Richard's satisfaction. For when Leopold died he was under sentence of excommunication, which the pope had imposed upon him for having held Richard captive while he was returning from the crusade. The pope reasoned, understandably enough, that since Richard as a crusader was under the protection of the pope, then Leopold in capturing and holding Richard was acting in defiance of the papacy. Hence the excommunication, which was still in force when Leopold died unexpectedly following the amputation of one of his legs. The Church remained adamant even after Leopold's death: his body was refused Christian burial until the hostages given to him by Richard were released.

The year's end was also brightened by another death: Count Raymond V of Toulouse expired at about the same time that Duke Leopold died. Count Raymond was an old enemy with whom Richard had often fought. The disappearance of such a foe could not help but augur well for Richard's chances of maintaining control of his lands in the south of France.

If Richard found the Church a useful ally in his dealings

with Duke Leopold, however, his attitude toward the Church establishment from this point forward was to become increasingly lukewarm. The Treaty of Tillières marked the beginning of Richard's wariness toward clerical politicians and diplomats, for that treaty had been negotiated in large part by ecclesiastics, especially by the papal legate, who brought increasing pressure on Richard to abandon, or at least to moderate, his wars with Philip Augustus. In truth, Pope Celestine III seems to have become increasingly suspicious and distrustful of Richard after his return from the crusade. While Pope Celestine looked upon Philip Augustus as a natural ally and a supporter of papal interests, he could scarcely be expected to harbor friendly feelings for Philip's major enemy. Moreover, the fact that Richard kept putting continuous and increasing military pressure on Philip meant that Philip by the same token was less amenable to papal requests for military assistance in Italy and elsewhere.

The political tensions between Richard and Pope Celestine III did not mean that Richard's personal attitude toward the practice of his religion was necessarily growing cooler. He was and remained throughout his life a religious man, at least in certain ways. The pomp and pageantry of the Church's solemn services appealed to him deeply and he seems to have delighted in attending ecclesiastical ceremonies through his adult life. In a more personal and intimate sense, too, he was capable of being influenced by considerations of piety. One such episode occured during the early part of 1195.

Of the precise circumstances we know little, not even the exact date. But sometime early in that year Richard was visited by a hermit; his name likewise is unknown to us. Richard had been separated from Queen Berengaria since before he had left the Holy Land and there is little doubt that during their separation he had again fallen in with homosexual companions. The hermit who visited the king chose the occasion to excoriate Richard's sexual diversions and warned him of the vengeance that God would take upon him if he persisted in imitating the wantonness of Sodom.

The immediate effect of the hermit's warning was negligible. Richard was annoyed and not at all inclined to change his habits or his friends. The hermit found it prudent to withdraw from the court as soon as he had preached his sermon and, indeed, went into hiding. Presumably he had reason to think that Richard might repay him rudely for the remarks that he had made. At the end of March, however, Richard fell gravely ill and on his sickbed the hermit's warning suddenly hit him with great force. He called the clergy to his bedside, confessed the details of his misdeeds, and received absolution for his sins. In shame and mortification he attempted to make amends. Queen Berengaria was summoned from Poitou, where she had been living in seclusion, to rejoin his court and to become once again a member of Richard's household. When she arrived at Richard's side in Normandy, the two were reconciled and shortly thereafter they found a spot which both of them liked at Thorée. There they bought a modest parcel of land and built themselves a house, the first permanent, private dwelling place they had had since their marriage in Cyprus.

Richard's reconciliation with his wife was followed by a flurry of grants to churches, monasteries, and convents. These were presumably inspired by Richard's desire to make amends for his recent misdeeds and to ingratiate himself both with the clergy and with God. His piety, like his rage, tended to be episodic and extreme. For a time, at least, he even changed his daily routine and that of the royal court. No longer did he linger late at night with his cronies, only to lie abed late the next day. Instead, he took to early rising, together with frequent attendance at Mass and other services. The courtiers who had previously amused him during the long evenings were abruptly banished from the household and Richard made a great show of opening the doors to the poor and needy. "Daily," we are told, "he ordered many poor

to be fed, both in his court and also in his cities and villages."
That there were plenty of destitute folk to take advantage of
Richard's generosity is attested by the chroniclers of his
reign. What they neglect to add—prudently perhaps—is that
a great deal of the suffering was caused, more or less directly,
by Richard himself. His continuous wars, especially those
against Philip Augustus, combined with the heavy tax bur-
dens which he imposed in order to finance all the fighting, in-
sured a steady and increasing supply of poor people to whom
Richard could show charity. During the period of fervent
piety which followed Richard's recovery from his illness and
his reconciliation with his wife, he also took the occasion to
make restitution to the churches for the sacred vessels of gold
and silver which he had ordered confiscated in order to raise
the money to ransom himself from captivity.

One of those who benefited from Richard's fit of remorse
in 1195 was his brother John. Richard had never taken John
very seriously—none of his family seemed able to do so—and
whatever pique he had felt at John's faithlessness during his
absence and captivity had long since evaporated. John was
the baby of the Angevin family. During his youth he had
been indulged by his father and his elder brothers to the
point where he apparently failed to develop any strong sense
of responsibility for his actions. His personality was marked
by a strong streak of sadism as well. John was undoubtedly
the least gifted child of an intelligent family and presumably
found it exceedingly difficult to compete with his peers. As
an adult he constantly strove to recapture the kind of sympathy and approval which he had enjoyed as a boy. His recur-
rent failures to manage affairs with even modest success
seem to have reinforced John's chronic sense of inadequacy.
His relationship with Richard was particularly ambivalent,
for John desired very strongly both to earn Richard's approval
and also to demonstrate his independence of his elder
brother. In May, 1195, six weeks after Richard had been reconciled with his wife, he moved to reinstate John in some of

the lands which he had confiscated from him the year before. John once again was placed in possession of Mortain and Gloucester and the Honour of Ely. He was also granted an annual stipend of £8,000 from the royal treasury. Richard's half-brother, Geoffrey, was another beneficiary of the king's new-found generosity. Richard and Geoffrey had been estranged for months over Geoffrey's misbehavior at York. His enemies accused Geoffrey of conduct unbecoming an archbishop and alleged that he habitually cursed the clergy of his diocese, imprisoned those who had the temerity to appeal his decisions, broke into churches with bands of armed warriors, and otherwise violated the normal rules of clerical conduct. Despite these complaints, Richard now welcomed Geoffrey back into the circle of his favorites and extended to him the protection of royal approval.

Richard was primarily occupied with household matters and more-or-less routine administrative actions during most of the first half of 1195. It was not until July that the records show any significant involvement in larger affairs.

The round of his domestic and personal concerns was broken in July by the arrival of a mission from the court of the German emperor, Henry VI. The imperial ambassadors brought with them a golden crown as a gift to the English king. Accompanying this splendid present was a request from Henry VI that Richard again take up his wars with Philip Augustus. Richard sent back an inquiry to Henry, asking what assistance he could expect from the emperor if he were to resume warfare in France.

The reasons behind the emperor's request for a renewal of the Anglo-French fighting had to do with problems of international politics. Although he was, of course, ruler of Germany, Henry interpreted his imperial heritage in a larger and more generous sense than had many of his predecessors. Thanks to the successful intervention of his father, Frederick Barbarossa, in the Italian peninsula, Henry enjoyed a considerable amount of prestige and actual political control in northern Italy. His specific concern at this particular moment in time was to extend that control to south Italy and Sicily. His claims to rule that area rested on the fact that his wife, Constance, was the heiress of the late Sicilian king, William II, who had died in 1189. Henry contended that the death of his wife's nephew, William, conferred a clear title to the Sicilian throne upon himself and his wife. In the realm of logic and the law, no doubt, his arguments were well founded. But in cold fact there was one major stumbling-block which Henry persisted in overlooking: the Sicilians, both noblemen and commoners, did not want him as their king. They looked upon Henry as a northern intruder who had no real right to rule south Italy and Sicily at all and those whom he claimed as his subjects were perfectly ready to resist Henry's attempts to subject them. Despite his proclamations, often reiterated, that he was the rightful ruler of Sicily, Henry had yet to make good his claims upon the land itself.

All of this was certainly in Henry's mind when he had held Richard as his prisoner and in the negotiations for Richard's release the Sicilian matter had been an important consideration. In the early stages of the negotiations, Henry had hoped to get both a cash ranson from Richard, which would help to defray the costs of a campaign to take control of Sicily, and also Richard's active cooperation and military assistance in such a campaign. When he found that he had no chance of getting Richard's military assistance, Henry had decided to settle for the money alone. In a very real sense, then, Richard had already provided Henry with one essential ingredient for the realization of his dream of bringing Sicily and south Italy under his effective rule. In 1194 Henry had launched a military campaign in Italy which he conducted very prudently and with overwhelming success. The domestic opposition to his rule in Sicily was swept aside and Henry and his wife were crowned as monarchs of Sicily at Palermo in November, 1194. On the day after Christmas Henry's joy was completed when his wife gave birth to a son, Frederick, thus assuring, as it seemed, that the united crowns of Germany and Sicily would be passed on to the next generation.

Now, in 1195, Henry was meditating a further enlargement of his already extensive domains. The time was propitious. His major domestic enemies in Germany were either dead or otherwise quiet. In Sicily he had just established a firm administrative control. He had plans—just how clearly defined they were is difficult to say—for creating a Mediterranean empire, based upon Sicily, and in this context he contemplated going on crusade. The conquests which he hoped to achieve on the crusade were to be stepping stones, it would seem, to a firm establishment of his imperial power in the Latin States of the East.

Before he could undertake a crusade, however, it was necessary to take precautions to safeguard his interests in Europe from attack while he was away. Richard's recent experiences had demonstrated plainly how serious this could be. From Henry's viewpoint it was extremely important to protect himself against possible French intervention in imperial affairs during his absence. The easiest and most natural way to achieve some guarantee of this, in turn, was to make sure that Philip Augustus would be amply occupied with fighting off Richard, so that Philip would have neither the leisure nor the men and money to launch an attack against the emperor's territories. Hence Henry's interest in securing from Richard some indication of his future plans and, if possible, a commitment that he would be at war with Philip during the next several years.

Given Richard's ambitions not only to maintain control of the land he already had in France, but also to recover what he had lost through Philip's machinations, it was very likely that he would soon renew the fighting in France, regardless of the situation of the emperor. Henry's invitation to carry on the struggle, however, and the intimation that the emperor might reward him for his initiative in that direction may have had something to do with the fact that in the middle of July,

1195, Richard resumed active warfare in France. The renewal of hostilities occurred first near Le Vaudreuil, where Philip and Richard camped on opposite sides of the Eure River, while representatives of the two monarchs discussed the possibility of agreeing on a permanent peace. While the negotiations were still going on, Philip Augustus, whose men were occupying the Castle of Le Vaudreuil, ordered the walls of the fortress to be undermined. Presumably Philip calculated that Richard was almost certain to take back Le Vaudreuil and wished to make sure that the castle would not be used in future as a base for attacks upon his own territories. As the parley was in progress, the wall of the castle suddenly collapsed. Richard immediately recalled his emissaries from the peace conference and commenced an attack upon Philip's forces. Philip, taken off guard by these sudden events, retreated and, as he was crossing a bridge in his flight, suffered the distressing experience of having the bridge collapse under him. Philip was thrown into the water, but escaped serious injury. The French forces then withdrew from the scene leaving Richard in control of Vaudreuil, and Richard immediately set his men to work rebuilding the castle that had just collapsed.

The next weeks saw a sporadic resumption of fighting. Richard was biding his time, waiting for an opportunity to inflict a really serious defeat upon the French forces, while the captain of his mercenaries, Mercadier, took the offensive in the south and occupied a part of the county of Berry. Mercadier, who had been with Richard in the Holy Land, played an increasingly large role in Richard's French campaigns. He was almost continuously in Richard's company and rose in the king's favor to the point where he enjoyed his full confidence. As Mercadier himself put it after Richard's death, "I fought for him strenuously and with loyalty, never opposed his will, and promptly obeyed his commands." He became virtually Richard's alter ego in the last years of the king's life and a genuine affection and trust seems to have grown up between them.

The flare-up of hostilities in July, 1195, failed to develop into general warfare, at least in part because both Richard and Philip seem to have been frightened by events in Spain. There the Muslim ruler of Morocco had invaded the peninsula and inflicted a dramatic defeat upon the Christian armies near Ciudad Real. Under the circumstances Richard and Philip found it wiser to stay their hands, in order to see if further disasters south of the Pyrenees might require them to join forces against a common foe.

Early in August another parley was held between representatives of the two kings and a new formula for settlement was proposed. This one involved concession by Richard to Philip of the disputed areas in Normandy, together with a payment of 20,000 marks. In return, Philip was to recognize Richard's claims in Angoulême, Aumâle, and Eu and to return to him the castles which had been confiscated during Richard's captivity in Germany. The terms of the agreement were reported to the two monarchs, but ratification was postponed until November. During the interval, Richard proposed to discuss the whole matter of his policy toward Philip Augustus with the emperor. For the next two months there was comparative quiet in France, while Richard dispatched emissaries to Germany to consult with the emperor. Henry proved unwilling to encourage Richard to agree to the peace terms which were proposed and, as an additional inducement to Richard to hold out against the proposal, agreed to write off the debt of £17,000 which Richard still owed him as a part of the ransom settlement.

On November 8 Richard and Philip were due to meet again at Verneuil to discuss the peace treaty. The interview did not take place, however, as a result of some intricate maneuvering on Philip's part. The French king had originally agreed that the meeting was to take place at midmorning, but on the stipulated day he sent a messenger to tell Richard that the interview would have to be postponed for several hours. After waiting impatiently through the morning and the early part of the afternoon, Richard finally appeared at the meeting place in midafternoon, only to find another representative of the French king awaiting him with the message that since Richard had failed to appear at the midmorning hour Philip Augustus would not honor the parley agreement. Both kings returned to their own camps and within three days general fighting had resumed. The French forces in the north invaded Normandy, where they captured and destroyed the town of Dieppe. Philip, meanwhile, had personally taken another portion of his army down to Issoudun, in Berry, and besieged the castle there.

In the opening phase of this campaign Richard concentrated his attention upon strengthening his defenses in Normandy. By the end of November he was sufficiently reassured about conditions there to divert part of his own forces, with himself at their head, into Berry, where he relieved the castle of Issoudun. Shortly after Richard's arrival on the scene, Philip asked for another parley on December 5. At that meeting the two kings, drawing apart from their advisers and courtiers, conferred together in private and managed to agree upon a temporary truce, which was to last until January 13. They also agreed that on that day they would meet at Louviers and arrange a permanent peace. As soon as this agreement was reached, both sides retired from the scene. Richard journeyed to Poitiers, where he spent the Christmas holidays of 1195 in the comfort of his mother's castle. He had grown up in Poitiers and the surrounding countryside. The Poitevin dialect spoken there was his mother tongue and his earliest memories doubtless centered in this region. This Christmas was the first he had been able to visit Poitou since his return from the crusade.

Shortly after the new year opened, Richard and a large contingent of his counselors set out on the road back to Normandy. They settled at Louviers, to the south of Rouen, about January 7, 1196, and spent the following week in consultations both among themselves and with Philip's representatives concerning the peace terms that were to be bargained for. The result of all these conferences was an elaborate peace agreement to which, at last, both kings finally consented. The agreement provided for territorial concessions by both sides. Richard gave up to Philip the territories of Gisors, Neaufles, and the Norman Vexin, while Philip yielded to Richard his claims to lands in Berry, Eu, and Gascony. A boundary line was agreed upon separating the French and Angevin territories. The frontier was to run halfway between the fortresses of Gaillon and Le Vaudreuil along the line connecting the Seine and the Eure rivers. The territories to the south of this line were deemed to belong to the French king, while the territories to the north were Richard's. Both Richard and Philip were determined to secure control over the little town of Les Andelys which belonged to the archbishop of Rouen but, after some futile bargaining, they could only agree that both would renounce their claims there—at least until one or the other saw the chance to secure it in some other way. The town was of considerable strategic importance for the control of traffic on the Seine River, and hence both Richard and Philip were anxious to secure it for themselves. The treaty also provided for restitution of church property which had been taken during the recent fighting and for the mutual exchange of prisoners and hostages.

For the time being, the Treaty of Louviers assured a relative peace in France, which allowed Richard to turn his attention briefly to other areas. During the month of April he was involved in an attempt to secure control of the County of Brittany, a territory which was formally subject to him but that was for many practical purposes autonomous and enjoyed a considerable measure of independence. Richard sought at this time to have the ten-year-old count of Brittany, Arthur, placed under his control. He claimed a right of ward-ship over young Arthur because of his feudal position as over-lord of Geoffrey, Arthur's deceased father, who was Richard's brother. The Breton nobility, jealous of their independence, opposed Richard's claims to be the guardian of the young count and when they refused to turn Arthur over to him, Richard invaded Brittany. Richard invited the boy's mother, Constance, to talk with him on the matter and, when she appeared, he had her seized and imprisoned. When Bishop Guénéhoc of Bannes, Arthur's tutor, saw what was happening, he determined that at all costs he would keep the boy out of Richard's hands. In desperation, Guénéhoc contacted Philip Augustus and secured his promise to take young Arthur into his household for safekeeping. Guénéhoc then delivered the boy secretly to Philip's men and he was brought to Paris, where he was brought up in company with Philip's son, Louis, who was just six months younger than Arthur.

In Brittany the fighting continued until Good Friday, April 19, when the Bretons finally conceded victory to Richard and made peace with him. Since Arthur was by this time safely out of Richard's grasp, however, he had to return to Normandy without having achieved his major objective in the campaign.

Richard was frustrated and furious. He was determined now to disregard the peace treaty which he had made at the beginning of the year and commenced work on fortifications in the Vexin, in direct contravention of the agreements he had made with Philip. At some undetermined time during the summer of 1196 he began construction of the grandest and most impressive of all of his many fortifications—the castle at Les Andelys which came to be christened Château Gaillard. Richard's plans for Château Gaillard were immensely complicated and were thought out with great care and sophistication. First the island of Les Andelys was fortified. Then a new town was built upon the adjacent river-bank and this, too, was walled in and elaborately reinforced. A stockade was built across the river. Far above the river and the lesser fortresses loomed the great rock that was the site of the main castle. This was laid out so as to give the garrison continuous overlapping fields of fire, thus permitting the defenders of the castle to control every inch of the surrounding territory. The commander of the garrison could interdict sapping operations most effectively and even the angles of the walls were scientifically calculated to deter both sapping and frontal assault. Given capable leadership, together with an adequate garrison and sufficient provisions, Château Gaillard seemed nearly impregnable to any of the offensive techniques of twelfth-century warfare.

While this long-term project was going forward, warfare in the field also commenced. By the beginning of July there was fighting at Nonancourt, where Richard succeeded in taking the castle from Philip's garrison. Philip, meanwhile, besieged Aumâle. As soon as Nonancourt was safe in his hands, Richard hurried to Aumâle to try to raise the siege. In this expedition he was unsuccessful and his attack on Philip's camp was repulsed. Richard then laid siege of Gaillon, which was held by a mercenary captain, Cadoc, in the employ of Philip Augustus. During the fighting at Gaillon, Richard was hit in the leg by a shot from a crossbow.

It was ironic that the weapon which wounded him should have been a crossbow, for Richard had been instrumental in bringing this weapon into general military use in France. The crossbow was considered a super-weapon in the twelfth century, because the velocity and impact energy of its missile far exceeded those of any other hand weapon then in use. The employment of crossbows in warfare among Christians had been forbidden by a Church council in 1139 and this ban had apparently been respected in France. While Richard was on crusade he had become familiar with the military potential of the crossbow, which the Church had ruled could legitimately be used against non-Christian foes. When he returned to fight in France against Philip Augustus, Richard continued to employ the crossbowmen who had been so

effective in the East and his enemies, naturally, had countered by hiring crossbowmen of their own. It was one of these
who wounded Richard in the leg at Gaillon. Richard was laid
up for a month recuperating from his wound.

During this time fighting was also going on in the
south, where Richard's opponents were led by the new count
of Toulouse, Raymond VI. While Richard was recovering
from his wound at Gaillon, however, the warfare in the south
came to a stop and Abbot Guillebert of Castres, acting for
Count Raymond, reached an agreement with Richard
whereby Richard gave up his claims in the County of Toulouse and agreed to a marriage between his sister, Queen
Joan, and Count Raymond. The point of this agreement lay in
the fact that Richard was preparing for all-out war with the
French king and needed to have a firm ally in Toulouse upon
whom he could rely. His concessions to Count Raymond
were designed to secure just such an alliance. He was also
working to create alliances elsewhere, notably with the
counts of Flanders and Boulogne, whom he was wooing at
the same time that he was concluding negotiations with the
count of Toulouse.

Once Richard had recovered from his wound, he
pressed forward still more vigorously with his preparations
for large-scale hostilities. Reinforcements were sought from
England and Wales. Castles were reinforced and new ones
built. Particular effort and expense was devoted to the construction of Château Gaillard, upon which Richard lavished
nearly £50,000 during the following year. Taxes and other
levies were imposed and treasure in large amounts had to be
shipped from England, where most of the money was raised,
to France, where Richard was spending it faster than it arrived. Before the end of the year Hubert Walter declared that
he had delivered 1,100,000 silver marks for Richard's use
during the past two years and wondered where more could
be got to meet the steadily growing royal expenditures.

The operations involved in building Château Gaillard

at Les Andelys was costing Richard more than just money. Archbishop Walter of Rouen, to whom Les Andelys belonged, was outraged at Richard's disregard of his rights there, but he protested in vain at what was going on. In November, 1196, the archbishop set out for Rome to bring his complaints before Pope Celestine III and, before he left, the archbishop laid the whole of Normandy under interdict. This meant that the services of the Church could no longer be publicly performed throughout the Norman duchy, a situation that troubled many of Richard's subjects there and that was designed to bring pressure upon the king to change both his plans and his behavior. Richard, however, was not prepared to acquiesce. He dispatched William Longchamp, his chancellor, together with three other bishops, to fight the case in Rome and to defend Richard's actions at the papal court. On the way, however, Longchamp died at Poitiers, which considerably crippled the party of Richard's supporters at Rome and hampered his defense.

Meanwhile Richard spent a worried Christmas at Bur-le-Roi in Normandy. He was vexed and unhappy because the archbishop's tactics seemed to be working only too well. His Norman subjects were upset and distressed. Masses could not be offered on Christmas, which disturbed a great many people. Even more disturbed were those whose marriages could not be solemnized because of the interdict. The families of those who died were, if possible, still more unhappy, since burial services could not be conducted during the interdict. In consequence of this, the lanes and streets of the cities of Normandy were littered with the bodies of the dead. The king's proctors at Rome, in the meantime, were defending his actions before the pope and the cardinals. They argued that Richard's actions were grounded in his right and duty to defend his subjects against external aggression and that, if he did not proceed with the building of his fortifications at Les Andelys, Richard would be hopelessly handicapped in resisting the encroachments of the king of France. The case was not finally settled until April 20, 1197, when Pope Celestine III delivered a verdict which essentially supported Richard's position. The pope ordered the archbishop to cease his resistance to Richard's work at Les Andelys and to permit the fortifications to be constructed without further hindrance. In return, the pope added, Richard must pay suitable recompense to the archbishop for the land which he had seized for this purpose and must grant him land of equivalent value elsewhere in reparation for the archbishop's losses. The pope also lifted the interdict on Normandy and dismissed both parties. Subsequently an agreement concerning the recompense to the archbishop was drawn up and the case was finally closed. The archbishop, incidentally, profited handsomely from the affair, for the lands which he received from Richard brought him an annual income of more than £1,400.

Richard had, in the meantime, continued with the construction of Château Gaillard and spent much of the first three months of 1197 supervising the building operations on the spot. In June, while he was still at Les Andelys, Richard brought to conclusion another lengthy project—the consummation of his alliance with the counts of Flanders and Boulogne. The alliance was embodied in a complicated treaty. Each of the parties furnished hostages to the others to stand as surety for the performance of their undertakings and Richard granted large sums of money to his new allies as a condition of securing their help in the sturggle against Philip Augustus.

At this point, Richard was in an excellent position for pursuing his feud with the French king. As a result of the fortifications rapidly going up at Les Andelys, his control of the main route of access to Normandy and the Vexin was infinitely superior to what it had been earlier. He was now in an ideal position to check at an early stage any aggressive actions against Normandy. The alliance with the count of Toulouse made his position in the south of France far more secure than it earlier had been and added measurably to his military resources in that region. The alliance with the Flemish count, Baldwin, secured his northern flank and at the same time gave him an admirable point of departure for diversionary attacks upon the Ile-de-France, the heartland of the French royal domain.

Active military operations in the first seven months of 1197 were scattered and comparatively minor. In April Richard captured and burned the town of Saint-Valéry. In May his brother, John, and Mercadier, the chief of his mercenary troops, captured Bishop Philip of Beauvais, Richard's longtime adversary. In June the castle of Dangu surrendered to Richard and in July he made a successful expedition into Berry, where he captured a number of Philip's castles.

The wars resumed with greater intensity during the month of August, when Count Baldwin of Flanders, Richard's new ally, attacked the city of Arras. In response to this attack, Philip Augustus brought a major army to the relief of the city and, as Philip's forces approached, Baldwin craftily withdrew ahead of them. Philip's army, scenting an easy victory against a retreating foe, followed Baldwin's withdrawal with more spirit than cunning. Baldwin was thus able to entice his enemies into the drained lowland regions near the coast. Then, when he had them where he wanted them, he opened the sluice gates in the dykes which lined the drainage canals. This flooded the lowlands, forcing Philip's army to move onto raised ground from which they could neither advance nor retreat. With the French army thus ignominiously trapped, Baldwin was master of the day. Since he had sworn to Richard that he would not make terms with the king of France, Baldwin could not take full advantage of the situation when Philip, in desperation, surrendered. Baldwin did insist, however, that Philip must agree to confer with Richard and himself at a place near Les Andelys between September 8 and September 16.

The meeting between the two kings and Baldwin of Flanders in September marked a new stage in the ongoing struggle in France. Philip at last seems to have realized how serious his situation had become and how greatly Richard had strengthened his position during the past several months. The three men agreed to establish a general truce for the coming sixteen months, ending on January 13, 1199. There was no attempt at an elaborate agreement concerning the possessions of the parties; apparently they simply agreed to maintain the territorial situation as it was for the period of the truce and to cease fighting with one another during the time that the truce lasted.

As such things went, this truce agreement was relatively successful and for almost a year there was a halt to further military activity in France. Presumably none of the parties to the truce was under any illusion that a permanent settlement had been reached, but the agreement gave all of them a breathing space they sorely needed.

Richard certainly used a large part of the time which he gained by this agreement to prepare for a resumption of the fighting. Within a few months he was sending for further reinforcements from England and his demands for money continued unabated. He continued to work at rounding out and finishing his fortifications at Château Gaillard, which Philip apparently saw for the first time during this peace conference. Richard was inclined to be boastful about his masterpiece in stone, bragging that he would be able to hold the position he had created at Les Andelys against the French king and all his forces, even if the stonework turned to butter. Philip responded with his own boasts and threats of vengeance, but he was obviously impressed by what he saw.

At the same time that Richard was concluding his peace treaty with Philip Augustus, the political situation was beginning to change in another quarter. The Emperor Henry VI fell ill in Sicily in mid-September 1197. As he grew worse, Henry became anxious to clear his conscience and to make his peace with the Church on a number of scores. One of the matters which troubled him was his treatment of Richard, for which he had subsequently been excommunicated in the same way as had Leopold of Austria. From his sickbed Henry dispatched his cousin, Bishop Savaric of Bath, to visit Richard and to offer to refund to him the ransom money he had collected. Henry's repentance came too late. While Savaric was still en route to Richard's court, the emperor died at Messina on September 28. The sentence of excommunication was still in effect and consequently the pope forbade Henry to be given a Christian burial.

To complicate matters further, Henry left a widow, Constance, and an infant son, Frederick, to succeed him. Constance might possibly have been able to maintain control of her late husband's Sicilian possessions, but she, too, died a little more than a year later and the situation of southern Italy and Sicily rapidly became chaotic. The infant heir, Frederick, became a ward of the pope, who was able eventually to secure a recognition of Frederick's right to rule Sicily when he should come of age.

The future of Germany was even more cloudy and there Richard's interests and ambitions were more directly involved than they were in Sicily. It was clear that Constance's young son, despite the strength of his legal and moral claims, stood no chance of controlling Germany at this point. A strong ruler was needed on the spot in Germany and Richard was determined to see that the man of his choice secured the German throne. He had a candidate ready at hand: his nephew, Otto of Brunswick. Not only was Richard linked by family ties to Otto, but in addition the two had already grown to be close personal allies. Otto had been raised at Richard's court in Poitiers, had served his apprenticeship in arms under Richard's command, and had become one of Richard's favorite subordinates. Richard had supported him consistently and even named him count of Poitou, making Otto his agent to rule his own home county. If Otto were to sit on the German throne, he required active support from Richard, since another serious rival was already on the scene.

This rival was Philip, duke of Swabia, the younger brother of Henry VI. Philip's candidacy for the throne was supported by the allies of the royal house of the Hohenstaufen, who constituted a potent political bloc.

Richard had his own friends and followers, however, among the German nobility. He had become acquainted with many of them during the period of his captivity and, upon his release, he had taken pains to cultivate their good will and respect. Geographically, Richard's friends were situated predominantly in the north and west of the German kingdom and these regions could safely be counted upon to back Otto of Brunswick. The southern and eastern portions of the kingdom, by and large, supported Philip of Swabia. Richard's problem was to secure some kind of preponderance on behalf of the candidate whom he favored and for this purpose he sought the aid of the papacy. The pope claimed the exclusive right to crown the emperors of the West, who were also the rulers of Germany. Papal claims to this right had been bitterly contested in the past, but the right was sufficiently well established to give the pope a significant voice in deciding who should become king of Germany and ruler of the empire.

While the problem of the succession to the imperial throne was still very much in flux, the reigning pontiff, Celestine III, suddenly died on January 8, 1198. On the same day, Cardinal Lothario dei Segni was elected to succeed him. The new pope took the title of Innocent III.

From Richard's vantage point these developments were all to the good. Innocent III was favorably disposed toward Richard. He had been well impressed by Richard's performance on the crusade and regarded him as, in some sense, a champion of Christendom against its enemies. Further, Innocent was convinced that the papacy's interests, both in Italy and elsewhere, required the reduction of the power of the Hohenstaufen family. In terms of the German political situation, this meant that Innocent was decidedly inclined to favor the candidacy of Otto of Brunswick for the throne in preference to the Hohenstaufen candidate, Philip of Swabia. Beyond this, Innocent was also at odds with Philip Augustus on another issue. In 1193, after his return from the crusade, Philip had married the princess Ingeborg of Denmark, daughter of the late Danish king, Waldemar. Shortly after the marriage, Philip had repudiated Ingeborg and had sought an annulment of the marriage, since his earlier scheme for a Danish alliance had not proved successful. Subsequently, in June of 1196, Philip had married Agnes, daughter of Duke Berthold IV of Bohemia. The papacy had been offended by the repudiation of Ingeborg, for the process was canonically very irregular, and the offense had been compounded by Philip's later marriage to Agnes. As things stood, relations between Philip Augustus and the Holy See were decidedly strained and Innocent III was all the more inclined to favor Richard of England precisely because Richard and Philip were at odds with each other.

Almost as soon as the news of Innocent's election reached France, both Richard and Philip Augustus were busily dispatching proctors to Rome to plead their interests before the new pontiff. Each of the kings sought papal decisions to strengthen his position on each of the areas of controversy in which they were involved and Innocent, like the skillful lawyer and politician that he was, patiently and deftly sifted through the mounds of pleadings and petitions that were laid before him.

By late April, the pope had satisfied himself on the question of the exchange which had been made to secure Richard's possession of Les Andelys and wrote to the archbishop of Rouen, to convey his approval of the settlement. Even before this decision had been handed down, Richard had appealed to the pope on the matter of the redress of his grievances against the late Duke Leopold of Austria and his successors. At the end of May, Innocent gave his answer on this matter and again his decision was favorable to Richard's cause. The pope's decision required Duke Leopold's son to refund to Richard the ransom money which the king had paid and warned him that if he failed to make restitution, the archbishop of Salzburg was being instructed to impose ecclesiastical censures upon him. In addition, Innocent admonished Philip of Swabia, as heir to the estate of Henry VI, that he must make restitution to Richard of the money which Henry had taken as his share of Richard's ransom. Moreover, the pope also informed Richard that he was taking steps to see that others who had benefited from Richard's imprisonment and ransom restored to him the profits which they had taken as a result of the king's capture.

In addition, Innocent took cognizance of the issues in the quarrel between Philip Augustus and Richard and promised to give a decision on that matter at a later date. Before he reached a conclusion on that affair, the pope said, he intended to visit both Philip's and Richard's kingdoms in order to inform himself more accurately about the points that had been raised by the representatives of the two kings. Meanwhile, Innocent warned both kings that they should make peace with each other and observe the agreements which they made, otherwise he would inflict ecclesiastical censures upon both of them.

The strenuous personal intervention of the new pope in Richard's affairs was a hopeful sign from the king's viewpoint. Since each of the decisions which had thus far been rendered had been distinctly favorable to Richard's interests, the chances seemed excellent that papal intervention might considerably improve Richard's chances of securing a favorable outcome in his other international problems.

A few weeks later Richard scored a further success. His nephew, Otto of Brunswick, was chosen as king of the Romans and emperor-elect by the German electors at Aachen. Richard had been busy behind the scenes, making known his wishes and using his influence upon his German friends and allies to secure Otto's election. Following the election, Otto married the daughter of the count of Louvain, who was one of Richard's major German allies. Then on July 12, 1198, he was crowned at Aachen by Archbishop Adolf of Cologne. From this point forward, relations between the German crown and Richard became extremely close and Richard was almost as closely involved in German imperial politics as he was in the politics of France. For Richard the securing of Otto's election meant, along with much else, a further triumph in his continuing quarrel with Philip Augustus. For with the German monarch on his side, Richard had added another major bloc to the series of alliances with which he was gradually but remorselessly hemming in the French monarch.

To be sure, Otto's grasp upon the crown was not yet certain, even after it had been placed upon his head. Philip of Swabia was still to be reckoned with and Philip had his own supporters who were eagerly pressing his claims to the German throne. Both Otto's supporters and Philip's sought the help of the pope in securing a clear title for their respective candidates and so once again Innocent III was in the position of giving judgment in an affair of enormous international significance. In August Richard wrote to the pope to bring his views of the contested imperial election to the pope's notice and made a spirited case for Otto's claims to the throne.

During all this time, up to September, 1198, there had been no significant military activity in the areas of France that were disputed between Richard and Philip. The peace was finally broken on September 6 by one of Richard's allies, Count Baldwin of Flanders. Baldwin laid siege to the castle of Saint-Omer, which surrendered to him three weeks later. This was the signal for the resumption of hostilities in other areas as well. Philip Augustus retaliated for the loss of Saint-Omer by invading Normandy in a purely punitive expedition. His objective was not to gain territory, but rather to terrorize the population, which he did very effectively by burning down towns and villages and by a calculated harassment of the population of the territories through which his forces swept. Richard, in turn, invaded the territory of the French king and on September 27, while Philip's forces were beginning to return to royal territory, Richard laid siege to Philip's castles of Courcelles and Burriz, both of which he captured. On the following day, Philip, who was unaware that Richard had taken Courcelles, brought up a force of three hundred knights to relieve the castle. Richard had advance information about Philip's approach. Anticipating that the French army would continue on its line of march toward Courcelles, Richard posted the main part of his army along the banks of the River Epte and then went forward in the company of his mercenary captain, Mercadier, and a small troop of other soldiers. Unexpectedly, Philip departed from his anticipated plan and turned toward Gisors, which brought Philip himself right into the path of Richard's small company. Philip and his men seemingly were quite unaware of the presence of Richard's men until suddenly they found the English king and his small force charging directly at them, like hungry lions upon their prey. Philip and his companions took to their heels, running pell-mell for safety toward the gates of Gisors. The shock of their pounding feet, as men and horses rushed across the bridge for the gates of the city caused the bridge to collapse suddenly under the mass of men and animals, as had happened three years earlier at Le Vaudreuil. Philip himself was on the bridge as it went down and, as Richard gleefully reported, "The French king had to drink of the river." Philip had to be dragged out of the river by the leg and, in fact, was very nearly killed. Even so, Philip was luckier than some twenty of his followers, who not merely sipped of the river water, but drowned in it. Another hundred knights or so were taken prisoner by the English king and Mercadier captured an additional thirty knights; the numbers of non-noble prisoners are not recorded, but they probably outnumbered the knights by a large margin.

Richard was elated at this success. It was precisely the sort of encounter he dearly loved: he had surprised the enemy and defeated them ignominiously, even though their forces far outnumbered his. Richard's joy was all the greater because it was won as the result of taking a foolhardy risk and, although he had failed to capture Philip himself, he had at least humiliated him personally. Furthermore, this adventure had cost him nothing and cheap victories were exactly what Richard needed at this point. The continual demands on his resources from the beginning of his reign left him financially embarrassed. The cost of building Château Gaillard, in particular, had involved him in extraordinary expenses during the past two years and the continuing outlays which were involved in maintaining his army in the field soaked up every penny he could lay his hands on.

Following this satisfying victory at Gisors, both Richard and Philip were involved during the next few weeks in a series of minor skirmishes, mainly in Normandy. About the middle of October, Archbishop Hubert Walter tried to mediate between the two kings. The archbishop's services as mediator were specifically requested by Philip Augustus and Richard consented to let him try his hand at negotiating yet another peace. The archbishop did his best and was able to secure major concessions on both sides, but the negotiations foundered on Richard's insistence that as a condition of the agreement Philip must guarantee that he would not attack Baldwin of Flanders and the other former adherents of the French crown who had gone over to Richard's side. This Philip adamantly refused to do and the negotiations produced only a temporary agreement to cease fighting until the Feast of St. Hilary, January 13, 1199. On that day the two kings agreed that they would meet again near Les Andelys and attempt once more to reach mutually agreeable terms.

Richard spent the remaining months of 1198 mainly at Les Andelys in his saucy new castle, which was virtually completed. During this time he was principally involved in the chronic search for additional money which had become such a pressing problem for him in the past several years.

The pope's efforts to secure a return of Richard's ransom met with scant success, while Richard's expenses continued to increase faster than his revenues. As a result, he was chronically short of funds. Richard had recently hit upon a new device for increasing his revenues. This was to destroy the great seal of the English kingdom and to have a new one, of different design, fabricated. The new seal was in use from the spring of 1198. Richard required those of his subjects who had received grants of royal favors authenticated by the great seal to turn their charters in and to have the impression of the new seal attached to them. Those which lacked this additional authenticating device were held to be invalid. For the authentication of documents with his new seal Richard required that a fee be paid and in this way he managed to create a new source of revenue for the crown. During the autumn months of 1198 a steady stream of charters passed through Richard's chancellery to be resealed and thus to augment the king's revenues.

Richard spent Christmas of 1198 at Domfront and during the holiday season welcomed the appearance of a distinguished visitor to his court. The visitor was Cardinal Peter of Capua, who had come from Rome as a papal legate, representing Pope Innocent III. The pope had earlier hoped to visit France in person and there to bring Richard and Philip Augustus to settle on permanent peace terms. Pope Innocent found himself too involved, however, in other pressing business to spare the time and energy required for such a mission and so had sent in his place the new papal legate. The cardinal visited both monarchs and then, on January 13, 1199, met with them jointly at a conference on the Seine to discuss peace terms. Richard came to the conference place in a boat from Château Gaillard and remained in his boat throughout the conference, refusing to disembark. Philip, who had come on horseback, sat upon his horse on the river bank and conversed with Richard, as he sat in his boat near the river's edge. At the urging of the papal legate the two kings agreed on yet another truce, this one, they said, to last for five years "with good faith and without evil intent." There were to be no territorial readjustments: the situation obtaining as of the date of the agreement was to be maintained for the five year period of the truce.

Whether anyone seriously expected this agreement to endure for five years is doubtful. In point of fact, it lasted at most a single month. Shortly after the conclusion of the treaty, Mercadier, Richard's mercenary captain, was attacked by French soldiers. Although Philip Augustus denied that he had ordered the attack and swore that it was made without his knowledge or consent, the incident indicated that the peace agreement was precarious from the outset. Still, Richard apparently believed that it was momentarily safe for him to leave Normandy and set out for the south. While he was in the County of Maine, he learned that Philip was at work on a new castle, named Gouletot ("swallow all"), in the vicinity of a small castle which Richard had recently erected, known as Boutavant ("push forward"). Moreover, Philip had caused a forest in that vicinity which was Richard's property to be felled. Straightaway, on St. Valentine's Day 1199, Richard dispatched his chancellor to Philip Augustus to deliver an ultimatum: either Philip must raze his new castle, or else Richard would renounce the peace agreement. Philip made a vague promise, but Richard found it unsatisfactory. Philip then made a counter-proposal, but Richard would not agree to it.

Still the situation did not seem critical enough to require Richard's presence back in Normandy and so he continued on his leisurely journey to the south. It had been nearly four years since he had visited his possessions in Aquitaine and even that visit had been a quick and hurried one. By March 11 he had reached Chinon, where he remained for the next two weeks. Sometime during that period he heard of an event which pricked his curiosity and also alerted him to the possibility of a quick profit.

A peasant plowing in fields which belonged to the castle of Châlus that spring had uncovered a valuable treasure: a set of gold and silver figurines. Just what they were it is impossible to say: perhaps a buried relic from Gaul's ancient past. Together with the figurines there were also some ancient coins. The lord of Châlus, one Achard, claimed the treasure hoard. The viscount Aimar of Limoges, in turn, claimed it from Achard as his overlord. Richard was Aimar's overlord: the right to the buried treasure, he was quick to claim, lay ultimately with him and, without ado, Richard demanded that the precious objects be turned over to him. Aimar apparently sent a part of the find to Richard, but attempted to keep the rest of it for himself.

Richard was outraged at this. He was inclined to be extremely sensitive, in any case, when he felt that his rights had been infringed upon and at this moment he was desperate for money and valuables of any kind. Gathering together the soldiers he had brought with him, Richard repaired to the castle of Châlus. The garrison of the castle were frightened. They had no desire to become embroiled with the awesome English king and offered to turn the place over to him if he would only promise to spare their lives. Richard was in a frenzy. He would not accept their surrender and let them go without punishment for having, as he saw it, defied him. The only promise he would give them, Richard declared, was that he would take their castle by force and hang everyone in it. As the two knights belonging to the garrison tried to put their defenses in order, Richard prepared for the assault. He set his sappers to work to undermine the castle walls, while his archers kept up a steady fire of arrows into the little fortress.

On March 26, Richard was preparing his forces for the assault on Châlus. One of the crossbowmen in the garrison was standing on the castle walls, holding a crossbow in one hand and a frying pan in the other. When Richard noticed this odd figure and inquired about him, he was told that the man had been standing there all day, fending off the missiles that were fired at him by using his frying pan as a shield. The audacity of the performance enraged Richard further. He approached close to the walls to try to get in a shot at the lone crossbowman with his own weapon. When the crossbowman saw the king approaching, he let loose a bolt from his crossbow. By chance the bolt hit Richard in the left shoulder, near the neck, and penetrated deep into the flesh.

Richard mounted his horse and rode back to his camp. On his way he ordered the army to begin the assault on Châlus and to keep it up until the castle was taken. Meanwhile, Richard sought a physician to treat his wound. While he was waiting for help to arrive, Richard worried at the missile, which was embedded in the rolls of fat on his shoulder, and succeeded in breaking off the shaft, leaving the iron barb buried. When at last a surgeon was brought to Richard's tent, he had to cut deeply into the king's shoulder in order to find and extract the iron head. Soothing lotions and medicines were applied to the wound and it was bandaged up. The wound immediately became inflamed and began to swell. Within a few hours the whole area was tender and discolored.

In the meantime, Richard's army kept up its furious assault upon the castle of Châlus. The garrison—two knights, a handful of peasants, a few women, and children, perhaps forty persons in all—realized that they were literally fighting for their lives and put up a desperate resistance. After two days, the defenses caved in. Richard ordered everyone found inside the castle, including women and their infant children, to be hanged at once, save for the crossbowman who had fired the shot that wounded him. He was to be saved until the king recovered enough to enjoy watching him suffer a slow death.

Richard's wound grew steadily worse. The infection spread and the king grew weaker. Then gangrene set in. Richard had seen others die by the hundreds, perhaps by the thousands. With all of his experience on the battlefield and in the aftermath of battle, he could not fail to recognize

the symptoms. He knew all too well the meaning of the dis-
coloration and the stench of gangrene. He knew that he
would not survive.

Methodically he made his preparations. He sent for
his mother, Eleanor, who was only a few miles away at Fontevrault. Then he began to dispose of his possessions. To his
brother John he bequeathed the kingdom of England and his
lands in France. He ordered those who were with him to
swear their loyalty to John and to promise that they would
carry out the king's will. They were to see that all of Richard's
castles were delivered into John's hands, together with
three fourths of the money and other valuables that were still
in Richard's possession, save for his jewels. The jewels were
to go to his nephew Otto of Brunswick, the emperor-elect.
The quarter of Richard's other valuables which was not given
to John was to be distributed among his household and the
poor.

Then Richard sent for the crossbowman who had
wounded him.

"What harm have I done to you, that you have killed
me?" Richard asked.

The crossbowman answered: "You killed my father
and my two brothers with your own hand and you intended to
kill me, too. Take any vengeance you think fit upon me. I will
endure any torments you can think of, now that you, who
have brought such evils on the world, are about to die."

At this, Richard ordered him to be released. "I forgive
you my death," Richard told him, and added that he should
be given a hundred shillings and sent away.

The man was taken outside, where Richard's mercenary, Mercadier, seized him and held him prisoner until
Richard was dead. Once the king was dead, Mercadier flayed
the crossbowman alive.

Richard sent for a priest, who heard his last confession
and gave him communion. By this time Queen Eleanor was
at hand. She remained with her favorite son in his last hours,

while he dictated his wishes about the disposition of his body. Richard willed that at his death his corpse should be divided up. His brains, blood, and intestines were to be buried at Châlus. His heart was to be interred at Rouen. His body, he directed, should be buried at Fontevrault, at his father's feet.

On Tuesday, April 6, Richard's condition grew rapidly worse and he was given the last sacraments of the Church. He died at seven o'clock that same evening, twelve days after he was wounded. He was forty-two years old.

Five days later, on Palm Sunday, April 11, Eleanor of Aquitaine was at Fontevrault to bury the eviscerated body of her son at the same spot where Richard had interred her husband's body eleven years before.

TEN

✠————————————————————✠

Epilogue:
The Character of
Richard Lion-Heart

What sort of person was Richard Lion Heart? Why did he stand out so flamboyantly among his contemporaries? Why has Richard been such an object of admiration both for his contemporaries and for later generations as well? Why did legends grow up about him, in particular? What set Richard apart from his father, Henry II, who was surely a far greater monarch and certainly was every bit as colorful in his personal life as his son? For that matter, why is Richard almost universally admired, when Philip Augustus, for example, has found scant sympathy among writers either of history or of fiction?

We must accept it as a fact that we can know only a tiny part of the story of Richard's life. His contemporaries knew him in ways that we cannot and only a small fraction of what they knew has been preserved in the historical records that we possess. We know little of Richard's private life and most of the little that we do know must be inferred from indirect and scanty evidence. What is known about him is almost altogether based upon the records of his public activities and even there are sources are incomplete and spotty. During the last ten years of Richard's life, while he was reigning as king, the evidence is naturally far more ample than it is for the earlier three quarters of his life span. Yet during that final decade, when Richard was one of the two or three richest, most powerful, and most important men in Europe, when he was engaged in affairs of the highest importance—even while he was in the international limelight of his day—there are still periods of almost half a year at a time when we have only a very foggy notion even of where Richard was, much less of what he was doing, or thinking, or saying.

Of the partial insight into Richard's life that the surviving sources do give to us, the greater part is more or less impersonal. Most of our evidence consists of records of routine kinds, showing that Richard was attending to one sort of business or another. These records tell us something about his administration, but they give us precious little information about his personal life or his character, except in the most indirect way.

We should also remember, however, even given all of these limitations of our evidence, that we know a great deal more about Richard than we do about any other king or major public figure of his era. His contemporaries may not tell us many things that we should like to know about him, but the very fact that they tell us as much as they do gives us one important lead in any attempt to assess Richard's life and character: he struck those who knew him as a colorful, memorable figure, as somehow larger than life. Richard was to them a most remarkable man and, whether they liked him or not, everyone who wrote about him acknowledged this fascination.

One aspect of Richard's career where the record tells us a great deal about his character has to do with his relationships with people. We find almost universal agreement among our witnesses that Richard's relationship with his father, to begin with, was thoroughly unsatisfactory on both sides. Richard was a bad son; and Henry II was, if anything, a worse father. So far as we can tell from our limited information, Richard spent scarcely any lengthy period of his youth in his father's company. Raised as his mother's heir, growing up in the heady atmosphere of Eleanor's court in Aquitaine, Richard was regarded during most of his youth merely as a younger son, who might inherit a sizable domain, but who would not inherit either his father's throne or his role in the higher spheres of politics. Beyond this, Richard certainly witnessed and almost certainly resented his father's rejection of Eleanor in favor of a varied and colorful galaxy of mistresses. Added to this was the virtual imprisonment of Eleanor during the last fourteen years of Henry's reign.

The period when Eleanor was imprisoned begins at precisely the point when Richard was coming into his own. He was sixteen years old at the time, bursting with energy and ambition, and resentful of the way in which his mother was being treated. Given these circumstances, it is scarcely surprising that he was a restless and rebellious prince and that he quickly became involved in schemes that gave him a chance to express his resentment of his father.

Richard was ripe to respond to the blandishments of those who fed that resentment, especially his older brother, Henry the Young King. The disillusionment which followed the failure of his attempt at rebellion in 1173 was probably directed as much against his brother, Henry, as it was against his father and the Aquitainian nobles who had refused to follow Richard's lead. His father, who only seems to have appreciated Richard's promise in the period of reconciliation following this uprising, was quick to capitalize on Richard's disillusionment and to bring the boy under his own influence for the first time. Certainly after the episode of 1173 there was a closer harmony between Richard and his father than there ever previously had been. They did not become extremely close to each other, however, and for this there seem to have been four reasons: Richard's continuing resentment of his mother's situation, the continuing rivalry between Richard and his elder brother, his resentment of Henry II's favoritism to John, and the matter of Richard's fiancée.

Richard's fiancée, Alice of France, had been at the court of Richard's father since she was a child. After Henry's break with Queen Eleanor, following the rebellion of 1173, he apparently introduced the young French princess into his bedroom and made her his mistress, despite the fact that she had long been engaged to marry his son. Although Henry made no particular secret of his numerous sexual escapades, he does seem to have tried to hide his affair with Alice. The Angevin court was no safe harbor for secrets, however, and rumors of the liaison circulated wide and far. It is virtually impossible that Richard could have been ignorant of what was happening.

It is most difficult to judge what effect this affair had on Richard's relationship with his father, or with other people in general, for the sentiments of Europeans in the twelfth century concerning marriage and sexual relations tended to be quite different from our own. The notion of romantic love was then just beginning its long career in European thought and society. Significantly, it was beginning to take shape precisely in the places where it would most affect Richard: at his mother's court and among the nobility of Aquitaine. Still, romantic love as it was then thought of was a type of love which had little to do with marriage. To the question of whether it was possible to be romantically in love with one's wife, most of Richard's contemporaries, if they understood the question at all, would have replied emphatically: "No."

It would be quite wrong, therefore, to think of Richard's reaction to his father's affair with his own fiancée as motivated by romantic sentiments. Marriage and romance had nothing to do with one another in Richard's society. Richard's sentiments had little in common with those of a spurned lover, for his engagement to Alice of France was a matter of diplomacy and politics, nothing more. Whether or not he married the lady was something he would have considered irrelevant to any personal feelings he may have had about her.

Still, it is also hard to escape the suspicion that in some sense Richard was wounded by his father's affair with Alice. It was at the very least a kind of personal humiliation to be in the position of having to accept as one's future wife a girl who had been one's father's bed-mate and there was an unpleasantly incestuous aroma about the whole affair. It is unlikely in the extreme that Richard's personal feelings had any significant influence in his final decision that he would not marry Alice. But his feelings about the way in which his espoused wife had been casually used by his father may well have stirred additional resentment of his father in Richard's mind.

When Richard ultimately did marry he selected his own wife, Berengaria of Navarre. But the choice was probably the result, again, of political calculation, not of romantic inclination. What Richard desired was not the person of Berengaria, but the aid of her brother, Sancho the Strong. Sancho turned out, in fact, to be a dependable, even indispensable ally for Richard. It was due to the presence of Sancho on the scene that Richard was able to maintain the cooperation of the hot-headed nobles of Aquitaine during his long absence on crusade and in captivity following the crusade. As for Berengaria, Richard's relationship with her was cool and casual.

The few weeks following their sudden marriage at Limassol marked the only period when Richard spent much time in his wife's company. During the crusade in Palestine they seem to have become definitely estranged. They did not even meet between September of 1192 and April of 1195 and following their reconciliation in 1195 they seem to have gone their separate ways for most of the remaining five years of Richard's life. Berengaria was not at Richard's bedside when he died and, even when he knew that he was going to die, he seems not to have thought of summoning her. Instead, he sent for his mother.

Eleanor of Aquitaine was the only woman for whom

Richard apparently held either respect or deep feeling, with the possible exception of his sister Joan. Richard seems to have had only one sexual liaison with a woman, and of that affair virtually nothing is known, not even the lady's name. All that is known of it is that the liaison produced a bastard son, Philip of Cognac, who was Richard's only child. Richard provided for his son, after a fashion, giving him the castle and manor of Cognac, but there is no evidence of any continuing association between Richard and his son. Some months after Richard's death, Philip of Cognac killed the viscount Aimar of Limoges, in vengeance, it was reported, for the viscount's implication in the death of Richard.

The relationship between Richard and Eleanor was a close one throughout Richard's life. He was clearly his mother's favorite child and the other members of the Angevin family eem to have sensed that special relationship between them. When she finally died in 1204 at the age of eighty-two, it seemed appropriate to bury her at Fontevrault between her husband, King Henry, and her son, King Richard. Richard was the Queen's protégé, the apple of her eye. He alone of all his brothers was raised in her domains as another Poitevin prince of the line from which Eleanor was descended, instead of as an Angevin, in his father's line of descent. From Eleanor, Richard received the upbringing and the value-system of the noblemen of Aquitaine. Richard shared with them the firm conviction that valor, military adventure, knightly honor, and physical prowess were supremely important, beyond anything else in life. Although these ideals were current among other noblemen throughout Europe, Richard and his fellow nobles in Aquitaine cultivated them more assiduously than did their counterparts elsewhere. This heritage took deep root within him as a boy and remained part of him to the end of his life. The accidents of his career carried him across Europe and into the Near East, but his home was in Poitou so long as he lived. Although he became king of England, he was never an English king.

Richard's relationships with his peers seem to have been formed in the likeness of his family relationships. He was uneasy and suspicious of the motives of other contemporary monarchs and popes—often with good reason—just as he was uneasy with his brothers and suspicious of their motives—also with good reason. The two monarchs whose careers were most closely entwined with Richard's were the emperor Henry VI and the French king Philip Augustus. Both were able, ambitious men, both were jealous of Richard on political and personal grounds alike, and both sought to better themselves at Richard's expense. With Henry VI, Richard was finally able to reach an uneasy and precarious understanding and in the latter years of Henry's lifetime the two monarchs occasionally found it profitable to cooperate with one another, despite their mutual suspicion and doubts about the other's motives. Richard's relationship with Philip Augustus, though habitually uneasy, was comparatively amicable during the last decade of Henry II's lifetime and the first years of Richard's reign, until the events which accompanied their crusade brought the latent hostility out into the open. From 1191 onward they became open enemies and during the last years of his life Richard appeared to be increasingly contemptuous of Philip, a contempt that probably arose from Philip's physical cowardice and his unwillingness to risk life and limb in combat.

Among his own circle of knights, warriors, and bishops, Richard achieved a genuine friendship and camaraderie with a number of individuals who served him, such as Mercadier, William Marshall, and Longchamp. His loyalty and affection for those persons whom he felt he could trust expressed itself primarily in lavish generosity. The bestowal of gifts was a normal, almost routine, function of medieval monarchs, who paid for the services of their helpers and administrators with gifts and presents, rather than with salaries and wages. But the scale and frequency of Richard's gifts to his personal retainers was exceptional and seems to suggest a genuine effort to show affection and favor, as well as to reward normal types of services. Richard was notoriously loyal to those who depended on him and who did his bidding. His partisanship for his favorites was well known.

On the other hand, Richard seems scarcely ever to have thought of his subjects, particularly his English subjects, save in terms of how much revenue he could extract from them. Of consideration or compassion for the inferior classes of his kingdom there is not a single sign in any of the records of Richard's reign. He simply did not consider them as anything other than a mass of people who owed him their loyalty, their service, and their money. If his attitude had been otherwise, it would indeed have been exceptional, for twelfth-century kings were not much inclined to consider the welfare of their subjects as a matter of great concern. Still, Richard seems to have been if anything even more callous toward his subjects than were most contemporary monarchs.

All in all there is something unsatisfactory about Richard's known relationships with most of the people with whom he came in contact. There is an element of coldness, of suspicion and distrust, often enough of jealousy, hatred and dislike, which color the relationships with his father, with his brothers, his wife, his bastard son, other kings and potentates, and with most of the officials and barons who served him. Richard reserved his affection for his mother, his sister, and for a small coterie of knights and warriors. Even of these, perhaps his closest companion and associate in the last years was the mercenary, Mercadier, a brutal and savage professional killer, who was despised and looked down upon by chivalrous knights and whose deeds are recorded with horror by monastic chroniclers.

Two facets of Richard's personality seem to have impressed his contemporaries most forcibly: his splendid physical presence and his extraordinary prowess as a warrior. Certainly Richard was accounted handsome and impressive by all of those who knew him. He was tall, muscular, and strong, to begin with, and his mane of gold-red hair set off his handsome features to advantage. Richard preserved his youthful strength and musculature throughout most of his life, although toward the end he seems to have curtailed his physical activity and, in consequence, he became grossly fat.

Combined with his natural physical strength, which was cultivated and enhanced by strenuous physical activity during most of his life, Richard also possessed a set of well-honed reflexes. These gifts he resolutely channeled toward the goal of becoming an outstanding fighter, an objective he attained early in life.

There can be no doubt that Richard was a peerlessly efficient killing machine, in an age that glorified and revered such attainments as one of the supreme goals of human activity. It was Richard's prowess in combat, more than any other single attribute, that underlay his heroic reputation. He seems to have been one of those persons who, for whatever reason, was a stranger to fear of physical danger. Speculation as to why he was instinctively courageous is probably fruitless: one can conjecture endlessly about some latent, unconscious death wish, which he may or may not have possessed, but we know so little about his personal life and feelings that a systematic psychoanalytical approach to an understanding of Richard is out of the question. The evidence on which to base such an analysis simply does not exist. But what we do know indicates that he was an extraordinarily brave man. To what degree he may have known fear and suppressed it, no one now can say; but we are reasonably certain that those who knew him believed that he was almost entirely free from the normal kinds of human fear and apprehension in the face of danger.

Richard's apparent freedom from fear seems to have given him the capacity for cool thinking and quick planning on the battlefield. The ability to adapt his plans to the unforeseen and unforeseeable contingencies of action was probably the most important element in Richard's reputation as a general. His crusading battles, particularly those at Arsuf and Jaffa, provide outstanding examples of Richard's extraordinary resourcefulness in action, as well as of his indifference to personal danger.

The tactical frame of the battlefield was the place where Richard showed off to best advantage. This was the setting in which he made the highest, most effective use of all of his gifts simultaneously. His capacity as a strategic planner, although considerable, was somewhat less than his capacity as a tactician. Richard was, without question, gifted with a greater than normal strategic insight, with the ability to anticipate the long-range course of a campaign and to allocate his resources to take the maximum advantage of time, terrain, supplies, manpower, and the weaknesses of his enemies. But even so, he was no Napoleon, much less a Clausewitz or Schlieffen. The patient, detailed planning of a campaign was not the kind of activity in which he most excelled and his overall planning, while creditable enough, does not match his supreme ability in the conduct of an individual battle. Moreover, he was too rash and impulsive to adhere consistently to a large-scale comprehensive plan of campaign.

In this context the contrast between Richard and Philip Augustus is particularly instructive. Philip and Richard were almost complete opposites in their talents and their characters. Where Richard was abnormally brave, Philip was a physical coward. Where Richard lived for battle and performed at his best in combat, Philip sought to avoid direct confrontation with the enemy whenever possible and sometimes seems to have frozen in action, unable to adapt readily to the changing situation on the field. But by the end of Richard's lifetime, Philip was learning something about strategic planning. If he avoided battle with the main forces of his enemies, Philip had learned that he could often gain far more by hitting at points where the enemy forces were light. More and more often in the last year or two of Richard's life, Philip seems to have caught him off-balance, to have made quick thrusts into Richard's territory and then to have withdrawn while Richard was still groping to locate the point for a counterattack. At times, of course, Philip failed to carry off his thrust-and-retreat pattern successfully, and on these occasions he fared ill. He was somewhat like a determined dancer who has no natural sense of rhythm but seeks to learn the movements by dogged observation and practice. In the course of learning the movement patterns he was stepped on several times, but repeated practice made him noticeably more skillful at it. By the time of Richard's death, Philip was becoming passably adept as a strategist, although he never seems to have learned a great deal of tactical sense. The tuition he received from Richard was costly, perhaps, but Philip made it pay off handsomely when he was faced with a less skillful opponent in the person of Richard's brother and successor, King John. He made even more valuable use of his painfully acquired knowledge in his campaigns against the barons of Aquitaine during the Albigensian Crusade.

In non-military matters, Richard's intellectual capacity shows off less well. There is no question but that he had an unusually keen mind, but it was narrowly channeled in one direction. True, he was literate and was even a passable poet. Two poems, at least, have been ascribed to him with reasonable certainty, one in the Poitevin dialect, which was his mother tongue, and one also in Provençal. He was reasonably fluent in Latin, too, although he was apparently not always certain of his grammar. But the poetry and music that he most loved centered about the themes of martial valor and military prowess in which he himself excelled.

In religious beliefs and observances he was reasonably conventional. He was certainly far from being overawed by his spiritual advisers, although he took them seriously enough to moderate his habits, sexual and other, on a few occasions in obedience to the precepts of religious morality. He abstained from receiving the eucharist for a long period before his death, because he felt unable, or at least unwilling, to forgive his enemy Philip Augustus for the treatment he had received at his hands. Under these circumstances Richard could not conscientiously receive the sacrament, since he was still seeking vengeance against his enemy. Still, before his death, Richard made his peace with the Church and he received the sacraments before his death. His theatrical instincts seem to have been most highly satisfied by participation in the solemn ceremonies of the Church, which he loved and looked forward to throughout his life.

Richard's interest in knowledge for its own sake was apparently slight or nonexistent. There is no indication that he was in the smallest degree interested in speculative philosophy or theology, in mathematics or science, or even in such applied sciences as law and medicine. The only areas of knowledge that elicited much real study and attention from Richard were those that dealt with military technology. He was a close student of military architecture and Château Gaillard was his masterpiece in this genre, a well-engineered fortress which incorporated in its design the latest wrinkles and novelities in the art of castle-building. In addition to Château Gaillard, however, Richard was also responsible for building a number of lesser fortresses in Normandy, as well as for renovating and reconstructing a sizable number of castles and walled cities in England, southern France, and Palestine. Collectively, the corpus of his buildings comprises a notable monument to Richard's achievement in this technological field and there can be little doubt that his own personal interests and ideas are incorporated in many of these structures. Richard was no mere passive patron when it came to the design and construction of fortifications. It was not a question of simply finding a master mason to whom he could assign the supervision of a given piece of work. On the contrary, Richard gave serious personal attention to these matters and, by and large, his buildings seem to reflect his own thought on the problems of defense which they posed, on their relationship to the terrain on which they were sited, on their strategic function, and even on the detailed problems of building and design.

Richard was lavish in his expenditures on military buildings, just as he was inclined to be generous in his dealings with those whom he liked and trusted. Far from being niggardly and hoarding his assets, as Philip Augustus was accustomed to do, Richard spent money and gave presents with scant attention to such sordid matters as account balances and estimates of income. These things he blithely ignored, apparently confident that some way could always be found to increase his income when he had spent whatever happened to be on hand at the moment. This is not to say that he was unaware of money problems: on the contrary, they cropped up so frequently in his career that he was constantly being pressed to find additional cash to make good his commitments. But the pressures of providing for the future were something Richard disdained—when he saw something that he wanted or needed, he acquired it, regardless of the fiscal implications of the action. "You know there's neither silver nor coppers at Chinon," he wrote in one of his poems, and the lines simply describe a chronic condition at his court. This was not something that worried Richard very seriously, but it was a fact of life with which he had continuously to deal. His continuing concern to make good any chance of immediate gain is characteristic of his whole career; and so he sold off Cyprus, although he never bothered to collect the full amount promised him in the transaction. So also, the final scene of his life was played out in pursuit of a gaudy bauble which could be converted quickly into cash.

Just as he was generous with his friends, so he was also disinclined to believe that those he trusted could betray that trust. Richard was unusually slow to suspect treachery from his friends, even when treachery was genuinely present. The record of his dealings with Philip Augustus is eloquent on this point and even more eloquent is the record of his relationship with his brother John. True, all of the Angevins found it difficult to take John very seriously, and Richard took him least seriously of all. Despite John's manifest betrayal of Richard's trust during the crusade, despite the fact that again and again he broke his word and connived at treason, Richard forgave him as soon as John came to him and professed sorrow for what he had done. First Richard gave him back his income, then his lands, and finally he bequeathed to John his kingdom. There was nothing foreordained in John's succession at Richard's death: there were others whose legal and moral titles to the succession were quite as good as his. It was Richard's final folly as a king to have designated John as his heir and successor; but this final action is wholly in keeping with Richard's characteristic inability to appraise men realistically.

Richard's shortcomings in this regard must be assessed in the context of a general emotional instability, which was clearly the gravest flaw in his makeup. If he was slow to be suspicious of those whom he trusted, Richard was also quick to anger at those of whom he was suspicious. His outbreaks of violent, unreasoning rage were notorious and occurred with embarrassing frequency. In this characteristic, Richard was very much like his father. Those who offended him, even without malice, were liable to the cruelest imaginable treatment, for Richard found no torture too unspeakable to practice upon those who incurred his wrath.

There was a strong streak, too, of unscrupulous dishonesty in Richard's character. Although he professed to abhor lying in others, he had no excessively tender regard for the truth when it was to his advantage to dissimulate. Nor was it unknown for him to break his pledged word behind a cloud of shabby pretenses. The record of his contest with Philip Augustus is full of such episodes. Richard was not above such maneuvers, either, when dealing with his subjects, as witness the sorry business when he replaced his great seal and then required those who had received privileges under the first seal to pay additional fees for authentication of their charters with the second seal. Richard pretended that the reason for the change of seals was that during his captivity his seal had been out of his control and hence, perhaps, might have been affixed to spurious documents. However, Richard was released from captivity in 1194 and yet continued to use his old seal until 1198 when, hard pressed for funds, he finally began to use his new one. The reason given for introducing the new seal in 1198 was a transparent fraud; but behavior of this kind was hardly unique in Richard's career.

We can see still another manifestation of Richard's basic emotional inconstancy in his well-known arrogance and excessive pride. That he should have boasted from time to time of his military achievements is not, perhaps, very surprising. He clearly had unusual talent in this line and, by his lights, had every right to glory in it. It is more disconcerting, however, to find him making an issue of his achievements at the least provocation and to see how easily his vanity was pricked by imagined slights. Richard was abnormally sensitive to criticism and reacted violently to the slightest hint that his conduct might be improved or that alternative measures to the ones he had taken might have worked out better than the ones he had chosen. He was clearly not a man who found it easy to take advice, no matter how well based the advice might be. Thus when he consulted the medical practitioners of Salerno on his journey to the East, he spent five days disputing with them, as well as securing their opinions about his own health and the sanitary precautions his army should take during its campaign. Richard seems to have found it most difficult of all to take advice in affairs of state, where he certainly was unusually inept himself and where the counsel of others was sorely needed. Yet despite one warning after another he stubbornly pursued his own courses, even when they led straight to disaster. Again, the history of his relationship with

John furnishes a sterling example of Richard's infirmity in this regard.

Richard's emotional immaturity shows through especially in the cloudy history of his homosexuality. His contemporaries were very unwilling to discuss the matter openly and contented themselves with dark hints about Richard's unnatural inclinations and his appetite for the vices of Sodom. Although they were unwilling to state the problem straightforwardly, they did not fail to make the nature of the charge clear. We know nothing of any significance about the details of his sexual conduct, save that he was widely suspected of homosexual inclinations and apparently confessed on at least two or three occasions to some homosexual episodes. This is as much as can be gleaned with any certainty from the witnesses. It is obvious enough that Richard had no deep feelings for women as a group. He had no mistresses, save for the anonymous woman who bore his bastard son. He waited until very late to marry, in an age where noblemen of all ranks customarily married early and frequently married often as well. When he did marry, he spent practically no time with his wife and was estranged from her for most of their married life. Even more serious, perhaps, was Richard's failure in one of the primary obligations of a medieval king: he produced no male heir, indeed no heir at all.

Richard's aversion to women was manifested at the outset of his reign: his coronation banquet was a bachelor party. Even Richard's fiancée, Alice, and his mother did not attend and no other ladies seem to have been invited. After he had left the predominantly feminine atmosphere of his mother's court at the age of seventeen, Richard by preference spent almost all of his life in male company. Overwhelmingly his companions were either soldiers, whose company he clearly preferred, or clergymen, whom he was prepared to tolerate.

This combination of factors—Richard's apparent aversion to women, his preference for exclusively male company, and the hints of the chroniclers about his addiction to unnatural sexual habits—points clearly to the conclusion that Richard was by preference a homosexual. The conclusion is, if anything, reinforced further by his known affection for his mother and his dislike of his father who rejected him, which modern writers about sexual aberrations have tended to link very strongly with homosexuality. We simply do not know who his sexual partners were, except possibly for Philip Augustus, nor do we know anything about his emotional attachments to his male friends.

The conclusions to be drawn from Richard's record as a ruler are almost uniformly negative. He was certainly one of the worst rulers that England has ever had. He visited the island only twice during the ten years of his reign and the total duration of those two visits amounted to about six months. During the other nine-and-a-half years of his reign he was absent from the country entirely, although he left it in the care of agents who were in many respects better fitted to rule than he was. Paradoxically, in fact, Richard's almost complete neglect of his English kingdom was more beneficial for the English than his presence on the spot might have been. For in the absence of the king, his English servants went far toward developing the institutions and instruments of government that were to serve so well and so fruitfully in the reigns of later monarchs. The growth of a sense of collective responsibility for the welfare of the realm on the part of the barons and administrative officers of England during Richard's reign is remarkable. In terms of institutional growth, the record of his period is less notable: the technical devices of law and administration which were in use throughout his reign were almost entirely those that were brought into currency by his father. What Richard's reign accomplished was to demonstrate conclusively that the presence and continuing care of the monarch was not essential for the orderly conduct of public life.

One of Richard's English agents, William Longchamp, bishop of Ely, chancellor of the kingdom, and justiciar, made himself widely unpopular during Richard's absence. In part this was due to Longchamp's inordinate greed and ambition, in part to a resentment of the man himself. None of these things is necessarily unusual in great officials. What is worth notice, however, is that when Longchamp was deposed as justiciar in 1191, the initiative for his deposition came from the English barons, not from Richard. The precedent set on this occasion was of great significance during the disorders of John's reign, when the barons, after being pushed far enough, dealt with the king just as they had earlier dealt with Longchamp during Richard's reign.

If many of the effects of Richard's regime were in the long run beneficial, it cannot be said that this was the result of any planning or foresight on Richard's part. Indeed he seems to have given very little consideration to what he was doing in England during the two brief periods when he was there. His wholesale auctioning of offices to the highest bidders was scarcely calculated to contribute to the welfare of anyone save himself.

In the short run, his careless provisions for the governance of his kingdom caused acute distress to a great many of his subjects. The rivalries between Longchamp, on the one hand, and on the other Richard's bastard brother, Geoffrey, whom he made archbishop of York, gave rise to acute difficulties in the orderly conduct of business. The intervention of Richard's other brother, John, to whom Richard had given a virtually independent segment of the kingdom, complicated matters further and sharpened the strife within Richard's disorderly realm.

For Richard, England was primarily a source of money, to be used to defray the enormous expenses of his crusade and of his struggles in France. The ingenuity of his officers in England was stretched to the utmost to devise new methods of raising the revenues Richard required. No expedient was too novel to be experimented with, so long as it gave promise of raising money, and fiscal innovations of many kinds were attempted. But try as they might, Richard's financial officers were never able to satisfy completely the demands for funds which the king made on them. Richard's ingenuity in spending outstripped their ingenuity in raising funds. The result was that the royal government hovered constantly on the brink of insolvency and when John came to the throne the resources of the monarchy were nearly exhausted. From this circumstance flowed many of John's troubles in England. In a very real sense John paid the price for Richard's extravagance.

One area where Richard's government was relatively liberal was the area of urban policy. Richard was unusually lenient and accommodating in granting the cities of his realm the right to govern themselves and to deal with their own internal affairs. In this he contrasted strikingly with his father, for Henry II had been extremely wary of yielding to his cities any rights of self-government at all and had sought to keep the towns strictly under royal control. Richard's chronic need for money, however, led him to reverse this policy and to grant town charters with a free hand, since the municipalities were willing to reimburse him generously for the liberties which they gained.

The picture of Richard which builds up as one reviews his record is necessarily a complex one. He was vain and arrogant, proud, combative, intellectually gifted, yet disdaining all kinds of mental exertion save for those that involved warfare. In combat he was brilliant and courageous; in the counsel-chamber he was a total loss, careless of his subjects' welfare, interested only in the satisfaction of his own needs; as a ruler he was a negligent king and the best that can be said for him was that his negligence was relatively benign. Personally his relationships were almost uniformly unsatisfactory, with very few exceptions. Richard's emotional instability and immaturity, manifested by his homosexuality, his ungovernable temper, his quick changes of moods, and the generally uneven tenor of his personal life, all contribute to a picture of an unhappy, unsatisfied, and unsatisfiable person. Yet Richard was widely revered during his lifetime and has enjoyed a posthumous fame such as no other English king has achieved. He quickly became a genuine folk-hero whose exploits were further dramatized and elaborated by numerous legends which, if they sometimes obscure the historical realities, nevertheless testify to his popularity.

Most of the legends which circulated concerning Richard dealt in one way or another with his military exploits and in the process Richard was popularly credited either with achievements which in fact belonged to others or which had never been performed by anyone. In part he was assimilated to other folk-heroes, particularly King Arthur, and feats which were supposed to have been performed by the legendary monarch were also ascribed to Richard as well. Richard was treated as a kind of reincarnated King Arthur by the story-tellers and folk-singers. In addition, some of Richard's real accomplishments on the battlefield were magnified and elaborated in the legendary treatments of him. At the same time, the mythologizers also colored their accounts of Richard's failings by creating stories to excuse them—thus Leopold of Austria becomes in the legends a sinister mastermind who took Richard into his power by treachery. In the same way, the evils and the suffering which Richard's wars and his fiscal policies alike created were assigned in legendary tales to other causes and the responsibility for them was shifted onto other shoulders, notably those of Philip Augustus and John.

If some of his contemporaries and some men of later generations mythologized Richard into a hero, there were others, even in his own period, who saw his reign in a different light. One such disillusioned writer put it this way:

Valor, avarice, crime
Unbounded lust, foul famine,
Unscrupulous pride and blind
Desire have reigned twice
Five years;
            all these
An archer did with art,
Hand, weapon, Strength
Lay prostrate.*

Modern historians and biographers who have dealt with Richard have been almost as sharply divided in their assessment of him as his contemporaries were. For a few he still remains a glorious, romantic warrior-hero, a paradigm of knightly virtues. Such paeans of Richard are less common now than they formerly were and nowadays are usually to be found in the pages of historians writing for school children or for large, popular audiences. A century ago Bishop Stubbs remarked that English writers, "while they have honestly recorded the crimes and excesses which on the face of it refute their views of his general character, seem to have thought it possible to show that, although in every relation of life he was found grievously wanting, he was, on the whole, a great and glorious king, to be defended against the calumnies of all the world." There are those who still feel this way. Thus, for Sir Winston Churchill, Richard remains "throughout the centuries the pattern of the fighting man. . . . His life was one magnificent parade, which when it ended, left only an empty plain." Sir Winston was closely attuned to Richard's heroic associations and he ends his hymn of praise to Richard's career with an explicit evocation of the legendary past, declaring Richard "worthy, by the consent of all men, to sit with King Arthur and Roland and other heroes of martial

* Roger of Howden, *Annals,* s.a. 1199, trans. H. T. Riley, 2 vols. (London, 1853), 2:54.

romance at some Eternal Round Table, which we trust the Creator of the Universe in His comprehension will not have forgotten to provide."

The professional historians have generally been considerably cooler in their admiration and for more than a century have commonly dealt rather harshly with Richard. "A bad son, a bad husband, a selfish ruler, and a vicious man" was Bishop Stubbs's pithy, if uncharitable, characterization in 1864 and not a few of the bishop's successors at Oxford and elsewhere have shared that view, although few of them have phrased it quite so bluntly.

The great problem of interpreting Richard's career, of course, is the question of what standards one should apply to his history. Judged by the standards of his own times and his own class of knightly rulers and warriors, Richard was indeed a fine monarch and a very great man, for he exemplified the virtues which they most admired and for them his vices and failings lay in areas of minor importance. The clergy and the merchants of his own time, however, were not particularly apt to agree with such a verdict. Their standards were somewhat different from those of the nobility and, while the clergy deplored Richard's moral failures, the bourgeoisie were appalled by the insanity of his fiscal policy.

Modern academic historians are rarely inclined to share the value systems of twelfth-century warrior-rulers and are much more likely to be sympathetic to the reservations felt by the clergy and the merchants of the Middle Ages. Certainly Richard shows up poorly by the criteria of modern statecraft; but of course he was entirely ignorant of those criteria and it is unrealistic to expect that he should have conformed to them.

Richard remains an enigma to the end: a valiant prince, mighty warrior, and a noble king, his character was strongly flawed by all too human vices. It is perhaps this very combination of great courage and great strength with common failings that endows him with perennial appeal.

A Note on Bibliography

This biography of Richard Lion Heart is based, as any histori-cal study must be, upon writings and records contemporary (or nearly so) with the subject studied. The medieval English kings were fortunate in that very considerable quantities of contemporary materials dealing with their reigns have sur-vived. The foundations for this biography of Richard have been built from the materials preserved by slightly more than a dozen narrative writers, who set down their accounts of Richard and his reign in the late twelfth and early thirteenth century. The basic accounts are:

Roger of Howden. *Chronica.* Edited by William Stubbs. 4 vols. London: Rolls Series 51, 1868–1871.

Gesta Regis Henrici II and its continuation, *Gesta Regis Ri-chardi I.* Erroneously attributed to Benedict of Peter-borough. Edited by William Stubbs. 2 vols. London: Rolls Series 49, 1867. This account was, in fact, the first draft of Howden's Chronicle.

Gerald of Wales. *Opera.* Edited by J. W. Brewer, J. F. Dimock, and G. F. Warner. 8 vols. London: Rolls Series 21, 1861–1891.

Ralph of Diceto. *Opera historica.* Edited by William Stubbs. 2 vols. London: Rolls Series 68, 1876.

Roger of Wendover. *Flores historiarum.* Edited by H. G. Hewlett. 3 vols. London: Rolls Series 84, 1886–1889.

William of Newburgh. *Historia rerum Anglicarum.* Edited by R. Howlett. 2 vols. London: Rolls Series 82:1–2, 1884–1885.

Robert of Torigni. *Chronicon.* Edited by R. Howlett. London: Rolls Series 82:4, 1889.

Richard of Devizes. *Chronicle.* Edited and translated by John T. Appleby. London: Nelson's Medieval Texts, 1963.

Itinerarium peregrinorum et gesta regis Ricardi. Edited by William Stubbs. London: Rolls Series 34:1, 1864. Book I of the *Itinerarium* has also been edited recently from a larger and more complete body of manuscripts by Hans Eberhard Mayer, *Das Itinerarium peregrinorum.* Stuttgart: Monumenta Germaniae Historica, Schriften, vol. 18, 1962.

Guillaume le Breton. *La Philippide.* In *Collection des mémoires relatifs à l'histoire de France*, edited by F. P. G. Guizot, vol. 12. Paris: 1823–1835; and also *Gesta Philippi II regis Francorum*, in the same collection, vol. 11.

L'histoire de Guillaume le Marechal. Edited and translated by P. Meyer, 3 vols. Paris: 1891–1901.

Ambroise. *L'Estoire de la guerre sainte.* Edited and translated by Gaston Paris. Paris: Collection de documents inedits sur l'histoire de France, 1897.

L'estoire d'Eracles empreur. In the *Recueil des historiens des croisades, historiens occidentaux*, vol. 2.

Ernoul. *Chronique.* Edited by M. L. de Mas Latrie. Paris: 1871.

In addition, for the period of Richard's crusade some valuable information is recorded by Arabic writers, particularly Bahā ad-Din, Imād ad-Din, and Ibn al-Athīr. The pertinent sections of their writings can be found in the volumes of the *Historiens Orientaux* section of the *Receuil des historiens des croisades*. There are convenient translations of some selections in *Arab Historians of the Crusades*, edited by Francesco Gabrieli (Berkeley, California: 1969). Two Greek writers furnish additional details concerning Richard's campaign on Cyprus. They are Leontios Makhairas, *Recital Concerning the Sweet Land of Cyprus*, edited and translated by R. M. Dawkins, 2 vols. (Oxford: 1932), and Neophytus, *De calamitatibus Cypri*, edited by William Stubbs in the prologue to his edition of the *Itinerarium peregrinorum*, as well as in the *Recueil des historiens des croisades, Historiens Grecs*, vol. 1.

All of the foregoing are narrative works, accounts set down by writers who sought to tell a connected story of their own period. Beyond these narratives, we also have a considerable quantity of documentary or record material for the period of Richard's lifetime. An old, but still useful, collection of such material is the *Foedera, conventiones, litterae, et cujuscunque acta publica inter reges Angliae et quovis alios imperatores . . .* , edited by Thomas Rymer, 3rd ed. (The Hague: 1745; rp. 1967). The principal financial records of Richard's administration in England are contained in the Great Rolls of the Pipe. These records have been edited by Lady Stenton and published by the Pipe Roll Society (London: 1925–1933), save for the roll for the first year of Richard's reign, which was edited by J. Hunter and published by the Record Commissioners (London: 1844). Many of the important documents of Richard's great Continental rival, Philip Augustus, are found in the *Recueil des Actes de Philipe Auguste, roi de France*, edited by H. F. Delaborde and others, 2 vols. (Paris: 1916–1943). Documents relating to the Latin East in the period of Richard's crusade are calendared by Reinhold Röhricht in his *Regesta Regni Hierosolymitani*, 2 vols. (Vienna: 1904; rp. New York: 1960). There are comprehensive calendars of papal documents edited by Philip

Jaffé and others (for the period up to 1198) and by August
Potthast (for the period from 1198–1304). In addition, for the
last fifteen months of Richard's life one should consult *The
Letters of Pope Innocent III* (1198–1216) *concerning Eng-
land and Wales,* edited by C. R. Cheney and Mary G. Cheney
(Oxford: 1967).

There have been a number of biographies of King
Richard in modern times. The only one of much value is Kate
Norgate, *Richard the Lion Heart* (London: 1924; rp. New
York: 1969). Miss Norgate's *England Under the Angevin
Kings,* 2 vols. (London: 1887; rp. New York: 1969) also re-
mains useful. One valuable study which has been referred to
constantly in the preparation of this book is Lionel Landon's
Itinerary of King Richard I (London: Publications of the
Pipe Roll Society, new series, vol. 13, 1935) which brings
together a great mass of useful information and references for
the ten years of Richard's reign as king. The problems and
vicissitudes of the English kingdom during Richard's reign
are described in detail in John T. Appleby, *England Without
Richard,* 1189–1199 (Ithaca, N.Y.: 1965); on this see also Ber-
tie Wilkinson, "The Government of England during the Absence of Richard I on the Third Crusade," in the *Bulletin of
the John Rylands Library* 28 (1944): 485–509.

For the general political history of England in this
period, Austin Lane Poole's *From Domesday Book to Magna
Carta,* 1087–1216, 2d ed., vol. 3 (Oxford: The Oxford History
of England, 1955, is invaluable. The governmental system
and its problems are dealt with by all writers on constitutional and legal history. The classical work is, of course, William Stubbs, *Constitutional History of England,* 3 vols. (Oxford: 1887–1891). On the law, the most important treatment is
Sir Frederick Pollock and F. W. Maitland, *History of English
Law,* 2d ed., 2 vols (Cambridge: 1968). Some provocative
views are expressed by H. G. Richardson and G. O. Sayles,
The Governance of Mediaeval England from the Conquest to

Magna Carta (Edinburgh: 1963). The governmental history of Anjou is dealt with by J. Broussard, *Le Comté d'Anjou sous Henri Plantagenet et ses fils* (Paris: 1938). For ecclesiastical matters the most useful work is C. R. Cheney's *From Becket to Langton* (Manchester: 1956). The complexities of Anglo-French rivalry in Normandy are dealt with in the magisterial work of Sir Frederick Maurice Powicke, *The Loss of Normandy*, 2d ed. (Manchester: 1961). Relations between England and the south of Italy have been examined by Evelyn Jamison, "The Alliance of England and Sicily in the Second Half of the Twelfth Century," in the *Journal of the Warburg and Courtauld Institutes* 6 (1943): 20–32.

Richard's crusade is treated by all of the standard histories of the crusading movement. See especially *A History of the Crusades*, edited by Kenneth M. Setton and others, 2d ed., 2 vols. to date (Madison, Wisconsin: 1969– ; in progress) and Sir Steven Runciman, *A History of the Crusades*, 3 vols. (Cambridge: 1951–54). Richard's involvement in Cyprus is described by Sir George Hill, *A History of Cyprus*, 4 vols. (Cambridge: 1940–1952). On this one should also consult Heinrich Fichtenau, "Akkon, Zypern und das Lösegeld für Richard Löwenherz," in the *Archiv für österreichische Geschichte* 125 (1966): 11–32.

A number of persons associated with Richard have been the subject of special studies. There is a charming and scholarly biography of his mother by Amy Kelly, *Eleanor of Aquitaine and the Four Kings* (Cambridge, Massachusetts: 1950; rp. New York: 1957). Richard's brother John has been studied by Sidney Painter, *The Reign of King John* (Baltimore: 1949) and there is a brief but helpful treatment of his bastard brother by Decima L. Douie, *Archbishop Geoffrey Plantagenet* (York: St. Anthony's Hall Publications, no. 18, 1960). Richard's crusading companion and later archbishop of Canterbury has been dealt with by C. R. Cheney, *Hubert Walter* (London: 1967). There is a recent and provocative treatment of Richard's father's reign, by W. L. Warren, entitled *Henry II* (Berkeley and Los Angeles, 1973). The best of the older ones is Louis F. Salzmann, *Henry II* (Boston: 1914). Another of Richard's close associates has been treated by Sidney Painter, *William Marshall* (Baltimore: 1933).

Index